A House Divided…No More
(Time for Indigenous Communal Healing)

Michael James Ph.D.
2011

HOPE
(Helping Oppressed People Emerge)

Chicago Illinois

i

TABLE OF CONTENTS

Part I: Unity Is the Key

Part II: Black Psychological Warfare

Part III: Divided...No More

Dedication
To Azalea

Poem by Dr. Michael James

When Can the Children Play Again?

The spirit of the Lord moved...on the planes of time. He has enlarged my territory. My daughter Sariese was blessed with a daughter, Azalea, a quiet, curious soul.

During formal family introductions, the Alpha and Omega, moved...upon my spirit, depositing an affirmation. This new arrival did indeed light up the room. I will call her Sparkle.

My mind, elevated by the moment, was challenged by the Creator, challenged with an existential question:
When Can the Children Play Again?

Immediately my previous public campaigns, HOPE (Helping Oppressed People Emerge) and Saving the Children, came full circle. The Creator once again charged me to take up shield and buckler, to stand up for the born and the unborn.

The Prince of Peace once again charged me to draw out the spear. To stop the enemy and the continuous unprecedented, unwarranted, unprovoked violence upon innocent children.
To suffer the little children, if you will.

Returning to the present moment...the Unmoved Mover's charge weighed heavily upon my soul. I made a promise to the Promise Keeper: To let judgment run down as waters.
To let righteousness flow like a mighty stream.

I will fight the good fight. I will finish my course.
I will keep the faith. But not only that!

I will stir a new consciousness upon the earth.
I will boldly address the question posed by the Creator:
When Can the Children Play Again?

Acknowledgements

The following short but necessary acknowledgements of men, women and marriages serves as a reminder of what John Donne so eloquently summed up:

> "No man is an island, entire of itself; every
> man is a piece of the continent, a part of the main...
> any man's death diminishes me, because I am involved
> in mankind, and therefore never send to know for
> whom the bell tolls; it tolls for thee."[1]

The bell tolls for...

Clarence Ross, a powerful brother, whose spirit of dedication to his students, coupled with an unwavering devotion to unconditional friendship during several turbulent years of discovery, deserves honorable mention. Brandon James' faith journey has inspired me. My brother George would be proud of the way you persevered and rose from the dust of despair with dignity and respect. Minister and soon-to-be-Rev. Dr. Nicholas Greer is a young, dynamic brother whose undying faith and commitment to the body of Christ represents an exemplary model of a young man groomed by a good family. Brother Nick is a light in the midst of the darkness of his generation. His unconditional friendship has blessed me over and over again. Mr. Mitchell Smith is a bother who is determined to empower the African American Village Community by highlighting the importance of educating minds. Your commitment to educate our people deserves honorable mention. Bill "Doc" Walls a drum major for political empowerment in juxtaposition to social justice eloquently represents the uncompromised courage to stand up to the political Goliaths in the land. The African American Village Community is a much better place due to your spirit of longevity and ability to create a grassroots movement.

The bell tolls for...

Tiffany (Norwood) James, the daughter of Andre James. In a short time span Tiffany's presence on this earth blessed the lives of those who watched this young lady battle insurmountable health issues. You will forever be on the tablets of my heart, mind and soul. Tracy Ruppman of Loyola University Chicago is a dynamic, knowledgeable professional whose invaluable assistance empowered me to successfully and competently complete the in-depth research requirements for my dissertation. Aunt Dora (Lofton) is a woman of faith who believed in my abilities to succeed prior to my own belief and confidence in myself. Your faith has instilled in me a lifelong thirst for excellence in education. Diane Carol Downs is a dynamic spirit filled sister whose prayers and words of encouragement have empowered me to stand and take on the shield of faith. Truly I am blessed to know you.

The bells tolls for...

Jennifer Tlusty, a teacher par excellence. Your friendship is truly a gift from the Creator. Your smile and spirit have blessed my life tremendously. Thanks for sharing your students with me; you are extremely graceful. Tamala Daniels' consistent wisdom and words of encouragement have empowered me to stand against the destruction that waits at noonday. Your character and beautiful spirit serve as a reminder to simply trust in the Lord. Ms. Susan Cole, teacher extraordinaire, the light from your soul not only enriches your students but your colleagues as well. Ms. Margaret Chris is a soul sister who has publicly and privately blessed me with her special friendship. Gwen Marie Burnett is a strong, quiet public servant who has humbly empowered an untold number of people (especially families) without taking a public bow or asking for recognition. My respect for your vocation has become immeasurable. Mrs. Theda Mambia is a woman I greatly respect and admire. Your spirit of fairness not only empowers students but your colleagues as well. Mrs. Juanita Robbins is a special friend and colleague, and I unequivocally believe she is a valuable asset to the educational arena. Your quiet confidence will inevitably prepare you for numerous future opportunities in administration. Dr. Philinda Coleman is an educator par excellence who listens to the voice of one crying in the wilderness. I am honored to know you.

Honorable mentions go to the following colleagues I have grown to love and respect as participants in the Beloved Community: Mrs. Chris Mitchell, a special colleague, has earned my respect, trust, and unconditional friendship. Her spirit of acceptance supports Dr. King's vision of the Beloved Community. Ms. Bernadine Edwards is a quiet, supportive spirit. Her devotion to children makes her a special addition to any creditable educational institution. Ms. Nicolette Jackson, a powerful teacher, serves as an example that those who wait on the Lord shall renew their strength. Mrs. Willa Foxx is a devoted woman of God whose prayers have enabled me to learn the lesson of patience. Ms. Athrell Evette Harris is a colleague I greatly admire for her sincere spirit of caring for those God placed in her path. Her devotion to the children of the community is outstanding. Mrs. Michelle Lee Jackson is a woman of great intelligence. I was blessed from day one when God, the Creator, placed her in my life. Mrs. Patricia Kroll is a dedicated leader who exemplifies the theme of No Child Left Behind. Shelia Wilson is a close colleague I trust to share my quiet moments with. The hand of God will always be upon you because your heart is in the right place. May God continue to use all of the mentioned educators' special gifts and talents to empower our students and develop future leaders.

I am honored to acknowledge a beautiful African American sister, Mrs. Kitty Fulce, for her in-depth assistance in the refining aspects of this important historical exegesis. Her tireless efforts to produce the best depiction of our cultural excellence prove to be exemplary of the concept that iron sharpens iron. Words cannot express my gratitude. May God keep you and heaven smile upon you and your loved ones.

The bell tolls for the following marriages. Marriage is the nucleus of the healing process in the African American Village.

Mr. and Mrs. Dr. Chaun and Natalie Johnson
Mr. and Mrs. Donald R. and Samantha Stone
Mr. and Mrs. Terry and Germaine Newsome

Mr. and Mrs. Alfonzo and Annie Kountz
Mr. and Mrs. Alfred and Dr. Brenda Little
Rev. Mr. and Mrs. Manuel and Alice Scott

Mr. and Mrs. Kerwen and Trina Whately
Mr. and Mrs. Brian and Stephanie Smith
Mr. and Mrs. Warren and Ruth Howlett
Mr. and Mrs. Craig and Deloris Watson

Mr. and Mrs. John and Alcine Arnett
Mr. and Mrs. John and Jackie Frazier
Mr. and Mrs. Jerry and Justine Scott

Mr. and Mrs. James and Diane Sibley
Mr. and Mrs. Wilbur and Verla Davis
Mr. and Mrs. Julius and Roslyn Scott
Mr. and Mrs. Todd and Joy Horton

Last, but certainly not least, it is with great pleasure that I honor a beautiful sister in Christ who has become an enormous source of inspiration. Dorothy K. Barton prayers and wise words of encouragement during my personal and professional struggles were truly God sent. She exemplifies and stands as a living testimony that we are our brothers and sisters keeper. Her smile and genuine concern for people proves to be her greatest assets. In the tradition of *A House Divided...No More* through the promotion of an olive branch between African American men and women she truly becomes the embodiment of *Time for Indigenous Communal Healing*.

INTRODUCTION

The primary purpose of this exegesis is to look inward for past and present footprints of the promotion of positive Black self-esteem and the creation and nurturing of the Beloved Community. It is a collective search for those who unapologetically launched a public vocation (moved by the Unmoved Mover) to rebuild, reclaim and restore the African American Village Community to a state equal to and greater than the Civil Rights Era. Most importantly, this indigenous search represents a catalyst for the authentic indigenous healing process to begin, thereby launching an investigative innate analysis: a critical self-analysis, if you will.

It is my intent to bring about a unification of our minds so that African American women and men can find common ground in our continuous fight for equality in America. Collectively our mothers and fathers faced the most brutal, evil system the world has ever known: Slavocracy via the Atlantic Slave Trade and the African Diaspora. *Collective* is the primary word. History teaches us that a people united can never be defeated. We must reflect on the historical words of Dr. Martin L. King Jr., who boldly proclaimed that we as a people will get to the Promised Land. Furthermore, Dr. King developed and supported what I refer to as the Inescapable Mutuality Paradigm: "Whatever affects one directly, affects all indirectly. I can never be what I ought to be until you are what you ought to be...and you can never be what you ought to be until I am what I ought to be".[2] This paradigm lends itself to the African American Experience and becomes definitive in a move toward a conscious unity. This unique historical experience was previously derived from the pluralistic tribes of Africa as we merged into one people during the long night of slavery to become African Americans. This in essence supports the hypothesis of the Inter-Related Structure of Reality and the cultural bridge connecting two imperative concepts: the African American Experience, an

xi

indigenous preternatural power base, and the Inescapable Mutuality Paradigm.

If our African American sisters achieve economic, social, political and educational parity without an agenda to address the similar needs of her oppressed African American brothers (the Black Alpha Males), how can the African American Village Community be restored? How can a Village Community survive when close to 80–90 percent of Black Alpha Males are either physically incarcerated and/or psychologically castrated? Moreover, if the Black Alpha Male similarly achieves emancipation and abandons his family and extended family, what will happen to the Village?

Collectively we must, by any and all means and resources available to us, engage the real enemy: the weapon of mass destruction (i.e., the furious greed of capitalists, the gatekeepers of wealth and power). I appropriately categorize this weapon as the Glass Ceiling. It is quite invisible to those who have been misled, had, took, hoodwinked, bamboozled, led astray and run amok, and quite formidable and effective in the economic, social, political, educational and psychological strangulation of African Americans.[3] Similar to the infamous Willie Lynch Initiative (i.e., Socialization of Division), this psychological weapon discourages any and all forms of Communal Initiatives that would address the social ills produced by capitalism. It is quite effective in the Rule of Containment, the silencing and corralling of the Black Alpha Male Constructionist.

During this contemporary and historical analysis we will revisit Ground Zero. Ground Zero can be defined in the following manner: a time in history when all slaves excavated from Mother Africa shared the common ideology of breaking any and all chains of human bondage. This hypothesis will give rise to a new Communal Initiative as we collectively and consciously embrace the Inescapable Mutuality Paradigm. The

xii

new Initiative is as follows: the unification of the African American Village Community, forming cultural solidarity to break all links of institutionalized oppressions in America (i.e., racism, sexism, classism, discrimination and inequalities, including any and all forms of marginalization). In doing so we will produce fertile ground for the indigenous healing process—indigenous Communal Healing, if you will. Within the parameters of this research, the contemporary and historical footprints of notable African American men and women in juxtaposition to indigenous-based organizations in America will be examined. The common thread of Empirical Hope, a hope based on the African American Experience, will be presented to the readers. Throughout this exegesis, the following (selective) appropriate terminology will assist in the clarification of the long overdue healing process: Historical Discipline, Historical Euthanasia, Laissez-Faire Entitlement Syndrome, Communal Healing, Communal Initiative, Village Concept, Socialization of Division, Cultural Utilitarianism, the Rule of Annihilation, Rule of Containment, Rule of Selective Engagement, the Constructionist, Objectionist, Destructionist, 2P's (Providers & Protectors), Generation E, the Ethics of Care and the Crystallization of Cause & Effect. After examining the contents of this book, we will be able to come to a collective agreement and will reach a consensus that capitalism has separated us; capitalism has interfered with our innate concept of cultural solidarity that once defined our relationships to our families, extended families and Village Communities.

The *Truth* is Black women from the African continent have been blessed with a natural beauty second to none. In retrospect, during the long night of slavery, the European Slave Traders found her to be irresistible. It became apparent that there must be a dividing line, an indigenous schism, if you will, between her and her natural mate, the Black Alpha Male. The house must be divided. The house of communal family values must be divided. The house that once supported the spirit of oneness that provided for and protected the Village Community must be divided. The house that once supported the fundamental activities of Continental African "first fruits" (ingathering, reverence, commemoration, recommitment and celebration) must be divided. The houses within the African American Village Community that embraced the Nguzo Saba, the seven principles of communitarian African values: (*Umoja*, Unity; *Kujichagulia*, Self-Determination; *Ujima*, Collective Work and Responsibility; *Ujamaa,* Cooperative Economics; *Nia*, Purpose; *Kuumba*, Creativity; and *Imani*, Faith) must unapologetically be permanently divided—divided and destroyed.[4] Moreover, any cultural values emphasizing the importance of African communitarian values stressing family, community and what it means to be human and of African descent must be destroyed! In retrospect, the imperative need for the promotion of division, the Socialization of Division among African American women and men, became an idea whose time had come. A weapon of mass human destruction.

Moving by the power of God I am convinced that after reading this exegesis the unction to revisit Ground Zero will become a categorical imperative. This preternatural amour (derived from the invaluable collective consciousness of our ancestors) will become a catalyst for my people, of the people and by the people to abolish any past and present forms of capitalistic ideology that promotes a schism between the Black man and Black woman. *A House Divided... No More (Time for Indigenous Communal Healing)* will answer the biblical questions: Is there a balm in Gilead? Is there no deliverance there? Why then is not the health of my people recovered? This book is representative of Empirical Hope: there is a balm in Gilead. There is deliverance from oppression in America. It is a message declaring that God is continuously raising up generational leaders (past, present, future). Evidence of things hoped for can be found in the contemporary and historic footprints of God's elect in America.

Part I: Unity Is the Key (Chapters 1, 2 and 3) will explore the heroic efforts of African American women who have labored tirelessly to unify our people. These noble women are model leaders of exemplary etiquette, grace and strength of character. Their individual and collective responses to grace under fire, the epitome of devotion for people under the tyranny of oppression, have set the precedent for all women of color. Chapter 1 will depict the lives and challenges of Michelle Obama, Mae Jemison and Rosa Parks; Chapter 2, Coretta Scott King, Ida B. Wells and Dorothy Tillman; and Chapter 3, Lyn Hughes, Margaret Burroughs and Yvette Moyo-Gillard. Collectively these leaders have decided there is a balm in Gilead, in America, and God, the Creator, has heard our cry by reason of the taskmasters.

Part II: Black Psychological Warfare (Chapters 4, 5 and 6) will examine the need to do battle against oppression by way of our intellectual talents. The ideologies of widely recognized and respected Black Alpha Males are a necessary corrective in restoring the African American Village Community to a state of respectability. Unity must be accompanied with countermeasures against the damaging indoctrination of complacency. Complacency with the 3/5 human label. Complacency with the unspoken rule that African Americans possess no rights that warrant respect from White America. Chapter 4 will examine the ideologies and leadership of Adam Clayton Powell, Sr., Adam Clayton Powell, Jr., John Lewis and James L. Farmer, Jr. Chapter 5 will continue the dialogue with notable scholars such as David Walker, Maulana Karenga and Dr. Jawanza Kunjufu. Chapter 6 will depict the Civil Rights activist Julian Bond and his award winning documentaries *A Time for Justice* and *Eyes on the Prize*, thus encompassing the historic footprints of Medgar Evers, Jimmie Lee Jackson, the historical Edmund Pettus Bridge Confrontation [Bloody Sunday] (including the three Selma-to-Montgomery marches), Project C (Confrontation), the D Day Children's Crusade and Emmett Till.

Finally, Part III: Divided...No More (Chapter 7) will examine past and present, local and national organizations and individuals who promote the continuous process of authentic Communal Healing throughout the greater African American Village Community. Inclusive in this concluding examination will be the National Association for the Advancement of Colored People (NAACP), Carter G. Woodson and the Association for the Study of African American Life and History (ASALH), Urban Prep Academies, Taki S. Raton (Blyden Delany Academy), Mrs. Gloria Jones (wife of Walter Jones, founder of Fathers Who Care), Alicia Archer (founder of CLEANkids) and the Deborah Movement (Mary Moore and Barbara Sanders).

This in-depth introduction, similar to my previous groundbreaking exegesis, *Brother to Brother (A Message of Hope),* will be followed by brief commentaries by my close friends and colleagues. Once again I am moved by the power of God, the Unmoved Mover (a Power greater than myself) to write another critical historical exegesis designed to empower the African American Village Community. It is with humility, the embracing of Empirical Hope, the unconditional belief in Cultural Utilitarianism, coupled with an uncompromised belief in the creation and nurturing of the Beloved Community that made this exploration possible. Through the bold presentation of two new Black liberation concepts (Communal Healing and Communal Initiatives) and a personal preternatural testimony of the African American Experience I present to my loyal readers of the Village Community *A House Divided... No More (Time for Indigenous Communal Healing).*

Glossary

2 P's (Providers & Protectors)
The God appointed human assignment of Black Alpha Males which consist of providing and protecting the inhabitants of the African American Village Community.

African American Experience
A unique historical experience derived from the pluralistic tribes of Africa who were forced to merge into one people during the long night of slavery to become African Americans.

African American Village Community
Indigenous group of African Americans whose preternatural ancestral bonds creates the promotion and the sustaining of the Village Concept in America.

Beloved Community
First coined by the 20th century philosopher-theologian Josiah Royce and used by Dr. Martin L. King and Mrs. Coretta Scott King: a global vision in which all people can share in the wealth of the earth…the unconditional promotion of an all inclusive spirit of sisterhood and brotherhood.

Black Alpha Males
The continuous lineage of male children derived from African descent representing the original (first) creation of humans by God.

Communal Healing
The spiritual restoration of cultural pride, self-esteem, and self-determination in juxtaposition to the complete absence of a bruised, wounded psyche caused by the implementation of institutionalized oppression.

Communal Initiative
The unification of the African American Village Community via the forming of cultural solidarity to break all forged links of institutionalized oppression in America.

Constructionist
A drum major for social justice representing the Talented Tenth (10%) of Black Alpha Males who embrace the human assignment of being the 2 P's (Providers & Protectors).

Crystallization of Cause & Effect
A rise in the consciousness of African Americans pertaining to the understanding of the destructive forces of capitalism and its agenda of global domination over the oppressed.

Cultural Utilitarianism
The promotion of the greatest good for the greatest number of people.

Destructionist
Black Alpha Males (70%) who embrace the title of public enemy number one due to his relentless violent assault upon his own oppressed people and Village Community.

Empirical Hope
A hope based on the African American Experience.

Ethic of Care
The need to nurture and support each other (the oppressed inhabitants of the African American Village Community) as we collectively struggle for racial equality in America.

Generation E (Entitlement)
Segments of the Village Community who are psychologically, socially, and spiritually detached from the past and present cultural struggles of their people. Allegiance and Black Pride is replaced with the arrogance of entitlement.

Glass Ceiling
A capitalistic weapon of mass human destruction and division which allows various forms of cultural strangulation.

Ground Zero
A time in history when the slaves excavated from Africa shared the common ideology of breaking any and all chains of human bondage…giving rise to a Communal Initiative.

Historical Discipline
The innate cultural awareness (specifically pertaining to African Americans) of the continuous communal struggle to obtain all levels of parity and respectability in America.

Historical Euthanasia
The categorical absence of Historical Discipline.

Inter-Related Structure of Black Reality
The cultural bridge (a collective consciousness) connecting the Inescapable Mutuality Paradigm and the African American Experience.

Inescapable Mutuality Paradigm
What ever affects one directly, affects all indirectly. I can never be what I ought to be until you are what you ought to be…and you can never be what you ought to be until I am what I ought to be.

Laissez-Faire Entitlement Syndrome
The negative mind-set of Generation E (claiming unearned rights) that perpetuates a total disconnect to the present and past struggles for (African Americans) equality in America.

Objectionist
Black Alpha Males (20%) who have consciously removed themselves from the allegiance and, or emotional attachment to the birthright of being born African American.

Rule of Annihilation
A capitalistic weapon of mass human destruction (political, social, economic, and educational castration) specifically targeting the Black Alpha Male Destructionist by promoting self-hatred and the encouragement of Black on Black violence.

Rule of Containment
A capitalistic weapon of mass human destruction (political, social, economic, and educational castration) specifically targeting the Black Alpha Male Constructionist who by nature will assume the role of being the Providers and Protectors of the African American Village Community.

Rule of Selective Engagement
A capitalistic weapon of mass human destruction (political, social, economic, and educational) specifically targeting the Black Alpha Male Objectionist who has removed himself from the continuous struggles of African Americans.

Slavocracy
A system of oppression supported by a ruling group of slaveholders or advocates of slavery, as in the southern United States before 1865.

Socialization of Division
The arrogant agenda (supporting cultural division) of the privileged White elite perpetuated by the continuous use of the Glass Ceiling.

Village Community
A sub-community within the greater African American Village Community who embrace the Village Concept.

Village Concept
The creation of indigenous self-reliant systems within the Village Community with the prime directive of addressing the unfinished task of emancipation in America.

Commentary: Timothy Johnson

A House Divided... No More is Dr. Michael James' most compelling work.

Dr. James' clarion call is being sounded so that present generations and those to come will feel and experience the vibrations and reverberations of his impassioned cry. In the pessimistic and lugubrious forecast for African American unity, Dr. James takes the painstaking steps to inspire us to the possibilities of what this unity can yield. He examines some of the splintered factions and begins to bring them together in order that The House is Divided No More. His keen insight and analysis on this subject matter is quite refreshing

"There are only two lasting bequests we can hope to give our children. One is roots, the other, wings" (Hodding Carter). Clearly, Dr. James, you have your roots. Now take your wings, and fly to your rightful place.

Pastor Timothy Johnson

Commentary: Kitty Fulce

Black American families and communities are divided and in crisis and their futures will be in limbo unless they take radical steps to change the status quo as it is today. The most effective changes should address existing conditions, habits, practices, policies and views within the African American Village Community. The following exegesis, *A House Divided... No More*, critically addresses the historical and cultural background of African Americans that led to past calls for change and reveals the need for a new call to action: to promote and achieve unity between Black males and females and ultimately the Village. Civil Rights activists and leaders, past and present, share a common belief that a people united will succeed. As a people, African Americans fought and struggled together because they had a sense of hope—hope entrenched deeply in our history. It is the responsibility of African American males and females to plant seeds of hope, to establish and maintain cultural pride, to elevate self-esteem, to educate, empower, equip, promote and strengthen families.

Aware that Blacks (former slaves) had no control over their lives and their existence was determined by someone else, Dr. James firmly believes that African Americans must take individual and collective responsibility for their own lives, for strengthening families and ultimately strengthening the African American Village Community at large. The time is long overdue for African Americans to stop perpetuating the Willie Lynch's theory. Instead it is time to embrace and activate the nurturing framework of family and build upon the foundation of the Nguzo Saba. It is time for African American males and females to break the divisive chains of oppression that have destroyed their self-esteem and contributed to the deterioration of the African American family unit.

Helen "Kitty" Fulce, MEd., CAS
Education Consultant & Advocate

xxii

Part I: Unity Is the Key

In a real sense all life is inter-related. All men are caught in an inescapable network of mutuality, tied in a single garment of destiny. Whatever affects one directly affects all indirectly...I can never be what I ought to be until you are what you ought to be, and you can never be what you ought to be until I am what I ought to be. This is the inter-related structure of reality.[1]

Dr. Martin L. King, Jr.

Chapter One	**Chapter Two**	**Chapter Three**
Michelle Obama	Coretta S. King	Lyn Hughes
Mae Jemison	Ida B. Wells	Margaret Burroughs
Rosa Parks	Dorothy Tillman	Yvette Moyo-Gillard

CHAPTER ONE

Shattering America's Glass Ceiling

Barack Obama was elected President of the United States on November 4, 2008. This historic landmark event awed and shocked America. Equally important to this unprecedented victory was that the President-elect was accompanied by his wife, Michelle Obama, and their two daughters, Malia and Sasha. The First Lady, an African American, serves as an inspiration to the preservation of Historical Discipline: this discipline can be defined as an innate cultural awareness of the past and continuous struggle of African Americans in their rise to respectability and parity over and against the tentacles of oppression. When the Glass Ceiling in America was shattered, the famous and historic words of Maya Angelou became applicable: "Bringing the gifts that my ancestors gave, I am the dream and the hope of the slave."[1] In retrospect, it was African American slaves and former slaves that provided the bulk of labor to build the White House, the United States Capital, and numerous other early government buildings.[2]

Construction on the White House (the President's house) originally began in 1792 in Washington, D.C. It is quite interesting that the building is strategically placed on land adjacent to two slave states: Maryland and Virginia.[3] It was African American slaves who painstakingly quarried and cut the rough stones to erect the walls. Freed men and slaves burnt bricks that lined the stone walls. Interesting and noteworthy, as they walk the halls of this mansion, the First Lady, her husband, mother and daughters represent years of blood, sweat and tears based on Empirical Hope. This hope is engraved and embedded in the African American Experience: a unique historical experience derived from the pluralistic tribes of Africa who were forced to merge into one people

3

during the long night of slavery to become today's African Americans. In retrospect, from the foundation of the first key cornerstones to the swearing in of President-elect Barack Obama, the First Lady and her family's presence in the White House reflect prior ancestral contributions to the challenging and final shattering of America's Glass Ceiling.

Contributions of prior drum majors for justice who embraced Empirical Hope derived from the African American Experience include Paul Jennings, born a slave on President James Madison's estate in 1799.[4] Jennings, "a body servant," found work at the Department of Interior. In 1865 he published *Colored Man's Reminiscences of James Madison*, the first memoir about the White House by one who lived side by side with the President.[5] Jemmy O'Neil, a Black doorkeeper and trusted servant, kept the keys to the White House during President's Andrew Jackson's term in office. During Lincoln's administration, Elizabeth Keckley, a former slave and talented seamstress, became Mary Todd Lincoln's close friend and confidante; Keckley made frequent visits to the White House to sew tailored garments. On October 29, 1864, Sojourner Truth, a respected abolitionist and advocate for women's rights, met and dined with President Lincoln. William Slade, a notable human fixture in the White House, not only became President Lincoln's friend and personal messenger but also became President Andrew Johnson's steward, friend and a Treasury Department employee.[6]

Empirical Hope, prior to the arrival of First Lady Michelle Obama and her family, accompanied the footsteps of abolitionist Fredrick Douglass. This drum major for justice not only advised President Lincoln on issues of emancipation and the treatment of African American troops during the Civil War, he also called on President Andrew Johnson in the East Room, appealing for support of voting rights for Black men.

President Rutherford B. Hayes made Douglass a Marshal of the District of Columbia, and in the year 1889, he was appointed American Consul General to Haiti. During his activism for social justice Douglass was regarded as the father of the early Civil Rights Movement.[7]

Michelle Obama serves as an embodiment of African Americans whose unique embrace of the African American Experience empowered their belief in God. God, the Creator, empowers the oppressed with Empirical Hope, a hope that would not allow the oppressed to lie dormant in a state of silent submission. Therefore, evidence of the confidence derived from this hope can be seen in the contributions of African American entertainers who made considerable contributions to the musical history of the White House. The accomplished pianist Blind Tom (Thomas Greene Bethune) created a sensation in the year 1859. This gifted African American, a musician who was blind and labeled mentally retarded, played the piano like Mozart, Beethoven and Gottschalk. The diva Marie (Selika) Williams presented a musical program, and the Fisk Jubilee Singers, who introduced the "spiritual" as an American art form, toured the White House in 1882. President Chester Arthur was moved to tears when the first Black choir to perform in the White House presented "Safe in the Arms of Jesus."[8] This tough act to follow was complimented by the great performer Matilda Sissieretta Joyner Jones (also known as Sissieretta Jones or the Black Patti in reference to Italian opera singer Adelina Patti) who sang opera arias and ballads for President Benjamin Harrison and his guest in 1892.

The shattering of and elevation over this unique Glass Ceiling (a capitalistic weapon of mass human destruction and division which allows various forms of cultural strangulation) at the White House encompasses the historic visit of Booker T. Washington. Washington walked the prestigious floors of the White House, including the basement where former slaves once lived. The basement, open at ground level on the south end (referred to as the ground floor today), had windows on the north facing a deep areaway that were intentionally hidden from view. Be that as it may, Washington walked proudly with his autobiography, *Up from Slavery*, in his hand to the prestigious Blue Room where he was greeted by President-elect Roosevelt. "The furor over the dinner—the first time that an African American was entertained at the White House—revealed the structure's symbolic power and the bigotry then at large in the nation."[9] Civil Rights activist and journalist William Monroe Trotter similarly caused a stir in 1914 when he challenged the president for allowing the segregation of Black federal employees in the workplace. Notably Trotter's nonviolent protest and demonstrations became a model for the Civil Rights Movement from 1940 to 1970.[10]

The same historic footprints made in Washington were followed by Oscar De Priest's election to Congress in 1928, thereby creating a social, political dilemma for the White House. During his three terms (1928–1935), De Priest was the only African American serving in Congress. Most importantly, he brought with him to the office his African American wife, Mrs. De Priest. During the traditional White House Tea for Congressional wives, controversy ensued. Because of the decision of several Southern members' to boycott the tea, Lou Hoover arranged a separate tea party for Mrs. De Priest at the White House with a few chosen, willing guests. Michelle Obama's marriage to Barack and her undisputed claim to the title of First Lady address the historic shame and bigotry of Southerners during the late 1920's "who did not want the impression conveyed that the nation would sanction the social equality of the races."[11]

Prior to Michelle and shortly after the shameful De Priest incident, the Glass Ceiling would be challenged by the wife of President-elect Franklin Roosevelt, Eleanor Roosevelt, in 1939 during the gala "Evening of American Music"[12]. White House history was made again in a most memorable performance by Marian Anderson's exquisite rendition of Schubert's "Ave Maria."[13] Anderson's powerful voice soared to the delight of King George VI and Queen Elizabeth of England. A few months prior to this event, the gifted African American moved an audience of 75,000 to tears at the steps of the Lincoln Memorial. Mrs. Roosevelt resigned from the DAR (Daughters of the American Revolution) when they adamantly refused to grant her an appearance at Constitution Hall. In defiance she arranged the event for Anderson at the Lincoln Memorial.

Needless to say, Michelle and her family stand on the backs of other first African Americans such as E. Fredrick Morrow, the first to serve in an executive position on a president's staff at the White House. As the sole African American appointed to the staff by President Eisenhower to deal with racial tensions related to integration, this lone drum major for social justice faced insurmountable (unspeakable) personal and professional struggles during his appointment. His autobiography, *Black Man in the White House*, leaves an invaluable testimony of the African American Experience.[14] Similarly, Rev. Dr. Martin L. King, Jr. walked to the East Room of the White House to witness a major victory in the struggle for racial equality when Lyndon B. Johnson signed into law the Civil Rights Act of 1964. President Johnson made history by appointing Robert Weaver as the Secretary of Housing and Urban Development and Thurgood Marshall as Associate Supreme Court Justice.[15] Noticeable cracks in the Glass Ceiling became apparent when President Johnson appointed more African American judges than any other president before him and opened the White House not only to select Black athletes and performers but also to Black religious, civic and political leaders in significant numbers.[16]

Prior notable ancestral contributions to the First Lady's occupation in the White House can be traced to Robert J. Brown, an African American member of President Nixon's staff assigned to promote Black colleges. John Calhoun, an African American assistant to President Ford, carried the torch for funding Black colleges.

On August 10, 1989, President Bush raised a few eyebrows as to the vulnerability of the Glass Ceiling when he appointed General Colin Powell as Chairman of the Joint Chiefs of Staff. Prior to this appointment, Powell served as White House Fellow in 1972 and worked as an executive assistant during the Carter Administration in the Energy and Defense Departments. Colin Powell was President Reagan's National Security Advisor for two years (1987–1989).[17] President George W. Bush appointed General Colin Powell to the office of Secretary of State. In addition, Rod Paige became the presiding Secretary of Education. Dr. Condoleezza Rice, an African American (the first ever), was appointed to the distinguished cabinet position of Assistant to the President for National Security Affairs.[18] Throughout the 20th century, distinguished African Americans such as Lillian Rogers Parks (seamstress/maid, 1929–1961), Alonzo Fields (butler and maitre d', 1931–1962), Preston Bruce (doorman, 1953–1976) and Eugene Allen (chief butler and maitre d', 1952–1976) have, similar to the slaves, believed that they had an inalienable God-given right to sit at the table of humanity and represent African Americans.[19]

The torch now has been passed on to the Obamas, and notably and deservingly Michelle will hold hands with one of the most powerful men in the world, Barack. She is the solid anchor of a strong African American family, chosen by God *for such a time as this.* In support of the Inter-Related Structure of Black Reality, it is believed that we are a total sum of our past. In addition, this historic connectedness encompasses African Americans who have directly and indirectly assisted in the shattering of the Glass Ceiling.

Michelle Obama's roots (historic family lineage) can be traced to a tiny wooden cabin lining a dirt road known as Slave Street (outside of Georgetown, South Carolina) during the early 1800's. Michelle's ancestors lived among the 200 slaves residents and remained there after the Civil War. "The last tenants abandoned the hovels about three decades ago and even they would have struggled to imagine a distant daughter of the plantation one day calling the White House home."[20]

The Glass Ceiling in America came face to face with a now famous speech on race during the Presidential primary when Barack stated, "He was married to a Black American who carry within her the blood of slaves and slave owners."[21] Jim Robinson, Michelle's great-great-grandfather who labored as a sharecropper in the mosquito-infested rice fields along the Sampit River and who could not read or write, can now rest in peace. Frances Cheston Train, the new owner whose family purchased the property during the 1930's and transformed the land into a hunting preserve, captures the moment (the shattering of America's Glass Ceiling) when she states, "It's beyond healing."[22] Train said of Obama's success, "What it has given everyone is a sense of pride that this amazing, intelligent and attractive couple could be connected to Friendfield."[23] The word connected explicitly supports the Inescapable Mutuality Paradigm. This paradigm supports the hypothesis that we are dependent upon each other to become what we ought to be. Healing takes place when the oppressed and the oppressor allow our innate commonalities to replace our differences and our differences to be embraced and accepted as a design implemented by God, the Creator. God never makes a mistake.

Furthermore, when Michelle Obama moved to the White House, *indigenous Communal Healing* began to transcend the pain caused by the dark years of Slavocracy. Moreover, as she embarked on a life that her great-great-grandfather never could have envisioned for his descendants, Empirical Hope greeted her and *the First Family* at the doorsteps of the White House. The long night of slavery, accompanied by the Socialization of Division (a weapon of mass human destruction designed to destroy the fabric of a binding union and Ground Zero communality between African American males, females and the family structure), had failed: it failed in its attempt to convey to the female that the Black Alpha Male could no longer perform his human assignment in the African American Village Community (i.e., to Provide and Protect.) Michelle publicly and privately affirmed her belief in a healthy, productive union between males and females of African descent, particularly African Americans.

Michelle has quietly and eloquently modeled the integrity and strength derived from the blood flow of former slaves and the extraordinary empowerment of the African American Experience. The strength of the Black family and supporting and honoring the leadership of the Black Alpha Male (her soul mate) became a categorical imperative in not only boldly approaching but shattering the Glass Ceiling in America.

In addition to the debut of Michelle at the White House, the Glass Ceiling would also be shattered in space. It is well to note that prior to Mae Jemison's historic flight, other women launched both an individual and collective assault on the ceiling in space. It is only proper and fitting that honorable mention of bold these pioneers be stated for recorded history. The list includes the following: Myrtle K. Cagle, Jerrie Cobb, Jan Dietrich, Wally Funk, Jane Hart, Gene Nora Jessen, Irene Leverton, Sarah Gorelick Ratley, Bernice B. Steadman, Jerri Sloan Truhill, Rhea Allison Woltman and for their families, the late Marion Dietrich and Jean Hixson.[24] Notably, Sally Ride shattered the Glass Ceiling at large for American women, and Eileen Collins extended the historic giant step for women in space by becoming the first woman to lead and command a NASA mission. Prior to Collins, Ride and Jameson, accomplished women pilots were tested in the 1960's. The women scored well and at times outscored their male counterparts, including the famed Mercury 7 astronauts. During the 11th hour NASA told the women (unapologetically) to simply go home.[25] Mercy 13 member Jerri Sloan Truhill was among the disregarded females during the summer of 1961. Her spirit was crushed. "Women (including women of color specifically) who struggle to open doors that have been closed to them know that the fight for equal rights takes many steps, not a single small one."[26]

In retrospect, from an African American perspective, Guion S. Bluford, Jr., born in Philadelphia on November 22, 1942, had previously set the stage for Jemison's debut by becoming the first African American to fly in space as a mission specialist on the Challenger Space Shuttle STS-8. It was 3:40 a.m. on September 5, 1983, when the Challenger landed smoothly within 300 feet of its target.[27] The humble Bluford responded rather gracefully to the extremely loud and continuous thunderous applause, acknowledging him as the first African American astronaut. Be that as it may, America's Glass Ceiling supporting the Rule of Containment and the Rule of Selective Engagement was still in place. Respectively, the former rule can be defined as a system that carefully monitors African Americans who promote self pride and dignity, offering them limited opportunities for advancement

11

in White America. The latter rule is a system that promotes, embrace and celebrate African Americans who publicly and privately disassociate themselves with their culture.

Faced with these formidable weapons of determent, Mae Jemison, born in Decatur, Alabama, on October 17, 1956, and whose family moved to Chicago, took her childhood dream of space flight to NASA (accompanied by the African American Experience and Historical Discipline) and shattered the Glass Ceiling. In addition, she was also the first African American woman to be admitted into the astronaut training program. On September 12, 1992, Mae Jemison and six other astronauts flew into space aboard the Endeavour flight, Mission STS-47. During the eight days of flight, the first African American female astronaut conducted weightlessness and motion sickness experiments both on herself and the crew. The successful flight returned to earth on September 20, 1992.[28] However, prior to her return, Jemison's satellite conference from space to the Museum of Science and Industry (Chicago) on Wednesday evening was groundbreaking. Needless to say, it held unprecedented value to the students attending Morgan Park High School, Jemison's alma mater. Moreover, as previously mentioned, her family moved to Chicago when she was 3 ½ years old. She attended Dumas School and Esmond School prior to her successful enrollment at Morgan Park High School. It was here (Morgan Park) that the now famous African American acquired and developed her critical skills in mathematics and science, excelling in these perspective subjects.[29]

Mae Jemison, in her own quiet way, promotes the concept of Cultural Utilitarianism, the greatest good for the greatest number of people. She is acutely aware that her achievements have shattered stereotypes, paving the way and making it easier for other women (including women of color) and other minority groups to succeed. Jemison affirms that:

> People don't see women particularly Black women in science and technology fields...my participation in the space shuttle mission helps to say that all people of the world have astronomers, physicists, and explorers.[30]

In juxtaposition to this candid affirmation, Jemison (similar to Michelle Obama) gracefully and eloquently carried the distinguished honor of first African American with dignity, pride and an unconditional commitment to remain humble. It would be safe to say that both women, whether consciously or unconsciously, became aware at some point that many of our predecessors endured and gracefully suffered unspeakable human atrocities for the liberation and advancement of our people. It was a result of the unselfish collective sacrifices and insurmountable perseverance (of the pluralistic tribes aboard the Mothership at Ground Zero) and their ultimate willingness to merge into a strong race of African Americans: African Americans who would ultimately fertilized this single moment in history for the daughters of the descendants of slaves to occupy. Notably, Jemison not only carries the torch of Empirical Hope humbly, but six months after her flight she resigned from NASA. In the tradition of the spirit of other dreamers, she proclaimed these words of hope: "I leave with the honor of having been the first woman of color in space and with an appreciation of NASA, the organization that gave me the opportunity to make one of my dreams possible."[31]

The Inescapable Mutuality Paradigm moved upon Jemison's spirit well after her historic space mission. The first African American female in space brought something new and innovative to the scientific arena: a blend of social and hard sciences, if you will. Mae Jemison believed that:

13

In today's technological world, it is imperative that the scientist is cognizant, concerned and active in social issues. It is also necessary for all people to have a feel for and knowledge of how science and technology affect their everyday world.[32]

Dr. Jemison founded the Jemison Group, Inc., located in Houston, Texas, to research, develop and implement advanced technologies suited to the social, political, cultural and economic context of the individual. Current projects of this unique foundation include Alpha ™, a satellite-based telecommunications system designed to improve health care in West Africa, and The Earth We Share ™, an international science camp for student's ages 12 years old to 16. This initiative utilizes an experiential curriculum. Furthermore, Jemison is committed to ensuring that science and technology fields become representative of the rich diversities of people in the United States, including full gender, ethnic and social diversities. By any and all means necessary, she is determined "to encourage all people, especially women and minorities, to pursue careers in science and any other field of their choice."[33]

In addition, to promoting the Inescapable Mutuality Paradigm, Jemison brought items on board the space mission that represented some of her primary concerns, such as racism, a consciousness for racial equality and access to a quality education. She carried a flag from the Organization of African Unity and proclamations from the DuSable Museum of African American History in Chicago and the Chicago Public Schools.[34] During the flight she displayed a poster advertising the Alvin Ailey Dance Theatre and was especially proud of a special banner from a special educational institution that teaches mathematics and science to children in preschool through second grade. The school bears the name, The Mae C. Jemison Academy (Detroit, Michigan).[35] "The children are the same age Jemison was when she first had to fight stereotypes to pursue her interest in science."[36] Prior to the historic Endeavour Mission in 1992, Cornell University (New York) Medical School presented her with the opportunity (via a financial grant) to travel to Kenya and conduct health studies. The Inescapable Mutuality Paradigm surfaced when she participated in solving the health care issues for people affected by disease and poverty on the African continent. "Jemison enjoyed living in the predominantly black society of Kenya (Africa), a place where she never encountered racial prejudice."[37] While studying at Cornell University she visited Thailand and Asia. During this assignment Jemison treated refugees for various diseases such as malnutrition, dysentery, tuberculosis and numerous other health issues.

The shattering of the Glass Ceiling in America by Jemison was accompanied by honors and awards that our slave ancestors at Ground Zero could have never imagined. Distinguished awards bestowed on the youngest child of Charlie Jemison, a roofer and carpenter, and Dorothy (Green) Jemison, an elementary school teacher, include the following: People Magazine's 50 Most Beautiful People/World (1993), CORE Outstanding Achievement Award (1993), Induction into the National Women's Hall of Fame (1993), Kilby Science Award (1993), Montgomery Fellow, Dartmouth (1993), Turner Trumpet Award (1993), Ebony's 50 Most Influential Women (1993), Mae C. Jemison Science and Space Museum, Wright Jr. College, Chicago (dedicated 1992), Johnson Publication's Black Achievement Trailblazers Award (1992), Pumpkin Magazine's (a Japanese monthly) One of the Women for the Coming New Century (1991), McCall's 10 Outstanding Women for the 90's (1991), Honorary Doctor of Letters, Winston-Salem, North Carolina (1991), Honorary Doctorate of Science, Lincoln College, Pennsylvania (1991), Gamma Sigma Gamma Women of the year (1989) and the Essence Award (1988).[38]

In examining the early life and education of Jemison it is well to note that her parents moved to Chicago during the latter part of the Great Migration to take advantage of better educational opportunities for poor and middle-class African Americans. The fertile ground of her parent's marriage (a unified African American family) produced a curious child who spent hours in the school library, reading books on astronomy and science. In an unspoken proclamation, the sky has always been the limit for Jemison. Her strong family structure empowered her to face all forms of racism and prejudice with dignity and honor.

Jemison unapologetically possessed the fortitude to excel in academics and stood up firmly, pushing forward and upward against the Glass Ceiling in America. Similar to Michelle Obama, she was mindful of her predecessors and consciously employed the use of uncompromised aspects of Historical Discipline, thereby never entertaining the negative aspects of the tenets of Historical Euthanasia, the absence of cultural awareness of the past and continuous struggles of African Americans in their rise to respectability and parity at every level of human intercourse. Jemison boldly claimed her right to a seat at the table of humanity when she stated:

> When I'm asked about the relevance to Black people of what I do, I take that as an affront. It presupposes that Black people have never been involved in exploring the heavens, but this is not so, ancient African empires, Mali and Songhai, had scientist, and astronomers. The fact is space and its resources belong to all of us, not to any one group.[39]

When asked to name the most influential people (heroes) in her life, Jemison insists on her website, "My mother and father, siblings, teachers, uncles, and aunts, next door neighbors and friends, because I knew them day to day."[40] In support of the Village Concept, she believed that each of their characters and values taught her important lessons about life. She commends her mother for taking the time to teach her the importance of intellectual challenges and lifelong learning. Grounded in her African American family values, Jemison, who dared to go where no woman had gone before, remained incredibly humble. She carries the torch of Empirical Hope in an eloquent way by stating:

> I want people to see that explorers can be from every gender and every ethnic group. I can't pay too much attention to being called a role model. If I do, I may become too self- conscious. On the other hand, I feel a tremendous amount of responsibility to provide an image that people can use. It's not only for young black girls but for everyone because the images you see affect the way you judge and relate to people.[41]

Notwithstanding Mae Jemison and Michelle Obama humbly relate their struggles to any and all oppressed people, they still possess an unapologetic Black Consciousness and remain loyal to the continuous struggles of their people. Therefore, this consciousness identifies and acknowledges the existence of the Glass Ceiling in America, a ceiling that represents a formable weapon of mass human destruction against their people, African Americans. African Americans (an extraordinary people) can best be distinguished from other oppressed people of color due to the uniqueness of the African American Experience, a preternatural experience. Moreover, their commitment (Obama and Jemison) to a higher calling beyond their respective lives supports the famous words of John Donne, "Any man's death diminishes me, because I am involved in mankind. And therefore never send to know for whom the bell tolls; it tolls for thee."[42]

In retrospect, prior to First Lady Michelle Obama and the first African American female astronaut, Mae Jemison, Rosa Parks, a seamstress, an experienced warrior, activist and drum major for social justice with a strong unapologetic belief in the *Beloved Community,* claimed her seat and a seat for her people at the table of humanity on December 1, 1955. Parks was arrested for her public defiance in the segregated city of Montgomery, Alabama, when she adamantly refused to surrender her seat to a White passenger.

Rosa Louise McCauley-Parks was born on February 4, 1913 in Tuskegee, Alabama. Her activism for Civil Rights was entrenched in the African American Experience. She was the granddaughter of former slaves and the daughter of James McCauley, a professional carpenter by trade, and Leona Edwards McCauley, a rural school teacher[43]. The mother of the modern day (now historical) Civil Rights Movement grew up in Montgomery, Alabama. She proudly attended the all-Black Alabama State College where her cultural pride and strength of character were nurtured. On December 18, 1932, Parks was wed to a barber, Raymond Parks. They both were active in the Montgomery Chapter of the National Association for the Advancement of Colored People (NAACP).

Parks resented that segregation was a way of life for the inhabitants of the African American Village Community. African Americans were required to enter the front of the bus to pay, however, they had to exit the same door and re-board through the back door of the bus. In retrospect, White drivers in the South were invested with police officers, and they publicly and routinely harassed African Americans. Many riders suffered the humiliation of paying their fares and prior to re-boarding the White drivers intentionally drove away. In addition to this oppressive practice, during peak hours, the boundary markers separating the White section from the colored section would be intentionally pushed back further, thereby allowing more White passengers to comfortably sit.[44]

The spirit and presence of a preternatural bond for a common cause (equality) similar to Ground Zero surfaced in the African American Village Community. The Montgomery Chapter of the NAACP braced itself for a test case, a case that would challenge the legality of segregated seating. It was time for a planned massive public protest to confront the Goliath of segregation. On the morning after the historic Parks arrest, all parties galvanizing for a movement agreed to let the NAACP take the case. Within 24 hours of the arrest, the WPC (Women's Political Council), led by Joann Robinson, passed the word through the African American Village Community to support a one-day bus boycott. WPC distributed more than 52,000 fliers, and on December 5, 1955, the Montgomery buses were virtually empty of African American passengers.

The city of Montgomery came to a standstill as African Americans begin to carpool, walk, bike and take cabs together (three to five passengers at a time) to work. Sadly, after her lawyer, Ed D. Gray appealed her case in the Circuit Court and (as planned) refused to pay the $14 fine, Rosa lost her job at the Montgomery Fair Department Store. Rosa Parks was also continuously and viciously harassed by those who opposed integration and threats to her life became common. However, the boycott became an important cornerstone of the Civil Rights Movement. Parks and her husband would later move to Detroit to work for U.S. Representative John Conyers, Jr.[45] During the initial protest, African Americans and other White sympathizers successfully organized and promoted a massive ongoing boycott of the city bus lines that last 381 days.

In addition, a young, powerful, energetic orator from Dexter Avenue Baptist Church became the spokesman for the Montgomery Bus Boycott. Martin L. King, in a wise, intellectual strategy, ushered in the philosophy of nonviolent protest. In retrospect, it saved thousands of lives on both sides of the color line. Most importantly, the final death warrant of Jim Crow came face to face with the embodiment of the uncompromised entrenched devotion to Historical Discipline encased in Rosa Parks. It is well to note that during the 1920's and 1930's, Montgomery, including the entire state of Alabama, was not a hospitable city. African Americans were faced with daily rounds of laws governing the acceptable oppressive conditions of all former slaves. The great-great granddaughter of former slaves always detested the practice of drinking from special water fountains and/or having to avoid lunch counters at restaurants designated specifically for Whites only. Eloise Greenfield, a contributor to *Ms. Magazine*, wrote:

> "With her mother's help, Rosa was able to grow up proud of herself and other Black people even while living with these rules...Rosa grew up believing that people should be judged by the respect they have for themselves and others." [46]

The hearse carrying Jim Crow accompanied Parks to the police station as she was booked, fingerprinted and jailed. The snapshot of Parks, now found in history books, stands as a testimonial caption of the final obituary (the official death) of the one of the most inhumane racial systems since Slavocracy. Prior to the decision of the African American Village Community to disconnect the life support of Jim Crow, E. D. Nixon called a liberal White lawyer, Clifford Durr, to represent Parks. After 381 days without life support (the daily ridership of thousands of African Americans who refuse to pump financial, social, physical and psychological life into the decaying corpse), Jim Crow was laid to rest in Montgomery, Alabama, on December 21, 1956. After more than a year of bus boycotting and legal battles, the Montgomery city buses were desegregated.[47] In promoting the African American Experience and Parks' efforts to initiate a city-wide movement, President Bill Clinton issued the following statement in the 1996 publication of *Jet Magazine*: "When she sat down on the bus, she stood up for the American ideals of equality and justice and demanded that the rest of us do the same."[48] Detroit Mayor Dennis Archer was quoted by *PR Newswire* in the following manner: "Her dignity and grace has inspired generations of freedom fighters and defenders of human rights."[49]

In moving upward, pressing against and shattering the Glass Ceiling in America, Parks was not, by any stretch of the imagination, consumed by the prospect of making history. She was consumed "By the tedium of survival in the Jim Crow South. The tedium had become unbreakable, and Rosa Parks acted to change it. Then she was an outlaw. Today she is a hero"[50]—a hero who promoted the Inescapable Mutuality Paradigm by calling to remembrance the 1954 Supreme Court ruling in the landmark case *Brown v. Board of Education* (Topeka, Kansas). This case sent a message to America that segregation in public schools was unconstitutional, thereby overturning the historic 1896 *Plessy v. Ferguson* ruling which sanctioned the separate but equal doctrine. Parks was a modern day hero who called to remembrance the Emmett Till tragedy when two White men, J.W. Milam and Roy Bryant, were arrested but later acquitted by an all-White jury for the brutal beating that led to the death of the 14 year-old African American from Chicago who was visiting his family in Mississippi. By virtue of her Historical Discipline, Parks almost single-handedly set in motion a revolution in the southern United States, a revolution moved by the collective spirit of Ground Zero that would eventually secure equal treatment under the law for generations of African Americans.

21

For those who lived through the unsettling 1950's and 1960's and joined the Civil Rights Movement, the soft spoken Rosa Parks was more, much more than a woman who refused to give up her seat to a White man in Montgomery, Alabama. Hers was an act that forever changed White America's view of Black people and forever changed America itself.[51]

Parks proved that the Glass Ceiling in America was not impenetrable. She proved that collectively, under the unifying goal to demand a seat at the table of humanity, emancipation and deliverance were obtainable and realistic goals. She proved that oppression and marginalization could be defeated through the preternatural collective empowerment of the African American Experience and the Inescapable Mutuality Paradigm. Needless to say, the lesson of the Montgomery Bus Boycott, inclusive of the well organized grassroots strategies, became a launching pad for the continuous assault against the Glass Ceiling. Throughout the years, the relentless assault against inequality would be witnessed in the following events:

- 1957 January, February. Martin Luther King, Charles K. Steele and Fred L. Shuttlesworth establish the Southern Christian Leadership Conference, of which King is made the first president. SCLC became a major force in organizing the Civil Rights Movement and its principles that were based on nonviolence and civil disobedience.

- 1957 September. Little Rock, Arkansas. Formerly all-White Central High School aggressively greets nine Black students during open enrollment. President Eisenhower sends the National Guard and federal troops to intervene on behalf of the students who became known as "The Little Rock Nine".

- 1960 February. Greensboro, North Carolina. Four determined African American students from North Carolina Agricultural and Technical College begin a sit-in at a segregated Woolworth's lunch counter. The event triggers many similar nonviolent protests in the South. The lunch counters were segregated six months later.

- 1960 April. Raleigh, North Carolina. SNCC (Student Nonviolent Coordinating Committee) is founded at Shaw University, providing young Blacks with a place in the Civil Rights Movement. Stokely Carmichael would later assume leadership of the organization.

- 1961 May. SNCC (Student Nonviolent Coordinating Committee) and CORE (Congress of Racial Equality) sponsor Freedom Riders and student volunteers to take trips through the South to test out the new laws that prohibit segregation in interstate travel facilities, which includes bus and railway stations.

- 1962 October. James Meredith becomes the first Black student to enroll at the University of Mississippi. Violence and riots surround the incident, and President Kennedy sends in 5,000 federal troops.

- 1963 April. Martin Luther King is arrested and jailed during an anti-segregation protest in Birmingham, Alabama. He writes his seminal "Letter from Birmingham Jail," arguing that individuals have the moral duty to disobey unjust laws.

- 1963 May. During a Civil Rights protest in Birmingham, Alabama, Commissioner of Public Safety

Eugene "Bull" Connor uses fire hoses and police attack dogs on nonviolent Black demonstrators.

- 1963 June. Jackson, Mississippi. Mississippi's NAACP field secretary, 37 years-old Medgar Evers, is murdered outside his home. Bryon De La Beckwith is tried twice in 1964; both trials result in hung juries. Thirty years later he is convicted for murdering Evers.

- 1963 August. Washington, D.C. About 200,000 people join the March on Washington. Congregating at the Lincoln Memorial, participants listen as Martin Luther King delivers his famous "I Have a Dream" speech.

- 1964 January. The 24th Amendment abolishes the poll tax, which originally had been instituted in 11 southern states after Reconstruction to make it difficult for poor Blacks to vote.

- 1964 Early-Summer. The Council of Federated Organizations (COFO), a national network of Civil Rights groups that includes CORE and SNCC, launches a massive effort to register local Black voters during what becomes known as Freedom Summer.

- 1964 July. President Lyndon B. Johnson signs the Civil Rights Act of 1964. This particular act becomes the most sweeping Civil Rights Legislation since the Reconstruction Era. The Civil Rights Act prohibits discrimination of all kinds based on race, color, religion or national origin. The law provides the federal government with the judicial powers to enforce desegregation.

- 1965 March. Selma, Alabama. Blacks begin a march to Montgomery in support of voting rights but are stopped at the Edmund Pettus Bridge by a police blockade. The incident is dubbed "Bloody Sunday."

- 1965 August. Congress passes the Voting Rights Act of 1965, making it easier for Southern Blacks to register to vote. Literacy tests, poll taxes and other such requirements that were used to restrict Blacks from voting are made illegal.

- 1965 August. Watts, California. Race riots erupt in a Black section of Los Angeles.

- 1965 September. President Johnson issues Executive Order 11246, which enforces affirmative action for the first time. All aspects of the hiring and employment of minorities are now monitored by the government.

- 1966 October. Oakland, California. The militant group known as the Black Panthers is founded by Huey Newton and Bobby Seale.

- 1967 April. Stokely Carmichael, a leader of the Student Nonviolent Coordinating Committee (SNCC), coins the phrase "Black Power" during a public speech in Seattle. Black Power would become the battle cry for the younger generation involved in Civil Rights.

- 1967 June. In *Loving v. Virginia*, the Supreme Court issues a ruling that prohibiting interracial marriages is unconstitutional.

- 1968 April. President Johnson signs the Civil Rights Act of 1968, prohibiting discrimination in the sale, rental and financing of housing.

- 1971 April. The United States Supreme Court, in *Swann v. Charlotte-Mecklenburg Board of Education*, upholds busing as a legitimate means for achieving the integration of public schools.

- 1988 March. Overriding President Reagan's veto, Congress passes the Civil Rights Restoration Act, which expands the reach of nondiscrimination laws within private institutions receiving federal funds.

- 1991 November. After two years of debates, vetoes and threatened vetoes, President Bush reverses himself and signs the Civil Rights Act of 1991, strengthening existing Civil Rights laws and providing for damages in cases of intentional employment discrimination.

- 2008 January. Senator Edward Kennedy introduces the Civil Rights Act of 2008. Some of the proposed provisions include ensuring that federal funds are not used to subsidize discrimination, holding employers accountable for age discrimination and improving accountability for other violations of Civil Rights and worker's rights.[52]

During the course of her life, Rosa Parks received more than 43 honorary doctorate degrees, many honorary keys to metropolitan cities throughout the U.S. and hundreds of plaques, certificates and citations, including a distinguished honorary degree from Soka University, Tokyo, Japan.[53] Notably, she was the recipient of the NAACP's Spingarn Medal, the UAW's Social Justice Award, the Martin L. King,

Jr. Non-Violent Peace Prize and the 1994 Rosa Parks Peace Prize in Stockholm, Sweden. In September 1996, President Clinton gave Mrs. Parks the Medal of Freedom, the absolute highest award given to a civilian citizen.[54]

Prior to her death on October 24, 2005, in honor of her late husband Raymond Parks (1903–1977), the Civil Rights activist (with the invaluable assistance of Ms. Elaine Eason Steele) developed the Rosa and Raymond Parks Institute for Self-Development's (Pathways to Freedom Program), which traces the Underground Railroad into the Civil Rights Movement and beyond. Mrs. Parks and other national leaders talk with youth, ages 11 through 17, as they participate in historic and educational research. Moreover, as they journey primarily by bus, similar to the Freedom Riders of the 1960's, the two categorical questions become, Where have we been? and Where are we going?[55] In a quiet exemplification of *courage under fire*, determination and dignity, Mrs. Rosa Parks approached the Glass Ceiling with a spiritual unction to survive and be recognized as an essential part of God's creation. She was acutely aware that the battle does not go to the swift or the strong but to those who endure until the end. She was acutely aware that at that particular point in time in African American history, the Glass Ceiling (a weapon of mass human destruction) had to be confronted by a people who would adamantly refuse to go silently into the night. The house, which was once purposely divided, was divided no more. Collectively we decided that a movement by the people, of the people and for the people shall never perish from the earth, and a house divided against itself cannot stand. She joined hands with her God appointed male counterparts and unapologetically declared to the world: we will, we must and we shall overcome, and we will use any and all resources available to us.

CHAPTER TWO

The Crystallization of Cause and Effect

The lives of Mrs. Rosa Parks and Mrs. Coretta Scott King became historically connected on December 1, 1955: Parks refused to yield her seat on a Montgomery city bus to a White passenger and was immediately arrested for civil disobedience. This brave stand by Parks ignited a citywide bus boycott. The bus boycott drew the attention of the world to the injustices of segregation and Jim Crow. In examining the crystallization of oppression (the causes) and its inhumane atrocities (the effects) on the oppressed, the debut of the historic U.S. Civil Rights Movement (inclusive of the Montgomery Bus Boycott) can be summed up in the eloquent words of Mrs. King who once stated:

> There is a spirit and a need and a man, woman at the beginning of every great human advancement. Every one of these must be right for that particular moment of history, or nothing happens."[1]

Moving by the power of God, Mrs. King, Dr. King and Mrs. Parks ushered in the spirit of nonviolent protest to combat the forces of segregation, bigotry and hatred. Mrs. King supported the ideology of the Beloved Community, a global vision in which all people can come and sit at the table of humanity and share equally in the wealth of the earth. This high tower philosophy stood against the present system of strife and racial division that continuously promotes what appears to be a permanent schism between Whites and the African American Village Community. In retrospect, the driving force of the evil schism surfaced daily on the public transportation systems throughout this nation. Mrs. Coretta Scott King believed that unity is the key, unity among African

Americans as well as unity among the pluralistic races of the earth. The effects of purposely holding a race hostage by intentionally denying their Civil Rights bestowed upon every human by God became unacceptable. The philosophy of unification surfaced again and again in her speeches prior to and after the assassination of her husband. Mrs. King continuously supported the belief that, "Freedom and justice cannot be parceled out in pieces to suit political convenience. I don't believe you can stand for freedom for one group and deny it to others."[2] This ideology on uncompromised equality and social justice coincidentally supports the hypothesis of Cultural Utilitarianism, the greatest good for the greatest number of people.

Mrs. King's marriage to such a great leader can never be understated. She alone, in their quiet moments of family life and away from the cameras and cheering crowds during the historic campaign for Civil Rights (including the March on Washington), created an environment conducive for the Black Alpha Male Constructionist to become a great leader and fulfill his destiny. She not only agreed with the Inescapable Mutuality Paradigm, she lived it! She was acutely aware of the negative effects it would have not only on her husband, family, friends and children if she became a personal stumbling block to her husband's vocation, but it would also have an enormous catastrophic (negative) effect on the Civil Rights Movement. She unapologetically modeled her marriage and the importance of the public and private spirit of unity on that of her in-laws. "Mama and Daddy King represent the best in manhood and womanhood, the best in a marriage, the kind of people we are trying to become." [3]

The spirit of Ground Zero nurtured, groomed and ministered to her during the quiet moments of life. She intuitively became aware that she could either become the catalyst for a great movement by standing side by side with a great man who was propelled by the hopes, dreams and prayers of our ancestors aboard the mothership, or she could become the self-serving wife who claimed her undisputed right to her husband. It is historically accurate and safe to say that she embraced the former.

Mrs. King walked with and endorsed not only the philosophy of nonviolence, but she also promoted the concept of the Beloved Community. In retrospect, after the forced separation of thousands upon thousands of slave time marriages, the house would be divided...no more. The effects of Willie Lynch, Jim Crow and modern day psychological weapons of mass human destruction (including the social, economic, educational and political strangulation of African Americans) would not cause a schism between Mrs. and Mr. King, between Coretta King and the Civil Rights Movement, between Coretta King and the creation and sustaining of the Beloved Community; a Beloved Community that nurtures an all-inclusive spirit of sisterhood and brotherhood. A special community where racism and all forms of discrimination, bigotry and prejudice will be replaced with an unconditional invitation to sit at the table of humanity. A special all-inclusive community where poverty, hunger and homelessness will not be tolerated; it will not, by any stretch of the imagination, be tolerated because new communal standards of human decency will not allow it! A community where international disputes will be resolved by any and all forms of peaceful resolutions and solutions saturated with the audacity of hope. A world community where all races will come to realize that love and trust will always triumph over hatred and fear, and justice and peace will prevail over war and the impromptu use of nuclear weapons.[4] In advocating the use of nonviolent protest as a means to defeat evil, Mrs. King realized that notwithstanding the oppression of her people was ethically and morally wrong and caused undue, unearned suffering, the effects of hate are equally damaging both to the oppressor and the oppressed.

In addition to this assessment, Mrs. King, in the support of *Unity Is the Key*, became an example, a living model, if you will, of Dr. King's vision of the Beloved Community. The Beloved Community addresses the role of three kinds of love: *eros*, *philia* and *agape*. In summary, *eros* can be defined as a sort of aesthetic or romantic love. *Philia* is affection among friends. *Agape* is considered to be a love that is understanding, redeeming and a form of good will for all, an overflowing, if you will, that is spontaneous, unmotivated, groundless and creative. It is the love of God operating in the human heart. Moreover, *agape* love:

> Does not begin by discriminating between worthy and unworthy people...It begins by loving others for their sakes and makes no distinction between a friend or enemy; it is directed towards both...Agape is a love seeking to preserve, sustain, and create community.[5]

Coretta Scott King possessed all three forms in accepting, embracing, nurturing and supporting her husband and the Civil Rights Movement. The crystallization of her role in addressing the causes and effects of racism, colonialism, all forms of oppression and discrimination became quite evident when she boldly and eloquently clarified the importance of her personal role in the movement. She said, "Women, if the soul of the nation is to be saved, I believe that you must become its soul."[6]

On April 8, 1968, approximately four days after the assassination of Dr. Martin Luther King, Jr., Mrs. Coretta Scott King took the torch of Civil Rights, and marched proudly in her husband's place during the sanitation workers' strike in Memphis, Tennessee, the city where he was brutally

31

ambushed and killed by a sniper's bullet. In retrospect, she was clear when she addressed the intent of his assassination: to kill the Civil Rights Movement once and for all. In retrospect she literally stunned a grieving America when she stated:

> And those of you who believe in what Martin Luther King stood for; I would challenge you today to see that this spirit never dies and that we will go forward from this experience, this to me represents the Crucifixion, on toward the resurrection and the redemption of the spirit.[7]

Mrs. Coretta King distinctly clarified and consistently promoted the definition and functional purpose of the Beloved Community. She unapologetically agreed with the philosophy that for a community to be great, it must be measured by the consistent acts of compassion enacted by its members. It is measured by a heart propelled to action by God's amazing grace, and it is measured by its soul that generates all three forms of love (*eros, philia* and *agape*) in the face of oppression, bigotry, discrimination and colonialism.[8] Mrs. King called for unity among women, especially women of color, to stand side by side with the Black Alpha Male and other oppressed males to create a unified front in the fight against the three evils of racism, poverty and war. Most importantly, she also encouraged others to take up the fight against oppression throughout the world communities based on the philosophical premise that "Injustice anywhere is a threat to justice everywhere."[9] Justice, she believed, was indivisible and unequivocally the inalienable birthright of every human being. Love that promotes, nurtures and is based on inclusiveness is stronger than hate. In retrospect, Mrs. Coretta Scott King, true to the mission and shared philosophy, ethics and moral teachings of nonviolent protest as the most potent weapon available for an oppressed people seeking a seat at the bountiful table of humanity, called for calm and true adherence to nonviolence after the assassination of her soul mate and husband.

The wife of the slain Civil Rights leader moved forward with a personal vision that freedom is never really won. You (the oppressed) have to earn it, and the struggle to sustain it is the responsibility of every generation. The struggle is never ending and tedious; it is an ongoing and necessary process in addressing all forms of social ills throughout the world. In her life after Martin Luther King, Jr., she became unapologetically active in preserving the memory and legacy of her husband, and she promoted the shared ideology of the creation of the Beloved Community. She initiated the start of a commemorative service every January 15 (at Ebenezer Baptist Church), the anniversary of his birthday, where he was co-pastor with his father. Finally, her tireless efforts were realized in 1986 when the first Martin Luther King Day was celebrated throughout the world. In juxtaposition to accomplishing this historic hurdle, she graciously paid her respects and tribute to her close friend, former President and contributor to the Civil Rights Act of 1964, President Lyndon B. Johnson during his state funeral. Similarly, she attended the funeral of President Ronald Reagan, who signed the historic, groundbreaking legislation that established the national observance of Dr. Martin Luther King Day.

During the 1980's Mrs. King, a drum major for social justice in her own right, reaffirmed her longstanding, uncompromised opposition to apartheid. She sojourned to Washington, D.C., the site of her husband's historic *I Have a Dream Speech*, and participated in a planned sit-in protest, thereby promoting nationwide nonviolent demonstrations against the racial policies of South Africa. Respectively, in 1986, she traveled to South Africa to meet with another phenomenal female leader, Winnie Mandela. In retrospect, at the time of this visit, Winnie's husband, Nelson Mandela, was still a political prisoner on Robben Island. She urged President Reagan to implement and approve sanctions against the reigning powers of South Africa and candidly declined numerous invitations from Pik Botha and the moderate Zulu Chief Buthelezi.[10]

Notably, in 1968, Coretta Scott King established the King Center. Its official name is the *Martin Luther King, Jr., Center for Nonviolent Social Change.* This nonprofit agency is dedicated to achieving the goals of Dr. King. The center is appropriately housed in Freedom Hall in Atlanta, Georgia, on Auburn Avenue, across from the National Park Service Visitors Center. The slain Civil Rights leader's gravesite is adjacent to a reflecting pool. It is located next to Freedom Hall. The National Historic Site consists of several blocks, including the leader's boyhood home.[11] In collaboration with other creditable organizations, the site respectively serves as an institutional guardian to Dr. King's legacy and supports the following mission objectives:

- Developing and disseminating programs that educate the world about Dr. King's philosophy, methods of nonviolence and ideas related to the service of mankind.

- Building a national and international network of organizations that, through sanctioned programs, promote, complement and help further the organization's mission and objectives of building the Beloved Community that Dr. King envisioned.

- Functioning as the clearinghouse for nonprofit organizations and government agencies that utilize Dr.

King's image and writings for programs and ensuring that the programs are historically and interpretively accurate.

- Monitoring and reporting on the impact of Dr. King's worldwide legacy.[12]

Mrs. King embraced the ideology of the Beloved Community both at home and abroad. She never wavered from teaching the concept both to the present generation and to our future leaders. She encouraged the Board members of the King Center to develop a wide variety of programs and services to address and fulfill the organization's mission of building and sustaining Dr. King's Beloved Community Concept. The programs and services developed include:

- The Beloved Community Network.

- Nonviolence Online Learning Program.

- Re-Ignite the Dream Campaign: Building the Beloved Community through Service.

- King and the Modern Civil Rights Museum Scholar and Historian Research Program.

- The King Papers Project.

- Education through Exploration Visitor Services Program.

- Annual Dr. Martin Luther King, Jr. Holiday Service Summit.[13]

On January 30, 2006, Mrs. King took her final rest. More than 14,000 people, including dignitaries, paid tribute to her during a six hour funeral at the New Birth Missionary Baptist Church in Lithonia, Georgia, on February 7, 2006. The mega church, with its seating capacity of 10,000 and where her daughter, Bernice King, is an elder, was better equipped to accommodate the huge crowd than Ebenezer Baptist Church where the leader was a member since the early 1960's. On January 31, 2006, President George W. Bush opened the State of the Union Address by paying tribute to Mrs. King. The President issued a special proclamation that all U.S. flags be flown at half staff throughout the day in honor of Mrs. King's internment on February 7, 2006.[14] Similar to Dr. Martin Luther King, Mrs. Coretta Scott King was carried on a horse-drawn carriage while a lone bag piper performed "Amazing Grace."[15] Mrs. King, representing the embodiment of the Beloved Community, became the first woman and African American to lie in state at the Georgia State Capital.[16] In a show of unity, the Atlanta City Council issued a special proposal in April 2006 to rename Atlanta's Simpson Street/Road after Coretta King. In the eloquent tradition of *A House Divided...No More*, Mrs. King expressed to her family and close friends that she wanted her remains to rest next to her late husband's body at the historic King Center. Respectfully, her children made arrangements to honor their mother's special request, and Dr. King's grave was altered to accommodate her remains.

On January 31, 2006, immediately following a moment of silence in memoriam to Mrs. Coretta Scott King, House Resolution 655 was presented to the United States House of Representatives in honor of Mrs. King's legacy. John Lewis (D-Georgia) moved the assembly to tears when he stated:

I first met Mrs. King in 1957 when I was only 17 years old. I was a student in Nashville, Tennessee. She was traveling around America, especially in cities of the South telling the story of the Montgomery Movement through song. She was so beautiful, so inspiring, she would sing a little, and she would talk a little, and through her singing and talks she inspired an entire generation.[17]

In retrospect, prior to Mrs. King, another solider for social justice, Ida B. Wells, led the way for her people and stood up against the evil system of segregation. The Inescapable Mutuality Paradigm motivated Ida B. Wells to similarly take the torch of humanity and represent her people. Wells, an African American, raised in Holly Springs, Mississippi, after the American Civil War, attended Rust College but was expelled for her rebellious behavior after challenging the president of the college. She taught school in Memphis, Tennessee, and was part owner of a newspaper, *The Memphis Free Speech*. Her father, James Wells, a carpenter by trade, and mother, Elizabeth "Lizzie" Warrenton Wells, a cook, were both former slaves who gained their freedom after President Abraham Lincoln signed the historic Emancipation Proclamation.[18] Her mother had experienced the harsh sting of slavery in America when she was torn apart from her family due to the common practice of White owners from nearby plantations desiring the sexual company and labor of young, innocent African American females.

In a strange twist of fate, while Ida Wells was visiting her grandmother in Mississippi Valley, her hometown of Holly Springs was hit by the Yellow Fever Epidemic. At the age of 16, she lost both parents and her 10 month old bother. However, Wells decided at this early stage in her life that unlike her mother, this family (house) would not be divided. "She was determined to keep her family together even under the difficult circumstances."[19] With the assistance of friends and relatives, the remaining six Wells children were unified.

She intentionally dropped out of high school and found employment as a teacher in a Black school. However, the double-edged sword of racism and discrimination greeted her during this crisis in her life when Wells discovered that White teachers were making $80 a month compared to her $30 a month salary. Notably, this double standard against her people sparked an interest in racial politics and improving education for Blacks in America.

Prior to the historic Rosa Parks incident in Memphis, Tennessee, on May 4, 1884, a Chesapeake and Ohio Railroad Company train conductor ordered Ida B. Wells to give up her seat on the train and move to the smoking car, a car that was crowded with Black passengers. In 1883, Civil Rights cases addressing the Federal Civil Rights Act of 1875 that banned racial discrimination in public accommodations were struck down by the Supreme Court 71 years prior to the Montgomery Bus Boycott.[20] Wells protested and physically refused to give up her seat. As a result, the conductor and two White men dragged her out of the car. Upon returning to Memphis, she hired an attorney and sued the railroad. Wells soon thereafter became a voice for her people against the evil tenets of segregation and racial oppression. Wells wrote a newspaper article for *The Living Way*, an African American church weekly paper, concerning the railroad incident and the continuous maltreatment of herself and all African Americans. Unfortunately, her lawyer was enticed by the railroad when a sizable amount of hush money was dropped off at his office. The tenacious Wells, more determined than ever, hired a White attorney and won the case on December 24, 1884. She received a $500 settlement.[21] When the railroad appealed the case to the Tennessee Supreme Court, the original ruling by the lower court was reversed in 1885. Wells was ordered to pay all court costs associated with the case.

Ida B. Wells held the belief that a people united shall never be defeated. She unequivocally believed in a Communal Initiative: the unification of the African American Village Community and the formation of cultural solidarity to permanently break any and all forged links of institutionalized oppression (racism, sexism, discrimination, inequalities and all forms of marginalization). While employed as a teacher at an elementary school, she accepted an editorial position on the staff of the *Evening Star* while simultaneously writing weekly articles for the *Living Way* under the pen name "Iola."[22] In an effort to stir a consciousness of pride to unite her people, she began to write about race issues in the United States.

In 1889, her reputation as a prolific journalist spread rapidly through both the White community and the African American Village Community: she became the distinguished co-owner and editor of *Free Speech* and *Headlight*, an anti-segregationist newspaper conveniently based at the Beale Street Baptist Church in Memphis, Tennessee. Two years after this inception, local racial tensions reached a fever pitch. The fight for racial equality would take on a synthesis involving a Communal Initiative and a personal crusade when her friends, Thomas Moss, Calvin McDowell and Henry Stewart, were shot and lynched by an angry White mob. The mob stormed the jail and, receiving absolutely no resistance from authority figures, they rode off into the Memphis night with a mind to murder and mutilate the three innocent African Americans who dared to fight back after being assaulted and fired upon by Whites. "The lynching was one of the most orderly of its kind ever conducted."[23] The People's Grocery Company, owned by the murdered victims at Curve Street where the public streetcars turned off to Mississippi Street onto Walker Avenue, was attracting new customers and competing with the White-owned grocery store across the street. One day, after a minor disturbance, White police officers shot at the owners.

They fired back, injuring one of the officers. The end for the trio came violently and swiftly.

In examining the fire behind Wells' insatiable thirst for social justice for her people, we find an unprecedented history of unprovoked assaults on African Americans in Memphis. Prior to the Lynching at the Curve, the Riot of 1866 reveals prior evidence of racial tensions. For reasons unknown, a White mob swept through the streets of Memphis, Tennessee, burning, pillaging, murdering and raping African American women. The three-day rampage was unprecedented in its relentless destruction and annihilation of African Americans. When the dust cleared after the rampage, 46 Black men, women and children had been killed, 75 wounded, 5 women raped, 100 robberies committed, and 91 houses, 4 churches and 12 Black schools burned.[24]

The Riot of 1866 and the 1892 Lynching at the Curve catapulted Ida B. Wells into an anti-lynching crusade that would consume her life. She began to write continuously and passionately about lynching, segregation, colored only railroad cars, laws against interracial marriages and unfair persecution in the courts.[25] Wells wrote an article in the *Free Speech* urging African Americans to leave the racist nest of Memphis:

> There is therefore, only one thing left to do; save our money and leave a town which will neither protect our lives and property, nor give us a fair trial in the courts, but take us out and murder us in cold blood when accused by White persons.[26]

The trumpet for justice coupled with the call for unity was heard by many. More than 6,000 African Americans fled the city of Memphis, and others organized mass boycotts of White-owned businesses. Ida B. Wells became the target for immediate extermination: the call for a Communal Initiative insulted southern Whites to no end. To add insult to injury, the public stand by Wells rejected the common argument that lynching was an understandable and legitimate response to Black men who routinely sexually violated White women. The terrible crime of rape was an excuse to kill, to exterminate the White man's competition. Wells contended that the majority of relationships between Black men and White women were consensual. Wells further concluded that, "A Winchester rife should have a place of honor in every black home, to be used for that protection which the law refuses to give."[27] With these strong words of defiance all hell broke out in Memphis. A White mob destroyed Wells' printing press, and she became a wanted fugitive from the unapologetic, violent, malicious, angry White mobs. She went into exile and eventually fled the city of Memphis and settled in Chicago, Illinois. To many African Americans, Wells was a hero, a modern day Joan of Arc of the race and a watchdog for social justice, equality and Civil Rights. In 1913, the *Chicago Defender* concluded, "The race has no greater leader among the feminine sex."[28]

Silence from the Village Community concerning the lynching, raping, burning and pillaging of her people meant division. A divided community, a divided house, a divided people. The anti-lynching crusade initiated by Wells gave people a voice. In the year 1896, Wells formed the National Association of Colored Women (NACW) and the National Afro-American Council (NAAC). The latter organization became the National Association for the Advancement of Colored People (NAACP). Wells also formed the first civic organization for African American women. This club, originally called the Women's Era Club, would later assume the name the Ida B. Wells Club in her honor.[29] Prior to these endeavors, in 1892, Wells published a pamphlet entitled *Southern Horrors: Lynch Law in All Its Phases* and *The Red Record 1892-1894*, which documented research on lynching. The tenacious and courageous Wells contended:

41

Having examined many lynchings accounts based on alleged rape of White women, she concluded that Southerners concocted rape as an excuse to hide their real reason for lynchings: Black economic progress, which directly threatened not only White Southerners' pocketbooks, but also their collective ideals about black inferiority.[30]

The Red Record, a 100-page (critically acclaimed) research pamphlet written, released and promoted by Ida B. Wells, specifically and candidly describes the lynchings of African Americans, especially Males, in the United States since the signing of the Emancipation Proclamation. The record also describes the Black struggle, the African American Experience, if you will. Wells addresses the ignorance of lynching (developed over a ten-year period) and describes the oppression of her people in the following manner:

The black man's body and soul was owned by the White man. The soul was dwarfed by the White man, and the body was preserved because of its value...ten thousand Negroes have been killed in cold blood, without the formality of judicial trial and legal execution.[31]

In collaboration with the famous abolitionist Fredrick Douglass, Wells agreed wholeheartedly with the explanation formatting the three eras of Southern barbarism (lynchings) and the presupposed excuses that accompany each deception:

- The first excuse that Wells explains is the necessity of the White man to repress and stamp out alleged race riots. Once the Civil War ended, there were many riots supposedly being planned by Blacks; Whites panicked and resisted them forcefully.

- The second excuse came during the Reconstruction Era: Blacks were lynched because Whites feared Negro domination and wanted to stay powerful in the government. Wells encouraged those threatened to move their families somewhere safe.

- The third excuse was that Blacks had to be killed to avenge their assaults upon women. Wells explains that any relationship between a White woman and a Black man was considered rape during that time period.[32]

In 1895, Wells married Ferdinand L. Barnett, a lawyer and editor of the *Chicago Conservator*. They had four children together (Charles, Herman, Ida and Alfreda). During the course of her marriage she not only carried the torch for justice and equality (Empirical Hope) for her people to audiences throughout the United States, but she managed to tour Europe twice: the first in 1893 and the second in 1894. After her retirement, Wells wrote her autobiography, *Crusade for Justice (1928)*. However, the manuscript was never finished; it ends in the middle of a sentence, in the middle of a word. The fiery drum major for social justice died of uremia in Chicago on March 25, 1931, at the age of 68.[33]

Prior to her transition, Wells addressed a house divided in the leadership arena through her famous writings, *Functions of Leadership*, published in the *Living Way* on September 12, 1885. Wells challenged African American leaders to help the masses by opening up businesses to employ young people. Under the auspices of Cultural Utilitarianism, Wells issued a mandate pertaining to cultural solidarity. She unequivocally believed that educated and privileged African Americans have a social responsibility to the less fortunate. Those who have acquired fame and wealth in their perspective callings (i.e., orators, teachers, preachers, officeholders, congressmen, etc.) and publicly declared themselves devoted to the interests of their people have a moral and binding obligation. Leaders of African decent who have acquired impeachable characters and are called representatives of the collective African American Village Community must unapologetically step up to the plate of humanity. Wells issued an uncompromised proclamation for those individuals to exert their talents and wealth for the benefit and amelioration of the condition of the masses.[34] She encouraged the upper class to use their earned capital for the purpose of opening business establishments and/or backing those who propose such ventures but have limited means to successfully do so. Most importantly, she encouraged them to employ young, educated African American men and women. Notably and unapologetically, Ida B. Wells reminds her race that Whites provide employment for their young people and routinely exclude young African Americans. Wells surmised that the house will continue to be divided if:

> The ambition seems to be to get all they can for their own use, and the rest may shift for themselves; some of them do not wish, after getting wealth for themselves, to be longer identified with the people to whom they owe their political preferment; if no more.[35]

Wells' anti-lynching campaign and self-empowerment philosophy is embedded in the writing of this exegesis: *A House Divided...No More*. This drum major for social justice was unafraid to lead the charge against the blatant and open insults against her people. In a most eloquent and nonviolent means of resistance she stirred a consciousness within the African American Village Community. The preternatural force generated by Wells empowered her people to collectively take a stand against the inhumane atrocities against the Black Alpha Male-an endangered human species.

On February 1, 1990, the United States Postal Service issued a 25 cents stamp in Wells' honor. In addition to this historic achievement, Ida B. Wells made the list of scholar Molefi Kete Asante's 100 Greatest African Americans.[36] Evidence of Empirical Hope can be found throughout her life. Wells can categorically be defined in the following manner:

> A woman born in slavery, she would grow to become one of the great pioneer activists of the early Movement for Civil Rights. A precursor to Mrs. Rosa Parks, she was a suffragist, newspaper editor and publisher, investigative journalist, co-founder of the NAACP, political candidate, mother, wife, and the single most powerful leader in the anti-lynching campaign in America. Wells can best be described as a controversial, powerful, courageous, tenacious drum major for social justice. This dynamic, temperamental, uncompromising African American (woman) broke bread and crossed words with some of the most notable movers and shakers of her time: Fredrick Douglass, Susan B. Anthony, Booker T. Washington, W.E.B. Du Bois, Marcus Garvey, Frances Willard, and President Mc Kinley. By any fair assessment, she was a seminal figure in Post-Reconstruction America.[37]

Ida B. Wells was the first Black woman to be a paid correspondent for a mainstream White newspaper, *The Daily Inter-Ocean,* a Chicago-based paper. Through her relentless efforts, *The Daily Inter-Ocean* was the only paper in America to persistently denounce lynching. Mr. William Penn Nixon, the editor, worked closely with Wells to document the horrors of lynching. Wells' column, the Ida B. Wells Abroad, slowly and surely won the sentiment of the inhabitants of Europe by revealing the inhumane atrocities of her people in America.[38] Her writings were supported by solid, indisputable evidence-based research, and she was successful in spreading the news.

Most importantly, influential people began to release public statements of their disapproval of the barbaric conditions afflicted upon African Americans. During her two tours of Europe, Wells became a major influence in the formation of human rights for her oppressed people: while writing abroad the advocate for social justice single-handedly became the catalyst for change in America. Years after her death, her words, writings and adamant uncompromised stand against racial inequality and segregation would be heard by a modern day drum major for social justice, Alderman Dorothy Tillman. Tillman humbly took the torch of Empirical Hope and similar to Wells began to lead a relentless campaign for equality in the form of a Communal Initiative in support of reparations for African Americans.

Dorothy Tillman was born on May 12, 1947. As the 3rd Ward Chicago Alderman (elected in 1985), she became a representative of the city's South Side and the first woman ever to hold that office. Tillman's *modus operandi* (MO) can best be defined as a fighter for the oppressed. Reparations for African Americans became the focus of her attention during the latter part of her political career. Prior to her political career, she was active in the Civil Rights Movement. She worked closely with Dr. Martin L. King and the Southern Christian Leadership Conference (SCLC) as a trainee and staff organizer in 1963. In retrospect, Tillman marched with Dr. Martin L. King and participated in the historic protest at the Edmund Pettus Bridge in Selma, Alabama, on March 7, 1965.[39] The plunge into Chicago politics occurred in 1965–1966 when Dr. King sent her on a personal mission to campaign in Chicago for equality in employment, fair housing and education specifically for African Americans. Tillman supported the Civil Rights Movement efforts to improve the socio-economic conditions in the African American Village Community. The Civil Rights activist was on the steering committee that initiated Dr. King's occupation as a tenant in the CHA (Chicago Housing Authority) project apartment in early 1966. This strategic move launched the End-the-Slums campaign in July of the same year.

After a brief stay in San Francisco and marriage to Jimmy Lee Tillman, a renowned blues drummer, she moved back to Chicago, Illinois and became a crusader for education. Tillman's grassroots organization, the Parent Equalizers of Chicago (PEC), became consistently active in 300 schools and set the precedent for strategic citywide public school reform in Chicago[40]. The momentum from this powerful grassroots effort enabled Dorothy Tillman to become instrumental in the successful election of Chicago's first African American mayor, Harold Washington. Needless to say, due to the Civil Rights and local civic efforts of this up-and-coming activist, Dorothy Tillman became a force to be reckoned with.

The powerful political influence of this drum major for social justice became quite evident as disenfranchised African Americans witnessed, first hand, the unifying agenda of the woman who walked with Dr. King. The miles of dirt along Garfield Boulevard and Martin L. King, Jr. Drive were restored to grass. Abandoned buildings, an embarrassment to the residents of the African American Village Community, were immediately and expeditiously boarded up, debris from vacant lots removed and abandoned cars were towed. The courageous African American alderman initiated a clean-up campaign entitled, "The Clean and Green Programs."[41] The Village, which was once referred to as "fly dump city" by the residents of the area, was restored to a noticeable level of respectability.[42] Using education, housing and homelessness as a major political platform, Tillman's Communal Initiative encompassed pioneering the first Tax Increment Financing (TIF) used in the African American Village Community with the construction of the 55th and Dan Ryan Shopping Center, thereby creating jobs and millions of tax dollars. In 2007, she recruited Quinton Primo, III of Capri Capital for the corner of 39th and State Street for a $155 million dollar retail and condo complex. In retrospect, due to her tireless efforts to restore the Village Community to a level of respectability, countless other multi-million dollar projects are presently still in progress in the 3rd Ward.[43] Furthermore, under the housing agenda, she is the founder of the historic African American Home Builders Association. This powerful grassroots organization serves as a watchdog group with a directive of making sure that African Americans receive a lion share, or at least a fair share, of the contracts in the Village Community. Tillman successfully advocated for an unprecedented 70/30 plan.

The vocal, courageous, bold, and unafraid advocate for social justice for African Americans became a major catalyst in addressing division, the Socialization of Division among the inhabitants of the Village Community. Tillman, in promoting the Village Concept, produced the stellar *Bring It on Home to Me Roots Festival* where more than 300,000 people annually support and attend this family-oriented event that attracts national and international mega stars that perform *pro bono*. Her support and belief in the Village Concept can also be seen in the successful initiation of the Annual Christmas Gifts for Children, Thanksgiving Family Affair Dinners and the Back to School Health Fairs.[44] Tillman's visionary insight and belief in the rights of African Americans to sit at the table of humanity led to the creation of the Chicago Blues District and the Harold Washington Cultural Center as well. Her numerous humanitarian efforts include an 80-bed homeless shelter, two hurricane relief drives and the Washington-King Resource Center.

Dorothy Tillman's (truly a force to be reckoned with) greatest voice in the plight for African Americans came in the form of the call for slave reparations from the United States Government. Under the promotion and implementation of

Cultural Utilitarianism, Alderman Tillman was noticeably more successful in having a number of resolutions passed in support of the concept as compared to others who took the torch prior to her arrival at the Chicago City Council. The co-founder of the Chicago Black United Community (CBUC), and the Black Independent Political Organization (BIPO), and the only woman elected to office in the United States who worked on Dr. King's staff, authored the groundbreaking Slave Era Disclosure Ordinance in the year 2000.[45] This ordinance requires companies to candidly disclose their past ties to slavery. Notably, this ordinance has been introduced and duplicated in several governing bodies internationally. While advocating human rights for her people under the all inclusive indigenous based agendas of the Village Concept, Cultural Utilitarianism, Communal Initiative and Communal Healing, Tillman's efforts have been featured in major books (including this historic exegesis) as well as documentaries and radio news features, thereby bringing worldwide recognition to her many years of fighting for the people.[46] Driven by an innate passion to improve the plight of African Americans at large, Tillman can best be described as a mother, Civil Rights Activist and radio host: an activist who is anointed by God to address the past and present oppression of her people.

The "Movement Baby," as she is referred to by her supporters, unequivocally believes that the struggle for Civil Rights, equality and liberation for African Americans extends far beyond the infamous "Bloody Sunday" confrontation for voting rights.[47] Reparations are an idea whose time has come. Furthermore, history was made on May 17, 2000, when the consistent advocacy of Tillman, who unapologetically yet adamantly represents the voices of our ancestors (Mothership voyagers who suffered through Ground Zero), led to the Chicago City Council's approval of a new resolution asking Congress to hold special hearings (on companies, businesses with past known ties to slavery) to consider paying reparations to living descendents of African slaves.[48] Tillman sponsored the resolution, with the assistance of scholars and emotional testimonies of how the catastrophic effects of slavery still manifest in the lives of African Americans (i.e., continuous Black on Black violence, dysfunctional families, single parent homes, *Mis-Education of the Negro*). The proposed measure was approved with a 46 to 1 vote. The lone republican, Brian Doherty, cast the opposing vote. Be that as it may, other White alderman, including Alderman Bernard Stone, not only favored the measure but issued a public apology to the African American Village Community. Stone insisted that when African Americans hear the words "I'm sorry," the importance of the moment could never be realized.[49] The apologetic White alderman went on to say, "Slavery didn't end with the Emancipation Proclamation. The residuals of slavery are still being felt today."[50] In retrospect, Stone's apology opened the floodgates for personal confessions and public affirmations from other White aldermen, including an apology from Mayor Daley. Mayor Richard M. Daley of Chicago stated:

> You apologize for a wrong, you apologize because it's the thing you were taught to do when you were young and you committed a wrong. It doesn't matter the race of the person, you just sincerely apologize because what happen was wrong.[51]

In addition to this historic apology, Chicago Alderman Burton Natarus stated:

> I want to go on record as saying I am in support of paying reparations to a people who have been disrespected for far too long. My only question is how do we determine who should be compensated and where do we get the resources to do it?[52]

During the 2005 campaign for reparations, Tillman launched a frontal attack against a $500 million refinancing deal with Bank of America due to its alleged links to slavery. The grassroots reparations organizers had recently traced indisputable slavery ties back to FleetBoston Financial, a company recently acquired by Bank of America in 2004. Providence Bank, a predecessor of FleetBoston Financial, was founded by a slave owner in 1791. Notably, this action by the well organized grassroots organization served as a warning to other companies that the issues over slave reparations were alive and well in Chicago.

In 2001, Tillman boldly and unapologetically hosted the first ever National Reparations Convention for African American Descendents of African Slaves in Chicago.[53] The 3rd Ward Alderman headed a steering committee whose task was to draft a universal platform to compel the federal government and American corporations that have historic links to slavery to provide reparations to the descendents of slaves. Dorothy Tillman contended that America was one of the cruelest nations in the world when addressing equality for African Americans. "Only reparations could atone for the cruelty. America would not be the America it is today without slavery."[54] In seeking Utilitarianism (the greatest good for the greatest number of people), Tillman supported the National Reparations Initiative by proposing that the freed slaves of descendants are at a gross psychological, social, educational, political and economic disadvantage. She further contended that these insurmountable disadvantages will unequivocally and absolutely never be adequately and properly overcome without the unconditional release of reparations. Tillman publicly declared, "America owes Blacks a debt and we will accept nothing less than full reparations as just recompense."[55]

Tillman's voice consistently stirred a consciousness in this country. John Conyers, a Michigan democrat, also worked diligently and tirelessly to establish a reparations commission. Virginia became the first state in the country to pass a resolution apologizing for the state's role in slavery. The house shall be divided...no more as supporters from several major cities have agreed upon the following ten reasons why Congress should support the commission to study reparations:

1. The U.S. Government and not long dead Southern planters bear the blame for slavery. They encoded it in the Constitution in Article 1. This designated a Black slave as three-fifths of a person for tax and political representation purposes. They protected and nourished it in Article 4 by mandating that all escaped slaves found anywhere in the nation be returned to their masters. In the Dred Scott decision in 1857, the U.S. Supreme Court reaffirmed that slaves remained slaves no matter where they were taken in the United States.

2. Major institutions profited from slavery. Several cities and states now require insurance companies to disclose whether they wrote policies insuring slaves. This is recognition that insurance companies made profits insuring slaves as property. The insurance industry was not the only culprit. Banks, shipping companies and investment houses also made enormous profits from financing slave purchases, investments in southern land and products, and the transport and sale of slaves.

3. The legacy of slavery endures. In its 2006 State of Black America, the National Urban League found that Blacks are far more likely to live in underserved, segregated neighborhoods, be refused business and housing loans, be denied promotions in corporations, suffer greater health care disparities and attend cash-starved, failing public schools than Whites.

4. Former Federal Reserve Board member Andrew Brimmer estimates that discrimination costs Blacks $10 billion yearly

through the Black-White wage gap, denial of capital access, inadequate public services and reduced social security and other governmental benefits. This has been called the "Black Tax".

5. Since the 1960s, the U.S. Government has shelled out billions to pay for resettlement, job training, education and health programs for refugees fleeing Communist repression. Congress enthusiastically backed these payments as the morally and legally right thing to do.

6. The reparations issue will not fuel more hatred of Blacks. Most Americans admit that slavery was a monstrous system that wreaked severe pain and suffering on the country. Also, there was no national outcry when the U.S. Government made special indemnity payments and provided land and social service benefits to the following: Japanese-Americans who were interned during World War II, Native-Americans whose lands and mineral rights were stolen and Philippine veterans who fought in the American army during World War II.

7. No legislation has been proposed that mandates taxpayers pay billions to Blacks. The reparations commission bill is primarily a bill to study the effects of slavery. The estimated cost of the study is less than $10 million.

8. There is a precedent for paying Blacks for past legal and moral wrongs. In 1997, President Clinton apologized and the U.S. Government paid $10 million to the Black survivors and family members victimized by the syphilis experiment conducted in the 1930's by the U.S. Public Health Service. In 1994, the Florida legislature agreed to make payments to the survivors and relatives of those who lost their lives and property when a White mob destroyed the all-Black town of Rosewood in 1923. Public officials and law enforcement officers tacitly condoned the killings and property damage.

The Oklahoma state legislature has agreed that making reparations payments is the morally right thing to do to compensate the survivors and their descendants for the destruction of Black neighborhoods in Tulsa by White mobs in 1921.

9. Oprah Winfrey, Bill Cosby, Michael Jordan and other mega-rich Blacks will not receive a penny in reparations. Any tax money to redress Black suffering should go into a fund to bolster funding for AIDS/HIV education and prevention, under-financed inner-city public schools, to expand job skills and training programs, drug and alcohol counseling and rehabilitation, computer access and literacy training programs and to improve public services for the estimated one in four Blacks still trapped in poverty.

10. A reparations commission may well conclude that reparations payments would do more harm than good. That slavery compensation would be too costly, too complex, too time consuming and too dated, and that it would create too much public rancor. Yet, a reparations commission that examines the brutal consequences of slavery and its continued tormenting impact on race relations in America is a good thing. We can all learn something from that.[56]

In addressing the Crystallization of Cause and Effect, Tillman have become a conscious reminder to America that the U.S. Government has indeed written African Americans a check marked insufficient funds. According to Tillman, that check is still being held by the African American Village Community and we are collectively waiting for America to own up to its historic wrong and do the right thing. The right thing is reparations. Reparations will allow the African American Village Community to invest in itself to create employment, training, housing and improve the quality of education. Reparations, if implemented properly, will ease the socioeconomic strangulation that presently has a death grip on the pulse of the African American Village Community. Reparations will be the fitting and proper thing to do after we have awakened from the long night of slavery to find a never ending nightmare in America. Reparations will represent the long overdue funds on the check we are still holding since the signing of the Emancipation Proclamation. Reparations will level the playing field in America and serve as a common public apology to the African American Village Community for the unspeakable inhumane atrocities of the past as well as the unapologetic oppression of the present.

Dorothy Tillman and the African American Village Community have come to realize that we can't wait. Waiting to African Americans has come to mean never, and this, according to Tillman and similar to the pronouncement of Dr. Martin L. King, Jr., is why we can't wait. Most importantly, in adamant defiance of waiting coupled with the demand for reparations, we unapologetically proclaim to the oppressor that *A House Divided... No More* is an idea whose time has come. Full and unconditional reparations will become a major catalyst for indigenous Communal Healing.

CHAPTER THREE

Promoting Cultural Utilitarianism

Unity is the key. It is the primary weapon used by noble African American women of the Village Community, a community whose bruised humanity stands in need of the immediate implementation of the Village Concept. Within the parameters of this concept is the preternatural healing balm of unity. Unity is a non-negotiable necessary human corrective in addressing the psychological, economic, political, social and educational strangulation of African Americans in America.

The Village Concept (a deterrent to oppression, racism, bigotry, and extreme marginalization) can best be defined in the following manner: the intentional and deliberate creation of indigenous self-reliant systems within the greater African American Village Community with the prime directive of addressing the unfinished task of emancipation in America. Furthermore, with the implementation of the Village Concept as a deterrent to institutional genocide of her people, noble and courageous African American women have engraved the Ethic of Care on the pages of history. The Ethic of Care is the need to nurture and support each other (the oppressed inhabitants of the Village Community) as we collectively struggle for racial equality in America. This special care was propelled by their unselfish, uncompromising and unconditional promotion of Cultural Utilitarianism, the greatest good for the greatest number of people. Utilitarianism accompanied by Empirical Hope therefore became a necessary corrective for a people who suffered throughout Slavocracy, (the long night of slavery) Jim Crow Segregation and beyond. Empowered by the preternatural connection to Ground Zero the concept of indigenous Communal Healing became the driving force of a leader who refuses to go silently into the night while her people suffer systematic extermination and daily oppression.

From the ashes and historic residue of oppression and unspeakable inhumane atrocities, we find the epitome of courage and undying commitment to become a catalyst for the cultural enrichment of not only the present generation but for generations to come as well. In a symbolic biblical gesture similar to the story of David and Goliath, we find evidence of courageous steadfast warriors (among many unsung heroes throughout history) who decided that they were spiritually and physically capable of facing and defeating the Goliaths of discrimination, bigotry, racism, sexism and marginalization, including all forms of economic, educational, psychological, cultural, political and social strangulations in America.

Three indigenous warriors (empowered by the African American Experience) will be discussed in this chapter: Lyn Hughes, Margaret Burroughs and Yvette Moyo-Gillard. These drum majors for social justice faced seemingly insurmountable odds, yet their enormous contributions to the unfinished task of emancipation are unprecedented. In the face of open and unapologetic sexism (in juxtaposition to communal suffering), their unique individual and collective strength of character and uncompromised faith in God have proven to be a formidable, undying, preternatural light that stands over and against the dark abyss of hopelessness; the abyss of hopelessness that encroaches upon the collective spirits of African Americans who presently reside beneath the Glass Ceiling in America.

Lyn Hughes listened attentively to the advisory words of Dempsey M. Travis, a prominent real estate developer and author who stated during an interview, "The best real estate investments are those in communities that have bottomed out or in an historic district."[1] During the early 1990's, the recent divorcee was supporting three children and decided that real

57

estate projects might be a good stream of revenue to pay for her offspring's college tuition. It was through a twist of fate, or perhaps God, the Creator's divine intervention, that she wandered into the Pullman Community on the far South Side of Chicago, Illinois after getting lost while trying to keep an appointment with a referral. The appearance of the community reminded Hughes of her hometown of Cincinnati, Ohio, and the community of Mount Auburn. The community looked pretty bad; however, an opportunistic spirit overwhelmed her.

During her extensive research, Hughes discovered that the Pullman Community was an historic district. As Hughes accompanied several tour guides and listened to the historic nature of the Pullman Community, the name George Pullman, its wealthy founder, surfaced continuously. The name became synonymous with the railroad sleeping cars. Not surprisingly, her own innate self-interest surged, and she put forth a burning question: "What role did African Americans play in the Pullman story and in the Pullman Company?"[2] Of course, silence was the answer. The group of about 20 people (all White) stared and dismissed the question as unimportant in comparison to the story about the rich founder. Finally, the tour guide, annoyed at Hughes' audacity, responded by saying, "Well, they worked on the trains."[3] Hughes' curiosity was highly elevated. After the tour, she sojourned to the local library to find material on Blacks and the Pullman Company. To add insult to injury, Lyn Hughes was handed a children's book that was written at about a sixth or seventh grade level.

As this drum major for social justice read the exegesis, *A Long Hard Journey*, she wept. "Reading the book literally changed the direction of my life."[4] The book, which told the largely unknown story of the Brotherhood of the Sleeping Car Porters, changed Lyn Hughes forever. Through the power of God, Hughes witnessed an early form of Communal Initiative. This initiative can be defined as the unification of the African

American Village Community via a collective preternatural forming of cultural solidarity that serves to permanently break all links of institutionalized oppression in America—racism, sexism, discrimination and inequality, including all forms of marginalization and strangulation. She discovered the story of recently freed slaves who were hired to work as the onboard crew on the Pullman Sleeping Cars; a job by today's standards would be categorized as menial minimum wage jobs if you will. However, through their innate strength of character and inalienable quest for a seat at the table of humanity, they transformed this station into a job of prestige in the African American Village Community at large. Through their unique creativity of par excellent service, they set a new standard, a standard of service excellence for the hospitality industry.

Lyn Hughes discovered that in the porters' quest for a respectable seat at the table of humanity in juxtaposition to their struggle for dignity and fairness and a right to earn a decent living wage, "They made history by forming the first Black labor union in America to be chartered under the American Federation of Labor."[5] By winning a collective bargaining agreement with a major U.S. corporation, they literally paved the way to improve labor practices in the United States, thereby opening the doors for generations of African Americans to come. Their collective communal actions set a precedent for the organizing and success of an indigenous Communal Initiative. At the nucleus of this well organized Communal Initiative that included more than 20,000 Black Pullman Porters, maids and other railroad personnel, the curious researcher found the name A. Philip Randolph. Randolph, a drum major for social justice, was the leader of the Brotherhood of the Sleeping Car Porters Union (BSCP), also known as the Pullman Porters.

Armed with this rich, hidden knowledge, Lyn Hughes wondered why she didn't know anything about this critical aspect of Black history, a history saturated by the humble pride of African American men who labored tirelessly and, similar to slavery, faced inhumane treatment by Whites, unfair wages and had no voice whatsoever to speak out against the daily oppression...*yet!* Through it all, these men managed to support their families and pay for their children's college education on tips in lieu of a decent living wage. Most importantly, these noble and dedicated men (Black Alpha Males) of impeccable character possessed the strength to stand up to a rich, powerful White man and his discriminatory practices. It is well to note that Lyn Hughes' second and third questions on the subject matter moved her to action: "Why was it that my children were not being taught this history as well?" and last but not least, "Why wasn't there some representation about these men?"[6] It was then at this precise moment in time that Lyn Hughes discovered her vocation. She started on a journey (similar to the Brotherhood's quest for a union) that would last 12 years. As she began to develop real estate, the researcher came face to face with God's plan for her life. Hughes candidly admits that founding a museum wasn't remotely entertained and her venture innocently began as an impromptu project under the auspice of *Cultural Economic Development* in the historic North Pullman Community. After initially introducing the idea of Cultural Heritage Tourism to the leaders of the community at large, Hughes testifies, "I was forced by a power greater than mine to focus on developing a museum."[7]

During February 1995, Lyn Hughes, the tenacious researcher, divorcee, historian and African American woman par excellence, founded the A. Philip Randolph Pullman Porter Museum. Under the directive of implementing an initiative based on Cultural Utilitarianism, it is the first museum in U.S. history solely dedicated to African American men. It honors their contributions to the community, organized labor efforts and uncompromised demands for Civil Rights.

Notably, the museum is a private, independently operated, nonprofit institution. It is not funded by federal, city or state funds. Under the direction and leadership of the founder Lyn Hughes, its yearly operational budget consists of funding derived solely from private contributions, fundraisers and memberships.

Moving again by the power of God, in the year 2000, Lyn Hughes decided to establish a living memorial, a historic documentation, if you will, about the descendents of the Pullman Porters. Hughes noted through fact finding research that the porters possessed strong characters. As previously mentioned, in the face of unspeakable cruelty and daily humiliation derived from the resentment of their release from physical slavery (the permanent abyss of plantation labor) their positive unselfish and unconditional impact as exemplary family men can only be categorized as unprecedented. Further research on the subject matter would prove to be educational and extremely worthwhile. Hughes began to collect primary and secondary source documents on and from the porters' descendents. Through this tedious process the concept of developing the book, *The Pullman Porters National Historic Registry of African American Railroad Employees*, came to fruition.[8] By any and all means necessary, Sister Hughes was determined to acknowledge and honor the unsung heroes of the African American Village Community 365 days a year. The registry portion of Lyn Hughes' book, *An Anthology of Respect: The Pullman Porters National Historic Registry of African American Railroad Employees* (preface by Lerone Bennett, Jr.), consists of African Americans who worked for the railroad between the years 1865–1969.

Through the establishment of the registry, the museum amassed a large amount of information that needed to be organized for use by community researchers. Close to 2,000 entries were made through the online registry, another 500 entries through the 1-800 number and another 500 that came through the U.S. mail. For example, there were 1,967 entries for jobs held by those registered. While 73 percent were listed as porters, another 14 percent were firemen, 3% were cooks and 1% percent each redcaps, attendants or trackmen. More than 40 other positions were listed, including maids and one nurse, representing the few Pullman maids registered. Of the 3,000 data entries, 1,500 were simply the names of the former employees, the routes run and the number of years worked. The remaining historic data, consisting of 1,500 entries, provided a few more details, and 1,000 data entries provided detailed recollections of a story or impressions of their descendants that respondents felt compelled to share with the researcher.[9]

Lyn Hughes, a researcher par excellence, instinctively noticed and identified five powerful, distinct, unspoken action-oriented themes that promoted a Communal Initiative among the Black Pullman Porters. These themes were:

- Self-pride

- Belief in unity

- Self-imposed standards of excellence

- Dedication to the Union's cause and existence

- Commitment to family.[10]

Historic figures (activists and advocates for early Civil Rights and social equality) such as Fredrick Douglass and W.E.B. Dubois equated manhood with the full humanity of first-class citizenship. Lyn Hughes, by any and all resources available to her, was determined to give these noble men their identities and proper recognition. When she discovered that White passengers routinely called all Black porters George (the first name of George Pullman, the founder), her resolve to right this historic wrong became a force to be reckoned with.[11] Ironically, the entrepreneur who invented the sleeping car and began hiring porters in 1868 strategically knew that there were large pools of cheap labor produced by the end of slavery:

> He was looking for people who had been trained to be the perfect servant, and these guys' backgrounds [were] as having been chattel slaves. He knew that they knew just how to take care of any whim that a customer had.[12]

Be that as it may, Lyn Hughes' fact-based research and the decision to establish the A. Philip Randolph Pullman Porter Museum were based on the underrepresentation of the indomitable human spirit, specifically that of the Black Alpha Male. Men of courage, faith and strength who stood gallantly (empowered by the African American Experience) to face the unprovoked insults hurled at them. They found dignity and respect in the reserves of their souls, strategically placed there by God, the Creator and Unmoved Mover. Moreover, this unexpected, innate, intrinsic evidence of unprecedented *courage under fire* can be found in the living testimonies of their children who witnessed firsthand their fathers' determination to be the Providers and Protectors of their families. Essentially, the Black porters (The Brotherhood of Pullman Porters) became extraordinary examples for their children and the African American Village Community. Their individual and collective abilities to persevere produced a message of Empirical Hope and proclaimed that no system of oppression promoted by the Glass Ceiling can define you as an individual or collectively as a people. John L.D. recalls his father's *courage under fire* in the following manner:

> My father was active in the movement of the Brotherhood of Pullman Porters of Chicago until his death. He was a positive role model in family and community life. He always reminded us of the dignified role of The Brotherhood of Pullman Porters in the struggle of our community. He wore his uniform with pride for 'The Brotherhood'. He was the first person to tell me that the Brotherhood of Pullman Porters, under the leadership of A. Philip Randolph, was very active in the Civil Rights Movement. He said that Dr. Martin Luther King was (strategically) drafted by the Brotherhood.[13]

Another documentation of this unique courage reveals:

> My father, James W. Mc-, was a member of the Sleeping Car Porters Union (Black Porters) for years, and worked as a Pullman Porter from approximately 1924-1960. Because of the teaching and foundation given to us by my father, we have achieved some degree of success in our careers. I am one of his seven children, which are all still alive. My father emphasized education and integrity to his children. He would have been proud to know that all his children have gone on to become professionals and, I believe, people of character. I am an attorney with licenses in Texas, Illinois, and several other federal venues, my two sisters both hold master's degrees, one brother previously served as assistant police chief in Centerville, Illinois, another brother retired from General Motors in Detroit, and a sister taught at Grambling University and currently works for the United States Government at Redstone Arsenal, Huntsville Alabama.[14]

Finally, a proud descendent writes:

> My father, Spencer B. B-, was a proud, hard working
> man, who instilled in his children a very positive work
> ethic. We all graduated from major colleges and
> reached high levels of achievement in our chosen
> fields. More importantly, my dad taught us how to
> negotiate through life's adversities and to meet each
> day in a positive manner. I contracted polio at five
> years of age and my parents were told I would never
> walk. My dad refused to accept that prognosis and
> found a specialist that was willing to perform
> experimental surgery on me. My dad's tenacity made it
> possible for me to walk and lead a normal life. Upon
> retiring I was one of the highest ranked Black women
> in my corporation. The Brotherhood of Pullman
> Porters gave my dad life choices that poor Black men
> seldom got and he, in return, provided opportunities to
> his children.[15]

Through the establishment of this museum, Hughes
answered the question: Who were they? They were fathers,
grandfathers, uncles and brothers, men who suffered through
Jim Crow and daily humiliations but cared enough to make
sacrifices and provide for their families. Family was first as
they endured racism, classism, hate, marginalization and
bigotry for their families. Be that as it may:

> They planted seeds, in a bloodline that would grow
> into the "I Can Spirit": a desire to want to know more,
> be more; they imparted in us the undeniable power of
> purpose embedded in our DNA, pride in oneself and
> gave us the understanding that with it, the human spirit
> (bestowed upon the living by God, the Creator) is
> uncrushable.[16]

65

Hughes insists that the indisputable evidence of that history-making DNA can be found in what she proudly categorizes as the Descendents of Distinction: Tom Bradley, Andre Braugher, Willie Lewis Brown, Jr., Ron Dellums, Whoopi Goldberg, Tom Joyner, Archibald Motley, Warner Saunders, Oscar Peterson, Roy Wilkins, Wilma Rudolph and the Neville Brothers.[17] In addition, notable Alumni Pullman Porters and Dining Car Waiters who later moved on to creditable careers include the following: Matthew Henson, James "Genial Jim" Knight, Malcolm Little aka Malcolm X, Thurgood Marshall, Benjamin Elijah Mays, Oscar Micheaux, E.D. Nixon, Gordon Parks, R. Eugene Pincham and J.A. Rodgers.[18]

The distinguished A. Philip Randolph Pullman Porter Museum (presently located on the south/east side at 10406 S. Maryland Avenue, Chicago, Illinois) serves as a reminder that the struggle for equality in America cannot afford sexism, separatism and in-fighting among African American males and females. There is now indisputable historical evidence that our families faced continuous overwhelming and inhumane obstacles in their quest to remain together. The innate power (preternatural in nature) of the African American Experience became a formidable weapon against the encroachment of division, selective hiring practices and the intentional targeting of Black Alpha Males for economic and social extermination. Although Lyn Hughes was a divorcee and the primary support for her children, she decided that she would not deposit any bitterness into the cup of division. She made an individual choice to serve as a chosen vessel of God, the Creator and Unmoved Mover to bring to the attention of the world the overlooked and purposely omitted contributions of dedicated African American fathers (the Black Alpha Males embracing the *modus operandi* (MO) of Constructionist) who were unequivocally and truly committed to the advancement and betterment of their families, devoted men who unconditionally assumed the role of the 2P's (Providers and Protectors) in their homes and the African American Village Community at large. Hughes, along with other supportive and empowered African American females such as Ida B. Wells (who graciously allowed A. Philip Randolph to speak in her house on what is now 3715 S. Dr. Martin Luther King Drive Chicago, Illinois), willingly stride toward freedom with the Black Alpha Male Constructionist; positive males who evolved from the shackles of slavery through the African American Experience.

In the struggle for equality at every level of human intercourse in America, it is clear that a house divided cannot stand. The Village Concept was and still is an idea whose time has come. Sexism and the continuous negative perpetuation of capitalistic ideologies occupy no space in Hughes' philosophy of solidarity between African American males and females. Let it be said, as Lyn Hughes affirms, "That the Brotherhood was a Brotherhood-Sisterhood of men and women, husbands, and wives, sons and daughters, communities and villages, like the Village of Harlem and the Village of the South Side."[19]

While embracing the spirit and passion of Cultural Utilitarianism, Hughes believes that the primary purpose of the monumental historic site is to provide educational and cultural enrichment, especially to African Americans who are not aware of the tremendous contributions of men who were former slaves. All past, present and future activities of this historic site will promote the study, perseveration, enrichment, interpretation and enjoyment of African American history and culture. The unique collections and exhibits represent the study of the Pullman Historic District, the era of the Great Migration, American labor history (from an African American perspective), A. Philip Randolph, the Pullman Porters and the historic Civil Rights Movement.[20] The museum and the unfolding discovery of a rich history of African American men, Black Alpha Males who stood the test of time, represents clear evidence that African Americans must continue to fight and struggle together because there is hope. Most importantly, this hope (Empirical Hope) is embedded in our history, the history of a people whose forgotten history is still being discovered, acknowledged and written. We will now proudly examine a powerful African American woman (Dr. Margaret Burroughs) who similarly uncovered Empirical Hope that had been purposely omitted from our history. Burroughs is an African American woman par excellence and founder of the Du Sable Museum.

Unity is the key, and as previously stated throughout part I of this exegesis, noble African American women of the African American Village Community supported the Village Concept and indigenous promotion of Cultural Utilitarianism to initiate a preternatural and imperative Communal Healing. The empowerment encompassed in the concept of Communal Healing can best be described in the following manner: the spiritual restoration of cultural pride, cultural self-esteem and self-determination in juxtaposition to the complete absence of a bruised, wounded psyche caused by the implementation, sustaining, and promotion of institutionalized oppression. The primary purpose of oppression (a weapon of mass human destruction) is to cause a cultural void in the past, present and possibly the future expectations of the oppressed. Effective oppression strips a culture, a people of their individual and collective attachment to any and all social contributions to society at large. The dark voice from the abyss of time emits negative connotations and discourages the oppressed from hearing, seeing, reading and learning about significant aspects of their history, a rich history consisting of individuals, groups and organizations that contributed to the betterment of humanity and/or championed the cause of their own liberation. Specifically for African Americans, any modicum of the surfacing of Empirical Hope, which is embedded in the African American Experience (from the oppressor's collective perspective), must be immediately addressed (discouraged if you will) by any and all means necessary.

It is a common practice of White European conquerors, as well as military conquerors throughout history, to rewrite any and all indigenous literature (records, documents, scrolls books, manuscripts) of the conquered. The spoils of war go to the victor, and oppression of a conquered people becomes an imperative corrective to keep the oppressed permanently subdued under the iron fist of rule. For example, servitude and total submission (similar to the conditions faced by the Black Pullman Porters) became the norm, not the exception to the rule. However, from the ashes of oppression and a total disconnection from our rightful place in history rose another drum major for social justice. She unapologetically decided that we would not be separated (divided, if you will) from our true history and the right to sit at the table of humanity and be rightfully and deservingly recognized. Propelled by the power of Ground Zero, the African American Experience, the Inter-Related Structure of Black Reality, Historical Discipline and an uncompromised commitment to a Communal Initiative, Margaret Goss Burroughs and her husband Charles Burroughs (as well as Gerard Lew and other supporters) decided to fill the void and abyss caused by the intentional agenda of cultural disenfranchisement promoted by the gatekeepers of wealth and power in America. On February 16, 1961, the Ebony Museum of Negro History and Art was established on the ground floor of the Burroughs' home at 3806 S. Michigan Avenue, Chicago, Illinois.[21] This humble gesture would set the precedent for the establishment of one of the greatest educational institutions celebrating the lives of great African Americans.

The idea of a museum surfaced in 1945, prior to the Burroughs' marriage. Mrs. Burroughs used her coach house located at 3806 S. Michigan in Chicago as the gallery for her personal exhibits. The Quincy Club members, a club of Black railroad workers who used the front building as a clubhouse, heard about the museum idea and sold the entire lot to the Burroughs. Charles and Margaret chartered the establishment in February 1961, during Negro History Week.[22] In 1968, the museum was renamed in honor of Jean Baptiste Pointe Du Sable, a Haitian fur trapper, a Black man, and the first non Native American permanent settler in Chicago. It was from this founding base that the city of Chicago formed its origin. The museum eventually outgrew the Burroughs' home, and in 1973, it was moved to a new facility located at 740 E. 56th Place, Chicago. Antoinette Wright is the present director.

The new edifice came by way of an agreement with the City of Chicago. The date was February 1973. In the presence of life long friends, several hundred guests, well wishers, city officials, faithful museum supporters and close family at the Educators Committee Annual Benefit Colloquium Luncheon, Dr. Margaret Burroughs formally announced that the DuSable Museum had been granted the use of the Washington Park building. Moving by the power of God, Burroughs and her skeleton staff and board members envisioned a major cultural establishment beyond the humble beginnings of the Ma and Pa original site. Through faith in a greater power, the floodgates for major funding soon poured in. The Chicago Community Trust granted the nonprofit organization $300,000 for the building fund. Notably, a successful proposal was submitted to the Oscar Mayer Company. The Woods Charitable Fund and the Field Foundation contributed $100,000 each. In addition, the Standard Oil Company donated $45,000.[23]

Burroughs' Communal Initiative fanned the cultural flames of Utilitarianism and the Village Concept. Believers and supporters of this new, innovative, educational institution moved full speed ahead with a commitment to light the torch of knowledge and shine brightly against the abyss of the oppressor's agenda to erase African American contributions from the pages of history. Supporters such as the late Representative Ralph Metcalfe, Dr. Ruth Fouche, Madeline Rabb, Audrey Tuggle, Charles Hightower, Mary Ellen Bell, Helen Fredrick, Leo Sparks, Bernice Walker, Gus Cherry, Irwin Salk, Eugene and Felicia Ford, and Lee Hillary just to name a few from the exhaustive list of major supporters, worked tirelessly with the Burroughs.

Dr. Margaret Burroughs (the principle founder of the distinguished DuSable Museum) unequivocally supports an all out indigenous based Communal Initiative to address the bruised psyches of African Americans. Margaret Burroughs (a force to be reckoned with) can be described as a tenacious person who knew how to successfully gather friends, how to gather money, how to gather books, papers, archives, photographs, tapes and rare hard-to-find documents. She institutively knew how to surround herself with a sound, solid core of volunteers who possessed a genuine shared love for Black History and for the work she was doing.

The DuSable Museum is recognized as the oldest and largest caretaker of African American culture in the United States. Through volunteerism, devoted supporters and major financial investors, the museum has expanded to reflect the continuous growing interest in African American culture. While other museums throughout the country have faltered due to decreased public support and a weakening economy, the DuSable Museum has historically and not surprisingly held its ground. Notably, it became the eighth museum located on Chicago Park District land. In a classic show of creating the Beloved Community, in addition to focusing on African American culture, "It is one of several Chicago Museums that celebrates Chicago's ethnic and cultural heritage."[24]

According to Antoinette Wright, the director of the museum (2011), the African American art exhibits have grown out of a need for African Americans to preserve their history both orally and in art form due to the historical obstacles hindering other important forms of documentation. Wright unequivocally believes that the DuSable Museum serves as a powerful motivational tool for African Americans at large. The museum continuously empowers African Americans, collectively and individually, to heal from institutionalized forms of continuous negative campaigns that demean any and all cultural contributions to their history and the world. This indigenous perspective highlighting the cultural contributions of an oppressed people serves as an awakening; African American history cannot, by any stretch of the imagination, be extracted or erased from the memory of this great nation. As time progressed and the residue of slavery began to lose its death grip, African Americans began to play vital roles in the political, educational and cross-cultural arenas, including the founding of the city of Chicago.[25] It is in this spirit and perspective that a new wing was built to house a permanent exhibit honoring the achievement of the late great Mayor Harold Washington, the first African American Mayor of Chicago, with memorabilia, personal effects and highlights of his political career. The museum similarly serves as the city's primary memorial to Jean Baptiste Pointe DuSable. Other notable highlights of various special collections include the desk of the great activist Ida B. Wells and the violin of the distinguished poet Paul Laurence Dunbar.[26]

According to a *Frommer's Review* published in *The New York Times*, the DuSable Museum possesses a collection of *rare* artifacts, books, photographs, art objects and historical memorabilia. The collections (acquired primarily from private gifts) emphasizes artists of African descent, themes, and topics pertaining to African American history, culture, and the historical African Diaspora, dating from the mid-nineteenth century to the present. The museum's collection includes United States slavery era relics, 19th and 20th century artifacts and archival materials, including the diaries of Sea Explorer Captain Harry Dean. Scholarly works include rare, memorable collections from W.E. B. Du Bois, sociologist St. Clair Drake and poet Langston Hughes. The special African American Art Collection contains works from South Side Community Art Center students Charles White, Archibald Motley, Jr., Charles Sebree and Marion Perkins. The collection also includes numerous works from the New Deal Works Progress Administration period and the 1960's Black Arts Movement. The museum successfully acquired prints and drawings by Henry O. Tanner, Richmond Barthe and Romare Bearden. The archives include an enormous collection of records and books specifically pertaining to African and African American culture and history.[27] The original north entrance was designed by Daniel Burnham, and the new wing encompasses 25,000 square feet. The auditorium seats 466 and hosts community events, including jazz and blues concerts, poetry readings, film screenings and other cultural events. The gift shop and research library have become a welcome destination for visitors of the DuSable Museum. The museum's funding of the new facility is partially dependent on a Chicago Park District tax levy. After the 1993 expansion of the new wing the museum encompassed 50,000 square feet (4,600 m2) of exhibition space. The $4 million expansion was funded by a $2 million matching funds grant from city and state officials.[28]

Dr. Burroughs' resume and endless campaign to revive the spirit of Empirical Hope is unprecedented. Notably, Dr. Burroughs joined other distinguished artists who publicly displayed their works at the South Side Community Art Center. This particular center was established in 1940 (located across the street from DuSable) by the Works Progress Administration (WPA) and dedicated by First Lady Eleanor Roosevelt in 1941. This drum major for social justice relentless campaign to bring authentic healing to the African American Village Community can be summed up in the following year-by-year dedication to excellence:

- **1946–69** DuSable High School, Chicago, art teacher

- **1961-84** DuSable Museum of African American History, Director and Founder; **1984** director emeritus

- **1968** Chicago Institute of Art, Assistant Professor of African American Art History

- **1968** Professor of African American art and culture, Elmhurst College; **1969** Barat College

- **1969–79** Kennedy-King Community College, Chicago, Professor of Humanities

- **1985** Founder and Director, The Burroughs Group

- Exhibitions of artwork include American Negro Exhibition, Chicago, **1940**; Atlanta Negro Art Exhibition, **1947, 1955**; San Francisco Civic Museum, **1949**; Leipzig, East Germany, **1965**; Friendship House, Moscow, USSR, **1967**; Evans-Tibbs Collection, Washington, DC, **1982**; Nicole Gallery, Chicago, **1986**; Museum of Fine Arts, Houston, **1988**.[29]

Dr. Burroughs' personal works were featured at the exclusive Corcoran Art Galleries in Washington, DC, and at the Studio Museum in New York. This drum major for social justice also served as the Art Director for the Negro Hall of Fame. Burroughs published several volumes of her elite poetry and illustrated the famous book, *What Shall I Tell My Children Who Are Black?* In 1975, Burroughs received the

Presidential Humanitarian Award. In 1977, the co-founder was named one of Chicago's Most Influential Women by the historical Black newspaper, the *Chicago Defender*. The late Mayor Harold Washington designated February 1, 1986, as Dr. Margaret Burroughs' Day. The social justice advocate was interviewed by *The History Makers* on June 12, 2000.[30]

In examining her life works, it becomes clear that Margaret Burroughs promoted Cultural Utilitarianism. The founder of the historical museum believed that:

> Every individual wants to leave a legacy; to be remembered for something positive they have done for the community. Long after I'm dead and gone the DuSable Museum will still be here.[31]

In support of a collective Communal Initiative and the African American Experience Burroughs states:

> A lot of black museums have opened up, but we are the only one that grew out of the indigenous Black community (the African American Village Community if you will). We were started by ordinary folks.[32]

In addressing, nurturing and sustaining the spirit of *A House Divided...No More*, Dr. Margaret Burroughs and her husband, Charles Gordon Burroughs, opened their home to the fledgling museum that was supported by an indigenous group of believers. This institution would begin the preternatural, indigenous process of healing the bruised and wounded psyche of African Americans; they unequivocally believed that the institution would become a healing balm and stand as an indomitable lighted torch of Empirical Hope within the parameters of the African American Village Community. Most importantly, in the spirit of Dr. Martin King's historic, philosophical question, Why we can't wait? the Burroughs "realized that if they wanted an institution for preserving and displaying Black heritage they would have to create it themselves."[33]

During the writing of this exegesis, Dr. Margaret Burroughs joined her husband and took her final rest on November 21, 2010. Unofficial records indicate that she was 93. However, her close relatives memorialized her officially at 95 years of age. I pray that she find rest after her earthly visit.

Unity is the key. Embedded in the actions and words of Margaret Burroughs we find evidence of an urgency to embrace the spirit of self-reliance and self-determination. It is in this spirit that we find another African American woman who decided to recreate, if you will, a true sense of community in the African American Village, especially in the arena of revitalizing the respect and honor due to African American fathers—an endangered human species targeted for extinction. African American fathers who are marginalized; African American fathers whose bruised spirits cry out for an olive branch and desire healing between themselves and the African American Village Community. With a similar spirit as the Burroughs' couple in their quest to enhance, empower, enrich and restore the Village Community to a level of respectability, Yvette Moyo-Gillard and Kofi Moyo (the name Moyo means soul or from the heart) took the torch of Empirical Hope. Through blood, sweat and tears, the couple fanned the flames, thereby igniting the collective preternatural spirit of a Communal Initiative to promote Communal Healing and usher in Cultural Utilitarianism within the parameters of the African American Village Community. The Village Concept became an idea whose time had come in addressing a divided and wounded Village Community.

Yvette Moyo-Gillard, a graduate of Eastern Illinois University, has a strong corporate experience that includes 11 years of magazine ad sales, promotions and marketing. She served as Senior Vice President of Sales and Promotion at Dollars & Sense Magazine, creator of MOBE (Marketing Opportunities in Business and Technology), launched the MOBE IT (Influencers and Innovators in Internet & Technology) and served as the host of a White House briefing on Blacks in technology.

Moyo-Gillard inevitably decided that Black-on-Black violence was unconscionable and a cry for help. According to Moyo-Gillard, what was missing was atonement and the only thing that could replace unprovoked violence upon one's own people was love. To change this unacceptable condition, our daily conversations must unequivocally change. Furthermore, the preoccupation of childhood scars and wounds, coupled with the negative connotations of Jim Crow (through the intentional promotion of the institutionalized marginalization of the oppressed), weigh heavily upon our psychological well-being. The relentless assault began with slavery and continues to this very day through the effective use of cultural brainwashing. It dominates our very lives and saturates our existence. We as a people must unequivocally (collectively) expose our children and grandchildren to what Yvette Moyo-Gillard defines as the *goodness of ourselves* and not be obsessed with the umbilical cord of negativity that has been attached to our psyche by greedy capitalists, the gatekeepers of wealth in this country. Y. Moyo-Gillard (personal communication, December 12, 2010)

This drum major for social justice decided to not only come to terms with the past, but in opposition to the negative psychological indoctrination, began to see each new day as a God-given opportunity to love, laugh and really live. In understanding the violence, you can come up with real life solutions. Moyo-Gillard reasoned that the misguided Black Alpha Male Destructionist are overwhelmed by the capitalist perception that a man's value is directly and intuitively tied to his ability to financially provide for his family. She began to notice undeniable trends in African American unemployment among African American males and the epidemic of violence that begin to consume and overpower the African American Village Community. She unequivocally believes that net worth does not, by any stretch of the imagination, equate to self-worth, but we must begin with self first. Y. Moyo-Gillard (personal communication, December 12, 2010)

Moyo-Gillard endorses the concept of self-love being used in the Freedom Schools (i.e., Urban Prep Academies), which will be discussed in the final chapter of this exegesis). The concept of self-love is nonnegotiable and should become a categorical imperative in the character curriculum of schools throughout this nation. Moyo-Gillard believes that self-love will cut down on the chaos both in the classroom and the community. Moreover, the evils of divorce, the American way of perpetuating more division, must not be systematically and continuously ignored but collectively addressed head on by the inhabitants of the Village Community. African American males and females are divided continuously by the greed perpetuated through capitalistic ideologies and money hungry lawyers who mimic the feeding of hungry sharks as they pit us against each other during divorce proceedings.

In addition to the above negative indoctrination we must begin to find amicable ways to address family disputes (divorce, separation, parental rights, etc). Instead of embracing the evil stepmother paradigm or the widely used your father is just no good mentality, Yvette Moyo-Gillard believes that we need to create new conversations where everyone matters. The authentic Communal Healing process can only begin when we change our conversations (especially negative ones) and our way of thinking. For instance, after an amicable separation (for the betterment of the children and all involved), she believes that we should embrace the extended family concept, which translates into increased opportunities for love, no matter what the configuration of the families. If love is in the midst of both families, the children will have a stronger foundation and not be torn into choosing between one parent or the other, between one family or the other, between one house or the other. We must not divide our children. Y. Moyo-Gillard (personal communication, December 12, 2010)

Yvette and Kofi pondered over the divided house paradigm in the African American Village Community and decided that the wounded, bruised image and psyche of the endangered human species, African American males, must be immediately addressed. The question surfaced, What about the good, humble, faithful fathers in the African American Village Community who, against insurmountable odds similar to the Black Pullman Porters, were being Providers and Protectors (the 2 P's) of their families and the Village Community? If these unsung heroes of the Village Community were publicly celebrated, this would serve as an olive branch to those fathers who lack (have turned away for whatever reasons) fatherhood responsibilities. This, Moyo-Gillard believed, would initiate an authentic healing process that would nurture the bruised, collective psyches of the indigenous Village Community at large, including women and children. Based on Judge Eugene Pincham's philosophy that you can't be what you don't see, the creation of Real Men Cook (RMC) began to successfully provide the disenfranchised families of the greater Village Community with continuous positive images of not only good male participants but visibly healthy, working relationships between the once divided African American males and females. Through eyewitness accounts from participants and news media, the event began to send a collective message to the public that through this Communal Initiative, the healing process had begun. Most importantly, the unsung heroes (dedicated African American fathers) who never took a bow publicly or privately for their commitment to their families and the community are now participants in a movement, the greatest movement since the Civil Rights Movement.

The sea of fathers, including fathers from other races throughout the communities, boldly and in an unapologetic voice proclaimed that we have earned a right to sit at the table of humanity. The 2 P's Providers and Protectors of the African American Village Community now stand side by side with White and Hispanic fathers. They stepped forward to become role models for those who continue to straddle the fence in their fatherhood responsibilities. Moyo-Gillard proudly yet humbly believes that the annual event has indeed become fertile ground for the healing process, a process that can only be initiated by God. She reports that not only have men gone on to connect with their fathers because of their participation in the event, but they have reconnected and mended broken relationships with their children, mothers, wives, ex-wives and significant others in their lives. In addition, men who are not biological fathers have become volunteer mentors-fathers. These positive Black Alpha Males are bringing some of the local neighborhood children to the event. The perception and role of fathers have taken on a new definition: to stand against the evil capitalistic perpetuation of the hunting down of men they call *deadbeat dads*. This humanitarian annual event has found a special place in participants' hearts; human hearts that were once broken due to failed and severed relationships within the family structure.

The subliminal message from the RMC event is quite simple: it's time to change our conversation. It's time for indigenous Communal Healing. From a historical perspective, Real Men Cook represents a special roll call for Fathers to step up and become visible in the lives of their children. It's an invitation, if you will, for men to become positive participants in the family structure. Real Men Cook has become the largest family celebration in the country. Father's Day 2011 will be the 22nd anniversary of the event, which has expanded to more than 10 leading cities in the United States.

The awesome preternatural healing power of this annual celebration goes far beyond the limits of the annual Father's Day event. The power of this day honoring fathers has far exceeded the expectations of the founders. It is now the catalyst for the creation of critical family services. The power of this family based event has expanded beyond the United States and become annual traditions in the Bahamas, London, Paris and on the continent of Africa.[34] Presently, Real Men Cook is the leading urban Father's Day experience. In addition to the in-person camaraderie enjoyed by the participants at the event, even more viewers share the experience through interactive news programming and media coverage. The event received more than 136 million media audience impressions in 2002 and more than 200 million during the 2010 annual event. "That's worth over $5 million in value in a single year."[35]

Beyond the media coverage is the importance of the intrinsic value of the event. The contributions and presence of males and the spiritual connections with their families and the community at large can best be described as unprecedented.

> RMC causes us to focus on not just the biological fathers, but men who make a difference in the lives of their families and communities. Men and women alike appreciate, celebrate, and collectively embrace this concept.[36]

This unprecedented gathering supports the hypothesis of the Village Concept, a concept that produces fertile ground for the initiation of the indigenous healing process. Most importantly, when there is a mass coming together, division, strife and unforgiveness cannot strangle the spirit of Empirical Hope in the lives and minds of the participants. Needless to say, this concept is conducive with indigenous and Communal Healing. This continuous, imperative, preternatural occurrence has become a necessary corrective for an authentic healing process: a human directive promoted by God, the Creator and Unmoved Mover. God is not pleased, by any stretch of the human or spiritual imagination, with the sustaining and promotion of schisms (evil intent) between African American males and females that are maliciously and intentionally perpetuated by capitalism, division, and greed.

Within RMC's Mission Statement and Real Men Charities, a year-round extension of the spirit of Real Men Cook (also founded by Sister Yvette Moyo-Gillard in 2003), the continuous creation, support and sustaining of Dr. Martin L. King and Mrs. Coretta Scott King's Beloved Community is paramount and unconditional. In addition to supporting and nurturing an indigenous Communal Initiative for the Village Community and Utilitarianism for the community, the themes of *agape* love, unity, and reconciliation are quite evident.

The ethical statement of intent for RMC Charities, Inc. supports a year-round human investment in the greater Village Community. RMC Charities, Inc. is determined to positively improve the way the world celebrates family and community by increasing the proportion of opportunities for committed and detached males to become involved, responsible and committed fathers for the good of all communities, families and youth. The mission directives include the following:

- Educating and inspiring all people through public awareness campaigns, research and other screenings.

- Equipping and developing leaders of national, state and community male, youth and family initiatives through curricula, training and technical assistance.

- Engaging every sector of society through strategic alliances and partnerships.

- Promoting public health, mental, physical, emotional and economics by disseminating medical information to the general public without charge, including healthy cooking, fitness and lifestyle.

- Strengthening the universal institution of family and encourage parents to practice Family First in their lives.[37]

As previously mentioned, the Father's Day event is no longer exclusive to the African American Village Community. Its expansion to other cultures has become the epitome of the concept of the Beloved Community. Furthermore, the event has assisted African Americans males in breaking the mental chains of enslavement caused by oppression that specifically target African Americans males (Black Alpha Males). The six chains of oppression addressed through a massive Communal Initiative supporting the complete emancipation of all African American males (according to a poster designed by WAK) can be categorized in the following manner:

Chain 1: From the lock (mid-body near the hips and pelvis) to the neck...This chain specifically and intentionally keeps the head of the African American male in a downward and negative position, stripping him of pride and self-esteem.

Chains 2 & 3: From the lock (mid-body near the hips and pelvis) to the wrists...Keeps the African American male from reaching for anything in life (i.e., his dreams and visions of becoming a Provider and Protector of the African American Village Community).

Chain 4: From the lock (mid-body near the hips and pelvis) to the ground...Keeps the African American male grounded and in his submissive place.

Chains 5 & 6: From the lock (mid-body near the hips and pelvis) to his ankles...Keeps the African American male, generation after generation, engaged in psychological mind games. This gives him the illusion that he can run from his problems, but he can only go so far before he is back where he started[38]—in an original state of servitude and oppression and into an abyss of hopelessness; completely separated from his God assigned role as the Providers and Protectors of the African American Village Community.

Moved by a greater power (the Unmoved Mover), countless African American males have gained the power of self-determination to rewrite their family history. These Black Alpha Males represent a new generation of fathers who are determined more than ever not to be a statistic in the dead pool of America's hypocrisy. They refused to be labeled with the unmerited title of *deadbeat dad*. Slowly but surely the six chains of oppression, one by one, are being broken on a daily basis. In the words of Maya Angelou, we will write our own history, we will take control of our own destiny.[39]

Each year during the Real Men Cook Father's Day event, the African American Experience reaches a new level of meaning, moving from the confines of the immediate family to what the co-founder categorizes as a preternatural family reunion. This is a spirit that absolutely cannot be divided. This is a necessary corrective, if you will. Moreover, where there is a spirit of unity and reunion, division cannot occupy the same space. Moyo-Gillard affirms that the RMC annual event is a classic celebration of family, no matter what the configuration. The family event is indeed an olive branch extended to the African American Village Community. Most importantly, this branch is extended to single moms who have not lost interest in the tradition of celebrating Father's Day. This community-based event can be used by single parents to highlight the existence and presence of good men, of real men, both in the family and the community. Yvette Moyo-Gillard emphasizes the intent of promoting the greater good, an all inclusive paradigm, in the concept of Cultural Utilitarianism:

> Let me emphasize that giving back is a very nationalist concept and I'm happy to say that Real Men Cook is an institution that has generated over $1 million to non profits, and not just Black organizations, but the food banks, blood banks, numerous YMCA's, Boys & Girls Clubs, various Museums and more. We give thanks everyday to the generosity of men and the sisters in the background (consistent dedicated yearly supporters and community activists) who volunteer to maintain structure and organization to the event. And, while we thank the men for cooking they know that the message is not about cooking at all but providing something that matters. We say, you come for the food and we'll feed the soul.[40]

Yvette Moyo-Gillard's honors include, but are not limited to:

- **1983** Black Achievers Award, YMCA
- **1985** Kizzy Award, Black Women's Hall of Fame
- **1988** 100 Women to Watch, Today's Chicago Woman
- **1998** Public Relations Advertising and Marketing Excellence Award

- **1999** Guest for the African American Leaders of the Internet
- **2000** Director of MOBE White House African American Business Briefing
- **2002** Women in Entertainment Pioneer Award
- **2002** Influential Women in Business, Network Journal
- **2003** V-103 Phenomenal Woman Award
- **2003** 50 Women of Excellence Award
- **2007** Guest on *Emeril Live* when company was featured for the full hour-long program reaching 800,000+ households.
- **2011** Drum Major for Social Justice Award-on behalf of RMC.[41]

Yvette Moyo-Gillard's personal testimony concerning the relationship with her father and the healing that took place serves as a reminder that this drum major for social justice is living her vocation: to bring children back into a rightful, healthy relationship with their fathers. Her father, Rudolph Sherman Jackson, was a dedicated Christian and followed her to Trinity United Church of Christ (Chicago, Illinois) in 1978 after falling away from the faith. After hearing Rev. Dr. Jeremiah Wright, he was moved by the power of God to return to the fold and became a deacon. He was widely known as Deacon Rudy for the final 15 years of his life. Yvette Moyo-Gillard confessed that throughout the years she harbored some differences with her father. However, after coming down off her know-it-all and judgmental high-horse she began to genuinely, soulfully and unconditionally love her father. During the last 20 years, her father was bestowed with the distinguished honor of delivering the opening prayer at the Real Men Cook events on Father's Day in Chicago, Illinois. He was routinely comical and virtually overwhelmed by the distinguished high honor. In retrospect, she could hear his commitment to their relationship in his prayers. Ironically,

Moyo-Gillard started the Real Men Cook event to address the dysfunctional relationships in families between fathers and their children. Truly, this drum major for social justice, whose steps have been anointed by God, has been tremendously blessed by this special journey. Given that the mission statement of RMC is to give all people the experience of being fathered, the annual Real Men Cook gathering has become a necessary corrective for so many participants and supporters of this extravaganza, including people who have been blessed with fathers and a close relationship with their parents.

Today, the Beloved Community includes almost 1,000 men (across the country) who willingly donate their time and resources to cook and serve the public. The RMC event (originating in Chicago) has expanded to major cities such as Atlanta, Baltimore, Benton Harbor, Columbia S.C., Dallas, Detroit, Houston, Miami, Los Angeles, New Orleans, New York, Philadelphia, Phoenix, East St. Louis and Washington, DC. Media coverage from *USA Today, USA Weekly, Southern Living, Ebony, Essence, Time Magazine* and *Black Enterprise* routinely televise and recognize the national Father's Day celebration.[42] This event dispels the myth that there are no real men in urban families and communities. The annual RMC event not only addresses the healing of the soul but the body as well. To that end RMC Charities, Inc. is committed to healthy families and communities. Partnerships with the South Side YMCA and the Community Mental Health Council and donations to each organization of more than $130,000 since the inception of Real Men Cook underscore the organization's primary mission and unfaltering, uncompromised commitment to restoring communities.

RMC Charities, Inc.'s Health & Wellness Pavilion, which is held as part of RMC events in every city, delivers between 500 and 3,000 free health screenings at the end of each day. Moyo-Gillard supports the mental health initiative and insists that silence is not an option. The socio-economic condition breeds mental health issues, particularly in the African American Village Community. She believes that the position the United States has taken on slavery and the corralling (the Rule of Containment, the Rule of Selective Engagement, and the dreaded Rule of Annihilation) of African American males have caused stress levels that consistently result in the mental imbalance of those specifically targeted for containment, assimilation or annihilation. RMC Charities, Inc. has decided to be proactive: proactive instead of reactive. This authentic consistent proactive stance, including the dualism (interconnectedness) of a Communal Initiative and indigenous Communal Healing, is quite evident in a newly developed public relations program appropriately categorized as *Gimme Five*. This special grassroots initiative focuses on healthy living and screenings to increase the life expectancy of African American males (an endangered human species) by five years. Gimme Five encourages Black males to become fully focused on what it takes to expand their life expectancy. The idea is to put at least five things in place to make the body strong enough to better fight diseases like cancer and to create a social environment that reduces stress. The five essential steps in this public health initiative are as follows:

- Get regular health screenings. Call Real Men Cook Charities, Inc. to find out how to get free screenings where you live.

- Eliminate stress with regular exercise. Begin with walking, yoga or martial arts. Just get started and create a routine.

- Add something green (daily) to every meal and double your water intake. You'll notice the difference within a week. Snack on fruits and vegetables. Real Men eat

healthy and avoid illnesses that cause friends and
family members to worry about them.

- Mend broken relationships, connect with those you
love and get love in return. Be a dad to a fatherless
child. Encourage others.

- Donate your time and talents. This increases your self
worth and delivers rewards that will have you looking
forward to each day.[43]

Additional RMC Charities events include Roast &
Toast, Real Men Love, Real Men Cook with Kids Program
and Real Men Charities Kids Carnival. The healing power of
the annual Father's Day event has proved to be magical under
the leadership and direction of co-founder Yvette Moyo-
Gillard. Leading women such as WGN TV's Merri Dee, Fox
TV's Robin Robinson and WYCC TV's Deborah Crable have
joined the ranks of other powerful and influential African
American women who support the efforts of this monumental
community gathering.

Similar to the No Child Left Behind initiative the RMC
event addresses the scars of children who feel left behind. The
event targets the preternatural void of children who are
fatherless (for whatever reason) and feel left behind when
compared to their peers. Moyo-Gillard insists that they need
not feel empty on Father's Day. Once again the healing
powers of unity surfaces and women have become the number
one purchasers of tickets to this festive event. Entire families
congregate and celebrate fathers beyond the biological
definition. A unifying air of acceptance filters down to uncles,
grandfathers and brothers. Children throughout the African
American Village Community and other communities benefit
greatly from the positive images, messages and pluralistic
array of role models. RMC is an event that women love and
attend; the positive spirit and experience last far beyond

Father's Day. The spirit promoting the concept of union, a family reunion, if you will, is virtually indescribable.[44] Sister Moyo-Gillard's effort (along with yearly faithful volunteers) to bring authentic indigenous Communal Healing to the African American Village Community at large (inclusive of other cultures and communities) has become a formidable weapon, a countermeasure (if you will) against the void, abyss of division and an indigenous, innate, humanitarian appeal and invitation to the Black Alpha Male Destructionist, the Black Alpha Male Objectionist and the noble believer and promoter of the fictive concept, the Black Alpha Male Constructionist.

In summary, according to the book entitled *Brother to Brother (A Message of Hope)*, seventy percent of Black Alpha Males fall under the Destructionist *modus operandi* (MO). Moreover, due to their asocial behavior they have become categorized under the auspices of public enemy number one. The Destructionist's indigenous assault upon his own family, his own village, his own mother, his own daughter and other Black Alpha Males has earned him the undisputed title of the sole promoter of Black-on-Black violence. Education, cultural unity and the advancement of his people mean little or nothing to this misguided, misplaced, confused and angry male. The anger from historical oppression is unapologetically released upon his own oppressed brothers and sisters in the struggle.[45]

In addition to the Destructionist, twenty percent of Black Alpha Males fall under the Objectionist *modus operandi* (MO). They have consciously removed themselves, through the process of time, from the allegiance and/or emotional attachment to their birthright as African Americans. The Objectionist's success within the hierarchy of the capitalist system represents his innate, selfish, self-centered, exclusive and individualistic defining moment. Neither the cultural loyalty of the Constructionist nor the genocidal tendencies of the Destructionist is important to this group. Money, success, power, inclusion and social acceptance are paramount goals to be achieved by any and all means necessary. In juxtaposition to this analogical indigenous assessment, cultural amnesia is the order of the day. The Objectionist perceives Blackness and his cultural placement (by God, the Creator) as burdens, a daily nuisance if you will. The apparent plight, suffering and daily oppression of his people are unapologetically non-issues in his life. Those who continue to struggle for human dignity below the Glass Ceiling in America are perceived as beneath his standards, a group of people to be avoided or at the very least, only included in general round table conversations with other above-the-ceiling close associates (Objectionist and/or successful Whites).[46]

The Constructionist distinctly represents the Talented Tenth. This drum major for educational, economic, political and social justice can routinely be found in the trenches of the African American Village Community throughout this great nation. This particularly proud Black Alpha Male will never compromise his spirit of cultural loyalty (bestowed upon him by God, the Creator and Unmoved Mover) in exchange for social acceptance, monetary advancement and/or house nigger status. Any and all personal gain is attributed to God, who has graciously allowed him to take his rightful place as the 2 P's (Providers and Protectors) of the African American Village Community. The overall and general welfare of his family, extended family, community and loved ones, coupled with the psychological, social, political and educational advancement of the African American Village Community (inclusive of his wife or significant other, children, neighbors, in-laws, etc.), is unequivocally a categorical imperative.[47]

The appeal for the Destructionist and Objectionist to participate in Communal Healing and a Communal Initiative is unprecedented by any standard. In juxtaposition to this innate and immeasurable cultural contribution, Yvette Moyo-Gillard's uncompromised belief in the indigenous nurturing, creation and implementation of Cultural Utilitarianism (an all-inclusive cultural event) through the communal gathering of the human family has become a force to be reckoned with—an effective, powerful, social force in defusing the continuous, negative, psychological indoctrinations and effects of the Rule of Containment, the Rule of Selective Engagement and the Rule of Annihilation. Under the auspices of Unity Is the Key, Moyo-Gillard has worked diligently to invite and extend an olive branch to Black Alpha Males from all three of the previously mentioned categories of males to the table of reconciliation; it is at this inclusive table that hundreds, maybe even thousands, of wayward males have reconnected with others as a result of this special gathering. The illumination of Empirical Hope (a healing balm derived from the power of prayer) generated through this indigenous grassroots human family reunion clearly stands over and against the abyss of the negative forces of separation, isolation, rejection and last, but not least, unforgiveness.

Moyo-Gillard's respect and philosophy of maintaining healthy dialogues with Black Alpha Males who are targeted for failure and desolation under the notorious Rule of Containment have proved to be successful. She reinforces and celebrates the activism of the Constructionist who never wavier from his uncompromised commitment to promote unity; these courageous and faithful Black Alpha Males are strong and active participants in the rebuilding and restoration efforts (atonement campaign) of the African American Village Community. They proudly represent God's voice crying in the wilderness; they are Black males who have been targeted by the gatekeepers of power and wealth: the primary purpose of the opposition is to silence the call for equality and liberation.

Similarly, Moyo-Gillard's uncompromised decision to include the Black Alpha Male Objectionist who falls under the auspices of the Rule of Selective Engagement have stood the test of time. These select Black Alpha Males have successfully shattered the Glass Ceiling in America; this privileged group has acquired a rare plateau of temporary generic acceptance. However, their temporary acceptance in mainstream America is based on a Jim Crow era prerequisite criteria: they must publicly and unapologetically remove themselves socially, physically, psychologically, politically, economically and, most importantly, culturally from any form of association with their disenfranchised brothers and sisters of the struggle. They must prove themselves worthy of this conditional acceptance by implementing a continuous public disassociation of their divine purpose for being. Be that as it may the RMC event unapologetically offers these prodigal sons an honest chance to reconsider, a chance to reconcile, a chance to sit at the table of humanity with his brothers and sisters of the struggle.

Finally, Moyo-Gillard, a woman of faith, supports the biblical concept that God will leave the ninety-nine to seek the one that is lost. In combating the dark, wicked forces of the Rule of Annihilation, a weapon of mass human destruction, she has repeatedly and tirelessly campaigned throughout the years to reach the Black Alpha Male Destructionist who have fallen into despair. These wayward males are encouraged by the gatekeepers of wealth to increase and continue their negative agenda of Black-on-Black genocide and self-hatred. Needless to say, these brothers have a special place in the secret chambers of her heart. Furthermore, the personal, historical and contemporary understanding of the bruised psyche of the Black Alpha Male and the need to promote a spirit of atonement have helped tremendously in bridging the schism caused by the evil tenets of capitalism, segregation and Slavocracy.

God, the Creator and Unmoved Mover, posed the existential question to Yvette Moyo-Gillard: Can these dry bones in the African American Village Community live? The daughter of Rudolph Jackson, a drum major for social justice, humbly answered, yes, Lord, they can, with your divine assistance! From the ashes of the dry bones and residue left by Jim Crow, Slavocracy and the tenets of economic, political, educational, cultural, social and psychological strangulation, Yvette Moyo-Gillard, moving by the power of God, a Power greater than herself, has become a human instrument of Empirical Hope. This special hope, based on the African American Experience, represents a gift from God, the Creator and Unmoved Mover, to the present and future generations of the African American Village Community.

Similar to the courageous, outspoken, and continuous efforts of Mrs. Coretta Scott King, Yvette Moyo-Gillard in a most bold yet humble manner has continuously, purposely, and successfully created vital fertile ground for a grassroots movement: an all-inclusive cultural summit, for the creation, promotion and sustaining of the Beloved Community. Yvette-Moyo Gillard's vision and belief in the Beloved Community has become a force to be reckoned with. With the assistance, love, respect and support of her male counterparts (ex-husband, Kofi and current husband, Derrick), her vocation and life's journey has become synonymous with the collective concept that Unity Is the Key and *A House Divided...No More*. Her grace, humility, determination and uncompromised fortitude to become an example for African American women not to invest into the self-destructive cup of hatred, bitterness, revenge, and unforgiveness was clearly shown when personal differences encroached upon her marriage to Kofi. By any and all means necessary, she remains friends with the co-founder and maintains a consistent, respectable and amicable working relationship. Her new husband is Derrick Gillard. Her belief in unity, healing and restoration confronts, dissect and destroys any and all myths pertaining to the perpetuation of permanent, irreconcilable differences among the inhabitants of the Village Community at large; myths of division that were planted and nurtured by the creation, sustaining and promotion of the infamous and notorious Willie Lynch Syndrome.

Yvette Moyo-Gillard's decision to rebuild all of her personal relationships with Black Alpha Males has restored hope in the collective philosophy of *A House Divided...No More*. As a result of her tenacious determination, young men strive to be real men, and mature men now stand up proudly to be counted. In the arena of Black Alpha Males, this event and the imperative year-round support programs implemented and supported by RMC Charities, Inc. have become a healing balm and an oasis that supplies critical social services, a necessary corrective to strife and division. This imperative corrective serves as an effective countermeasure to the Glass Ceiling that addresses the bruised psyche of the human male species: an endangered species branded under the oppressive sub-human title of expendable human commodities. It is well to note that more and more men (African Americans) have reclaimed their seat at the table of humanity, staking claim to their God-inherited rights as Providers and Protectors. Most importantly, they are consistently bringing their wives, significant others, sons, daughters, students, nephews, nieces, cousins, stepsons, stepdaughters and extended families with them. Moving by the power of God, the Creator, a Power greater than themselves, houses that were once divided are divided...no more. The time for *indigenous* Communal Healing in the Village Community is now an idea whose time has come. Because of Sister Yvette Moyo-Gillard, it is an unfolding reality.

We will now examine another critical necessary human corrective to be used in combating all forms of oppression and marginalization in America. In Part II of this exegesis the notable Constructionist (intellectual Black Alpha Males) of the African American Village Community instruct and invite us as a people united to engage the enemy of negative indoctrination with the cultural defenses of Black Psychological Warfare.

Part II:

Black Psychological Warfare

The ultimate measure of a man is not where he stands in moments of comfort and convenience, but where he stands at times of challenges and controversy.[1]

Dr. Martin L. King, Jr.

CHAPTER FOUR

Dismantling Generational Laissez-Faire Entitlement

Black Psychological Warfare, human resistance if you will, can best be defined as a necessary corrective to the indoctrination of permanent servitude. It is an innate demand; an uncompromised demand from the depths of the soul derived from the power of the African American Experience. This preternatural innate experience supports the indigenous belief that the African American Village Community not only possesses the physical ability to resist the inhumane atrocities of the oppressor, as was proven by our survival during the Middle Passage, but the intellectual prowess as well.

Black Psychological Warfare exists at the nucleus of the nonviolent resistance movement. It is well to note that this special, intellectual, preternatural, human weapon allows the oppressed to boldly and unapologetically approach the table of humanity and demand an inherent seat. From this strategic vantage point African Americans can effectively elaborate (in an articulate manner) on the inheritance claim to his/her Civil Rights that are bestowed upon every member of the human family by God, the Creator. These inalienable rights include life, liberty and the pursuit of happiness.

In retrospect, Adam Clayton Powell, Sr., Adam Clayton Powell, Jr., John Lewis and James Farmer effectively employed and elevated the implementation of nonviolent resistance to the next level. In a most eloquent fashion these noble Black Alpha Males supported the cause of Civil Rights by intellectually employing the formidable weapon of Black Psychological Warfare, an indigenous form of Black Power and Black Pride. However, prior to investigating these noble generational leaders who faced the Goliaths of discrimination, oppression, marginalization and inequality, we must inevitably address the schisms of today's younger generation, which we will instinctively and appropriately categorize under the shameful auspice of Generation E (Entitlement Generation). In addition, we will instinctively and appropriately categorize the destructive forces of their collective *modus operandi* (MO) under the Laissez-Faire Entitlement Syndrome. The Laissez-Faire Entitlement Syndrome can specifically be defined as the negative mind-set of Generation E (claiming unearned rights) that perpetuates a total cultural disconnect to the present and past struggles of African Americans for equality in America.

If African Americans plan to continue to make strides toward freedom, we must revisit and employ the power and effectiveness of Black Psychological Warfare. Historically, this powerful weapon of resistance produced a spirit of unity which undoubtedly propelled the participants of the historical Civil Rights Movement to a new higher level of respectability. Notably it was the African American youth of this great nation who refused to sit by passively and allow their parents to fight for Civil Rights alone. In major news paper clippings and TV broadcast from that era you will find baby boomers, young teenagers or even younger children standing side by side with the elders of the African American Village Community. Most importantly, a sizable numbers of generational leaders from that historical era were young African American males and females. With the hard to find exception of a small percentage of dissenting clergies and passive, frightened Negros who still embraced the wait-and-see philosophy, the houses, and the villages of the African American Community were, for the most part, unified and moving by the power of God.

Be that as it may, today's younger African Americans have sadly lost their historical connectedness as well as their inherited right to sit at the table of humanity. Generation E, the

Entitlement Generation, presently suffers from a chronic case of Historical Euthanasia. This social impediment can best be described as a noticeable lack of historical, generational respect for the blood, sweat and tears of those who suffered courageously, fought and died, for the collective advancement of their people. Generation E can be defined as the segment of the Village Community who are spiritually, socially and psychologically detached from past cultural struggles. All allegiances and pride in one's race (Black Pride) have been replaced with the misplaced arrogance of entitlement. The negative greed-centered effects of capitalism have destroyed their soulfulness and replaced this quality with a need for immediate gratification. Our youth have been diagnosed with the sociological, psychological symptoms of the notorious and shameful Laissez-Faire Entitlement Syndrome. The negative self-centered and egotistic mindset of Generation E (claiming unearned cultural rights merely through cultural association) perpetuates a total disconnect from the past and continuous struggles for equality in America for African Americans.

Evidence of this negative effect can be seen on street corners, in our schools, on the news due to the shameful epidemic of Black-on-Black violence and in the nation's penal system. An unacceptably high percentage of our young Black Alpha Males are not only at war with themselves and each other (peers) but also with their families and the Village Community. An unacceptably high percentage of our young women are pushing strollers and making all the wrong choices by seeking love in all the wrong places. African American males and females who successfully complete high school and attend college rank at the bottom cellar when compared to other minorities in this country. I won't bore you with statistics; however, it is quite clear that there is a disparity between the generation of the Civil Rights Era and today's Generation E. The latter house is certainly divided, and we must declare a state of emergency.

Most importantly, we must learn from history and not discard historical lessons as rhetorical nonsense irrelevant to our present conditions. Generation E must excavate, dismantle and abandon their embrace of the Laissez-Faire Entitlement Syndrome. As previously mentioned, this sociological scar is indeed shameful and does not support the continuous struggle for Civil Rights—rights that must be earned and fought for by each succeeding generation. It is the inherent duty of each generation of African Americans (with no exceptions) to keep the torch of Empirical Hope visible and well illuminated, otherwise all of the past struggles to acquire human rights guaranteed by the U.S. Constitution will be systematically taken away by the powers that be. We must learn from those who fought the good fight before us how to fight the good fight. In creating the Beloved Community we cannot become our own worst enemy, disregard our history and publicly disrespect the unselfish sacrifices of our people.

We must not, by any stretch of the imagination, forget the Communal Initiative, the implementation of the Village Concept and the promotion of Cultural Utilitarianism by the Black Alpha Male Constructionist who became extraordinary leaders in the face of insurmountable opposition to their claim for Civil Rights. These young men, empowered through the African American Experience, became a force to be reckoned with during the unfolding torrid history of our people. They, however, were acutely and proudly aware of their rich history and displayed an uncompromising respect for the sacrifices and commitment of their elders. The division caused by the weapons of mass human destruction (capitalism and the Glass Ceiling) did not deter their cause. When Dr. King eloquently proclaimed, "So let freedom ring from Stone Mountain of Georgia, from Lookout Mountain of Tennessee, from every hill and molehill of Mississippi, from every mountainside let freedom ring,"[1] the younger generation (encompassing Black males and females) stood in solidarity with their elders in unison. Their only claim to entitlement was God-given; it was not based on rights and privileges passed down from former slaves: on the contrary it was considered an entitlement to an inherent duty to continuously fight for human rights, not only for themselves but for generations to come.

Cultural Utilitarianism became the order of the day. In contrast to Generation E, the younger leaders of that era pledged respect for the elders and learned from example how to employ an array of powerful weapons available to oppressed people in their struggle for equality: nonviolent protest and the individual and collective intellectual capacity of Black Psychological Warfare. Spanning two generations, Adam Clayton Powell, Sr. and Adam Clayton Powell, Jr. serve as historical examples of *A House Divided...No More*. Most importantly, the Laissez-Faire Entitlement Syndrome was nonexistent. However, a God-given entitlement bridged the gap from one generational leader to the next generational leader. Cultural Utilitarianism was the common thread. Empirical Hope for the African American Village Community was an idea whose time had come.

On July 28, 1917, in New York City, Adam Clayton Powell, Sr., the NAACP and other civic leaders stood up to the uncontested violence that was being waged against African Americans around the country. The lynchings and murder of African Americans became commonplace during and after World War I. In response, African Americans migrated North to escape the unprovoked and rampant wave of violence and racial oppression in the South. However, riots broke out in East St. Louis when Whites went on a rampage; African Americans were employed by a factory holding government contracts. Forty African Americans were killed, more than $400,000 worth of property was completely destroyed, nearly 6,000 African Americans were driven from their homes and countless men, women, and children were beaten, stabbed, hung and burned.[2]

The activist knew that a physical confrontation would promote more violence against his people. Powell invested his grassroots energies in organizing an early form of Black Psychological Warfare; moreover 8,000 African Americans, primarily from Harlem, silently marched in an organized procession down Fifth Avenue. Dressed in their finest clothes, the participants marched to the sound of muffled drums. The power of their message to end the violence against African Americans (especially endangered Black males) was silently communicated through signs while literally thousands of New York bystanders witnessed the unique spectacle.

In a show of African American solidarity, the children, dressed in white, marched with the adults. The children were flanked by the women who were also dressed in white. The men, dressed in black suits, followed the women and children. This psychological weapon (nonviolent protest) would be similarly used by the leaders of the 1960's Civil Rights Movement. Some of the signs and banners read: "Mothers, do lynchers go to heaven?" "Mr. President, why not make America safe for democracy?" "Thou Shalt Not Kill." "Pray for the lady Macbeths of East St. Louis." "Give us a Chance to Live."[3]

The *New York Age* reported on the march:

They marched without uttering one word or making a single gesticulation and protested in respectful silence against the reign of mob law, segregation, "Jim Crowism" and many other indignities to which the race is unnecessarily subjected in the United States.[4]

Today's misplaced attitudes derived from Generation E and the continuous negative, thoughtless promotion of the Laissez-Faire Entitlement Syndrome stand over and against all previous movements demanding cultural entitlement and Civil Rights at every level of human intercourse. Adam Clayton Powell, Sr., born in Franklin County, Virginia, to Sally Dunning, a woman described as mulatto but whose heritage is unspecified, courageously and unapologetically engaged the evil tenets of marginalization, discrimination, inequality and capitalism with the spirit and support of his people.[5] The house, according to this drum major for social justice, would be divided...no more as African Americans nobly faced any and all forms of institutionalized oppression.

As a respected charismatic preacher of the Abyssinian Baptist Church Clayton Powell, Sr. bought land in Harlem for the establishment at West 138th Street. In 1923, a new church building was constructed and the first community recreation center was established in Harlem. During the1930's, moving by the power of God, the wise Powell, Sr. established a highly successful social/religious education program. Powell, a force to be reckoned with, claimed the undisputed right to minister over one of the largest Protestant congregations in America; it had a staggering membership of more than 14,000.[6]

In contrast to the self-destructive, socially defiant devices employed by Generation E, Powell, Sr. campaigned to feed the poor during the turbulent years of the Great Depression while simultaneously leading a personal campaign for better jobs and city services. This young, dynamic preacher championed the cause for equality (early Civil Rights) and was actively involved in the continuous struggle against racism, lecturing on the issue of race relations at Colgate University, City College of New York and Union Theological Seminary. He was a distinguished co-founder of the National Urban League and an early leader involved in the continuous organizational Civil Rights events of the National Association for the Advancement of Colored People (NAACP).

Embedded in his use of Black Psychological Warfare against racism, oppression, discrimination, marginalization and inequality was an uncompromised belief in striving for excellence in education and the ethic of hard work. Through Powell, Sr.'s efforts and philosophy, Abyssinian's educational program reflected both the spiritual and social sides of Powell's mission. His God-anointed mission was straight-forward and unhindered by rhetoric: he desired to build the world's largest religious, social and educational institution. Powell, Sr. stated, "I want to establish the kingdom of social justice."[7] Adam Clayton Powell, Sr. was strategically wise in his approach towards a liberation agenda involving nonviolent protest for African Americans: supporting the potent weapon of Black Psychological Warfare he embraced the philosophy that a people united can never be defeated.

Most importantly, he led by example and through the strength of his union with Mattie Shaffer [nee Mattie Buster] (married on July 30, 1889). Two children, Blanche and Adam Clayton Powell, Jr., were born to witness firsthand their father's resolve and strength of character for the cause of Civil Rights.[8] The once wild and reckless Powell, Sr., whose early life consisted of heavy drinking, bar fights, gambling and general wantonness, became a major catalyst and advocate for innate authentic Communal Healing by promoting a clear and concise Communal Initiative for the African American Village Community at large. By having children march in the silent parade and grooming his son for leadership (a changing of the generational guards, if you will), Powell, Sr. intentionally and consciously set the stage for the passing of the torch to the next generation, the Black Power and Civil Rights generation.

Powell, Sr. effectively and in an articulate manner demonstrated the importance of Historical Discipline; this discipline (a necessary corrective) is specifically the collective awareness of a people to sustain the continuous (generational) fight for Civil Rights and liberation. Unfortunately, the self-destructive Generation E adamantly refuses to carry the Civil Rights torch or actively preserve acquired rights for the next generation. This is the catastrophic result of a divided house; there is no empirical historical evidence of an individual or collective agenda to promote a movement of cultural and/or historical investment into our posterity. Be that as it may, Powell, Sr. (an early advocate for human rights) consciously and intentionally passed the Civil Rights torch to the next generation through his son, Adam Clayton Powell, Jr. This drum major for social justice challenged the Glass Ceiling and unapologetically demanded a seat at the table of humanity.

Adam Clayton Powell, Jr., a handsome and charismatic figure, succeeded his father in 1937 as the senior pastor of Abyssinian Baptist Church. Similar to his father (who used the power of the Silent Protest Parade), this drum major for social justice strategically employed the intellectual aspects of Black Psychological Warfare to combat, confront and defeat the evil tenets of discrimination, oppression, marginalization, sexism, racism and inequality. The ambitious son on Adam Clayton Powell, Sr. developed a formidable public following in the Harlem community through his relentless, unconditional and unapologetic crusades for employment and housing for the poor. As the chairman of the Coordinating Committee for Employment, he organized numerous and ongoing mass meetings, rent strikes and public campaigns, which forced major companies, local utilities and the Harlem Hospital to hire overlooked, unemployed African American workers.[9]

This Black Alpha Male Constructionist, truly a force to be reckoned with, took the Civil Rights torch from his father and stood against the unfair and unequal hiring practices of the 1939 New York World's Fair. Powell staged a nonviolent protest at the Fair's executive offices in the Empire State Building similar to the silent parade used by his father. As a result of this psychological warfare, the number of African Americans hired by the executives increased from 200 to about 732. Similarly, a bus boycott in 1941 led to the hiring of 200 African Americans by the city's transit system. Powell, Jr. stood gallantly against the discriminatory hiring practices of African American pharmacists by White-owned drug stores in Harlem.[10]

At the nucleus of Powell, Jr.'s Black Psychological Warfare was the use of mass action. The drum major for social justice asserted, "Mass action is the most powerful force on earth. As long as it's within the law, it's not wrong; if the law is wrong, change the law."[11] With the proper use of this effective weapon, coupled with the strategic involvement of young school-aged children, teenagers and up-and-coming future leaders, the early movement for equality and human rights (a precursor setting the stage for the Civil Rights Movement) gained national attention. The younger generation stood in solidarity with their parents and elders of the African American Village Community.

In 1941, Powell was successfully elected to the New York City Council. He became the first African American council representative. In 1944 Powell carried the torch for equality and human rights to the next level: this torch would reach Congress when he was elected as a Democrat to the U.S. House of Representatives; the distinguished son of Powell Sr. represented the 22nd Congressional District, which included Harlem. Moving by the power of God, he became the first African American congressman from New York and the first from any northern state other than Illinois in the Post-Reconstruction Era. As the spirit of cultural entitlement surged again and again, Powell, Jr. challenged segregation policies and practices on Capitol Hill. One of only two African American congressmen, Powell, Jr. challenged the informal ban on African American representatives using the Capitol facilities reserved for Whites only. He intentionally invited numerous African American constituents to dine with him in the Whites only Capitol Hill House Restaurant.

Powell, Jr. became the embodiment of Empirical Hope, and in 1961 this drum major for social justice became the chairman of the powerful Education and Labor Committee. Justice would flow like a mighty river when he presided over federal programs and advocated for minimum wage increases. The powerful orator was acutely and instinctively aware that a countless number of African Americans living below the poverty line (in America) would directly benefit. In this surge for inherit human rights, he monitored Medicaid programs, the minimum wage increase for retail workers, equal pay for women, education and training for the deaf, nursing education, vocational training and standard wages for hours worked. He was also extremely mindful of the need to assist minorities in acquiring aid for elementary and secondary education.

In addition to the above Powell, Jr. was instrumental in the passage of President Lyndon B. Johnson's Great Society social programs, including the renowned War on Poverty. As Powell, Jr. engaged the enemy through Black Psychological Warfare, millions of poor Whites living below the poverty line as well as the inhabitants of the Village Community was positively affected. Powell also orchestrated the passage of President John Kennedy's "New Frontier" legislation.[12]

Powell, Jr. remembered the Silent Protest Parade and the violent acts against his people. Holding the torch of Empirical Hope representing the continuous struggle for the advancement of early Civil Rights, Powell, Jr.'s committee passed a record number of bills for a single session (notably as of 2008 the record still stood). He steered 50 bills through Congress.[13] In promoting Cultural Utilitarianism, the energetic Powell, Jr. was instrumental in passing groundbreaking legislation that made lynching a federal crime. Focusing on inequalities in education, he sponsored a bill that addressed the desegregation of public schools. "He challenged the Southern practice of charging Blacks (the inhabitants of the African American Village Community) a poll tax to vote and courageously stopped racist Congressmen from freely and arrogantly saying the word 'nigger' in sessions of Congress."[14]

Powell, Jr.'s first wife, Isabel Washington, was a nightclub singer and entertainer, and he adopted her son Preston from a previous marriage. Powell, Jr. and his second wife, the singer Hazel Scott, named their son Adam Clayton Powell III. Powell III is Vice Provost for Globalization at the University of Southern California and one of the leading authorities on the use of the Internet for journalists. Powell and his third wife, Yvette Diago Powell, had a son named Adam Clayton Powell Diago. This son later changed his name to Adam Clayton Powell IV when he moved to the mainland from Puerto Rico to attend Howard University to honor his family legacy. Adam Clayton Powell IV (the politician) named his son Adam Clayton Powell V. [15]

It is well to note that the strong, unbreakable bond Powell, Jr. established with his wives and children held the families together spiritually long after the separations. The powerful influence of their father would surface in their lives when a section of Seventh Avenue, north of Central Park, was renamed Adam Clayton Powell, Jr. Boulevard. One of the landmarks along this street is the Adam Clayton Powell, Jr. State Office Building. In addition, two schools were named after him: P.S. 153 Adam Clayton Powell at 1750 Amsterdam Avenue and a middle school, I.S. 172 Adam Clayton Powell,

Jr., Education Complex at 509 W. 129th Street which closed in 2009. Both schools were located in Manhattan, New York.[16]

In the arena of Black Psychological Warfare, Powell, Jr. perfected the role of agitator. "Whenever a person keeps prodding, keep them squirming...it serves a purpose. It may not in contemporary history look so good, but...future historians will say, They served a purpose."[17] At the forefront of Black Psychological Warfare was the Powell Amendment. The Black Alpha Male Constructionist who represented Harlem nearly two dozen times used this weapon as leverage for his people to acquire access to a quality education. The Powell Amendment, one of the most dangerous legislative weapons employed by this skillful politician, was a rider attached to proposals requesting federal funds. The beauty of the Amendment was that if successfully attached to a bill, it would nullify federal grants to state or local government agencies that practiced discrimination. This meant that even school districts in the deepest South had to open their doors to African American teachers and students or risk losing the funds set aside for them.[18]

Powell, Jr. paved the way for many African Americans to stand up and fight the good fight. It is safe to say that the succeeding generation of young up-and-coming Civil Rights leaders gracefully accepted the historical torch handed down by Adam Clayton Powell, Sr. and Adam Clayton Powell, Jr. Notably, James Farmer and John Lewis stood among these up and coming generational leaders; leaders in succession who respectfully continued the struggle for the advancement of African Americans. Moved by a greater power (the Unmoved Mover) the young leaders graciously found themselves among a distinguished coalition of leaders who were not afraid to pass the torch for Civil Rights to the next generation.

The big six organizers of the historical March on Washington were indicative of the preternatural connection and respect for generational leadership. The potential for a divided house among the leaders of the African American Village Community was met head on with the balm of indigenous Communal Healing. James Farmer of the Congress of Racial Equality (CORE), Martin Luther King, Jr. of the Southern Christian Leadership Conference (SCLC), John Lewis of the Student Nonviolent Coordinating Committee (SNCC), A. Philip Randolph of the Brotherhood of Sleeping Car Porters (BSCP), Roy Wilkins of the National Association for the Advancement of Colored People (NAACP) and Whitney Young, Jr. of the National Urban League (NUL) all found common ground under the auspices of various Communal Initiatives.[19] Several generations of distinguished leaders joined forces and unapologetically stated their demands. The stated demands of the March on Washington included the passage of meaningful Civil Rights legislation, the elimination of all forms of racial segregation in public schools, protection for demonstrators against police brutality, a major public works program to provide jobs, the passage of a law prohibiting racial discrimination in public and private hiring, a $2.00 an hour minimum wage and self-government for the District of Columbia, which had a Black majority.[20]

John Lewis, along with Dr. Martin L. King, delivered a noteworthy speech. In respect for his elder leaders and in the spirit of *A House Divided...No More,* Lewis, who represented SNCC, a younger yet more radical Civil Rights organization than Dr. King's SCLC, agreed to tone down and omit specific inflammatory portions of his speech. For example, one portion called President Kennedy's Civil Rights bill "too little, too late" and asked, "Which side is the federal government on?"[21]

Be that as it may, the revised version was hard hitting and to the point as John Lewis unapologetically stated that it was time for a revolution.[22] (The text that John delivered will be examined later in this chapter). When the dust of disagreement cleared, the young drum major for social justice agreed with Dr. Martin L. King, Jr. that the mass of oppressed people were in Washington to cash a check for life, liberty and the pursuit of happiness. Most importantly, John Lewis and James Farmer agreed with the Communal Initiatives of their elder leaders that we as a people must not allow our creative protest to degenerate into physical violence: again and again, we must collectively rise to the majestic height of meeting physical violence with soul force.[23]

Unlike Generation E and the unapologetic promotion of the Laissez-Faire Entitlement Syndrome, John Lewis and James Farmer's generation stood side by side with elders who promoted Empirical Hope, Communal Initiatives and Cultural Utilitarianism. John Lewis repeatedly used the all inclusive word *we*. In retrospect, *we* became synonymous with the generational and unconditional acceptance of the Inter-Related Structure of Black Reality as well as the binding ties of the Inescapable Mutuality Paradigm discussed earlier in this historical exegesis. Notably, in contrast to Generation E, Lewis and Farmer's Baby Boom Generation did not embrace the negative aspects of the Socialization of Division. The bond between the various African American generations during the torrid Civil Rights Era was specifically derived from the power of Historical Discipline; this special cultural discipline was encompassed within the parameters of the uniqueness of the African American Experience and the imperative belief that a house divided...cannot stand.

In the midst of the Civil Rights Movement, James L. Farmer, another up-and-coming young leader (as previously mentioned in the big six organizers), surfaced and joined ranks with other generational leaders. Carrying the torch passed on by leaders prior to his birth, Farmer stood up against the tyranny of oppression and aggressively participated in various and numerous movements associated with Civil Rights, including the Congress of Racial Equality (CORE), the Freedom Riders and the Fund for an Open Society. In addition, to support and empower future leaders beyond his generation, he paved the way for many African Americans in politics when he served as the Assistant Secretary of Health, Education, and Welfare during the Nixon Administration.[24]

In direct defiance of the inappropriate philosophy of Generation E's cultural entitlement, Farmer's generation joined the struggle for Civil Rights. In contrast to today's divided generation who adamantly refuse to assist the elders and leaders of the African American Village Community, Farmer's generation played a towering role in the movement via direct action during the historical Civil Rights Movement. Notably, four Greensboro, NC, students turned to CORE after staging the first series of sit-ins that swept the South in 1960. It was the young leaders of CORE that supported the issue of desegregation on interstate transportation and forced the issue with the Freedom Rides of 1961. It was CORE's James Chaney, Andrew Goodman and Michael Schwerner (a Black and two Whites) who became the first fatalities of the Mississippi Freedom Summer of 1964. The three were murdered by a vicious gang of Klansmen and buried beneath an earthen dam near the town of Philadelphia.[25]

In a recalcitrant society dominated by Whites, Farmer used the discipline of Mohandas Gandhi. Similar to the elder generation of the Civil Rights Movement, he strategically used Black Psychological Warfare (i.e., nonviolent direct action). Farmer's public campaign, which was a direct action strategy against discrimination, bigotry, racism and other forms of marginalization (social, political, economic and educational inequalities) became embedded and saturated with nonviolent resistance. Furthermore, when asked by his critics, "When are we going to fight back?", the young and energetic Farmer eloquently answered with the intellectual response, "We are fighting back, we're only using new weapons."[26]

Similar to Adam Clayton Powell, Jr., Farmer's innate drive to foster unity in the divided African American Village Community can be traced back to his parents' generation. The house he lived in was filled with books, and the conversations with his father, James Leonard Farmer, Sr. (the son of a slave, a minister-scholar who became a college professor) were about the ideas embedded in those books. Farmer's initial encounter with racism came when he was three or four years old, living in Holly Springs, Mississippi, where his father was on the faculty of Rust College.

One day, Farmer's mother delayed buying him a soft drink and instructed him to wait until later. However, a White child immediately entered the drug store and departed with a drink. The young Farmer witnessed his mother cry and was determined to do something about the passive acceptance of second-class citizenship in America. In retrospect, he began to remember when Black children and White children played together peacefully, but when puberty arrived, the real separation between the races became apparent. Farmer stayed away from the ministry because, as he said, "I don't see how I could honestly preach the Gospel of Christ in a church that practiced discrimination."[27]

The employment of Black Psychological Warfare to address racial inequalities came full circle in the 1950's. Farmer worked assiduously to bring an end to segregation in southern schools. As the head member of CORE, he planned and organized protests, including a Pilgrimage of Prayer in 1959, protesting the closing of public schools in Richmond, Virginia. These schools were determined to avoid complying with the *1954 Brown v. Board of Education of Topeka*

Supreme Court decision outlawing all forms of segregation in public schools. Most importantly, CORE and Fellowship of Reconciliation (another Civil Rights organization) held a *"Journey for Reconciliation Event"* in 1947. CORE and Farmer were fit to be tied due to the fact that a year earlier, the Supreme Court of the United States ruled that all forms of segregated seating of passengers on interstate buses were unconstitutional. This ruling by the high court was virtually and maliciously ignored by the South.[28] The generational houses of the African American Village Community would not be divided. The courage of Farmer's CORE volunteers (African Americans and Whites) captured the imagination of Civil Rights supporters throughout this great nation. The Black Psychological Warfare of direct action through nonviolent protest "aroused the conscience of many Whites both in America and abroad."[29] The interstate discriminatory war was finally won when Bobby Kennedy convinced the Interstate Commerce Commission to issue an order banning segregation in interstate travel.

With the collective assistance of his generation and elders, Farmer's war against injustice, inequality, bigotry and discrimination continued as he turned his attention to the lack of employment for African Americans. Quotas were never the issue, just a fair chance at employment. Farmer and his constituents targeted major construction sites, specifically those financed by public funding. During the early 1960's, he ordered sit-ins at Mayor Robert F. Wagner's office in New York and Governor Nelson A. Rockefeller's office. In retrospect, when CORE and other Civil Rights organizations discovered that the White Castle Hamburgers establishments adamantly refused to hire and retain African Americans, Farmer organized the continuous, orderly picketing of White Castle Hamburgers stands in New York. Farmer's use of Black Psychological Warfare supported and strengthened the nonviolence philosophy of Dr. Martin L. King and other elders. This young, dynamic drum major for social justice boldly declared, "We are not pressing toward the brink of violence, but for the peak of freedom."[30]

In the tradition of Adam Clayton Powell, Jr., James L. Farmer's use of Black Psychological Warfare was elevated to the political arena. It had always been Farmer's public and private position that in the continuous struggle for liberation in America, African Americans, no matter what their position was on racism, should be part of the U.S. Government and influence policies and laws that affect the Village Community at large. In 1969, Farmer readily accepted an invitation from President Richard M. Nixon to become the Assistant Secretary of the Department of Health, Education, and Welfare. Farmer unequivocally agreed with activist Adam Clayton Powell, Jr., that African Americans should strategically place themselves into positions of authority within the U.S. Government in order to shape and influence national policy on race issues.[31]

To that end, Farmer's words became synonymous with other dynamic generational leaders. It is well to note that all three generational leaders—Adam Clayton Powell, Jr., James L. Farmer and John Lewis—shared the ideology of the following famous words spoken by Thomas Jefferson:

> When in the Course of human events it becomes necessary for one people to dissolve the political bands which have connected them with another and to assume among the powers of the earth, the separate and equal station to which the Laws of Nature and of Nature's God entitle them, a decent respect to the opinions of mankind requires that they should (boldly) declare the causes which impel them to the separation. We hold these truths to be self-evident, that all men are created equal, that they are endowed by their Creator with certain unalienable Rights, that among these are

Life, Liberty and the pursuit of Happiness. That to secure these rights, Governments are instituted among Men, deriving their just powers from the consent of the governed, That whenever any Form of Government becomes destructive of these ends, it is the Right of the People to alter or to abolish it, and to institute new Government, laying its foundation on such principles and organizing its powers in such form, as to them shall seem most likely to effect their Safety and Happiness. Prudence, indeed, will dictate that Governments long established should not be changed for light and transient causes; and accordingly all experience hath shown, that mankind are more disposed to suffer, while evils are sufferable, than to right themselves by abolishing the forms to which they are accustomed. But when a long train of abuses and usurpations, pursuing invariably the same Object evinces a design to reduce them under absolute Despotism, it is their right, it is their duty, to throw off such Government, and to provide new Guards for their future security. Such has been the patient sufferance of these Colonies; and such is now the necessity which constrains them to alter their former Systems of Government.[32]

In light of these words, Generation E's epidemic of unprovoked violence upon their own people and the African American Village Community at large, coupled with the embarrassing strangulation and void of any civic or political activism, pale in comparison to the young generational leaders of the Civil Rights Era. For example at the age of 23, John Lewis became a veteran of many Civil Rights battles. On August 28, 1963, during the March on Washington, this young drum major for social justice took his place in history and stood among the great leaders of that era. He stood with a sense of entitlement that his generation had earned a right to stand on the frontline of the Civil Rights Movement. He stood with an undeniable sense of earned entitlement that he had visibly supported the elders of the movement and the African American Village Community. Lewis boldly proclaimed:

> We march today for jobs and freedom, but we have nothing to be proud of, for hundreds and thousands of our brothers are not here. They have no money for their transportation, for they are receiving starvation wages, or no wages at all. In good conscience, we cannot support wholeheartedly the administration's Civil Rights Bill. There's not one thing in the bill that will protect our people from police brutality. This bill will not protect young children and old women from police dogs and fire hoses, for engaging in peaceful demonstrations: This bill will not protect the citizens in Danville, Virginia, who must live in constant fear in a police state. This bill will not protect the hundreds of people who have been arrested on trumped-up charges. What about the three young men in Americus, Georgia, who face the death penalty for engaging in peaceful protest? The voting section of this bill will not help thousands of black citizens who want to vote. It will not help the citizens of Mississippi, of Alabama and Georgia, who are qualified to vote but lack a sixth-grade education. "ONE MAN, ONE VOTE" is the African cry. It is ours, too. It must be ours.

> People have been forced to leave their homes because they dared to exercise their right to register to vote. What is there in this bill to ensure the equality of a maid who earns $5 a week in the home of a family whose income is $100,000 a year?

> For the first time in one hundred years this nation is being awakened to the fact that segregation is evil and

117

that it must be destroyed in all forms. Your presence today proves that you have been aroused to the point of action. We are now involved in a serious revolution. This nation is still a place of political leaders who build their careers on immoral compromises and ally themselves with open forms of political, economic and social exploitation. What political leader here can stand up and say, "My party is the party of principles?" The party of Kennedy is also the party of Eastland. The party of Javits is also the party of Goldwater. Where is our party?

In some parts of the South we work in the fields from sunup to sundown for $12 a week. In Albany, Georgia, nine of our leaders have been indicted not by Dixiecrats but by the federal government for peaceful protest. But what did the federal government do when Albany's deputy sheriff beat Attorney C. B. King and left him half dead? What did the federal government do when local police officials kicked and assaulted the pregnant wife of Slater King, and she lost her baby?

The revolution is at hand, and we must free ourselves of the chains of political and economic slavery. The nonviolent revolution is saying, "We will not wait for the courts to act, for we have been waiting for hundreds of years. We will not wait for the President, the Justice Department, nor Congress, but we will take matters into our own hands and create a source of power, outside of any national structure, that could and would assure us a victory." To those who have said, "Be patient and wait." We say that "patience" is a dirty and nasty word. We cannot be patient; we do not want to be free gradually. We want our freedom, and we want it now. We cannot depend on any political party, for both the Democrats and the Republicans have betrayed the basic principles of the Declaration of Independence.

We all recognize the fact that if any radical social, political and economic changes are to take place in our society, the people, the masses, must bring them about. In the struggle, we must seek more than Civil Rights; we must work for the community of love, peace and true brotherhood. Our minds, souls and hearts cannot rest until freedom and justice exist for all people.

We will not stop. If we do not get meaningful legislation out of this Congress, the time will come when we will not confine our marching to Washington. We will march through the South, through the streets of Jackson, through the streets of Danville, through the streets of Cambridge, through the streets of Birmingham. But we will march with the spirit of love and with the spirit of dignity that we have shown here today. By the force of our demands, our determination and our numbers, we shall splinter the desegregated South into a thousand pieces and put them back together in the image of God and democracy. We must say, "Wake up, America. *Wake up*! For we cannot stop, and we will not be patient."[33]

John Lewis would take the weaponry of Black Psychological Warfare to the next level by entering politics. Similar to the words of Thomas Jefferson, John Lewis, a Democrat and member of Georgia's 5th Congressional District, began to affect policy due to the long train of abuses and usurpations. Lewis was often called:

One of the most courageous persons the Civil Rights Movement ever produced...and dedicated his life to protecting human rights, securing civil liberties, and building what he calls the Beloved Community in America.[34]

John Lewis, the son of sharecroppers, grew up on his family's farm outside of Troy, Alabama. The young energetic Civil Rights leader attended segregated public schools in Pike County, Alabama. The activism surrounding the Montgomery Bus Boycott and the powerful words of Rev. Martin L. King, Jr. inspired him as a young boy. In retrospect, it was in those pivotal moments that God, the Creator, began to plant the seed of Empirical Hope in his soul, and Lewis made a critical decision early in his life to become a part of the Civil Rights Movement. Walking stride for stride toward freedom with his elders, he has faithfully remained a vanguard of progressive social movements and the human rights struggle in America.

While attending Fisk University, John Lewis organized numerous sit-in demonstrations at segregated lunch counters in Nashville, Tennessee. In 1961, he volunteered to participate in Freedom Rides, which challenged segregation at interstate bus terminals in the South. "He was beaten severely by angry mobs and arrested by police for challenging the injustice of Jim Crow segregation in the South."[35] As a young Civil Rights activist, the bold and outspoken Lewis became a nationally recognized leader and as previously stated was part of the big six leaders of the Civil Rights Movement.

In 1964, John Lewis, using the potent nonviolent form of Black Psychological Warfare, coordinated the grassroots efforts of the Student Nonviolent Coordinating Committee (SNCC) to organize voter registration drives and community action programs during the Mississippi Freedom Summer Campaign. Lewis and Hosea Williams, another notable Civil Rights leader and activist, led more than 600 peaceful, orderly nonviolent protestors across the Edmund Pettus Bridge in Selma, Alabama, on March 7, 1965. The peaceful march was met with unprovoked violence from Alabama State Troopers and became known as "Bloody Sunday."[36]

Lewis became the embodiment of courage for his young generation. He would not be deterred from his God-given inheritance (an unconditional entitlement, if you will) to acquire full Civil Rights. Despite more than 40 arrests, serious injuries and physical attacks, his generation, with the support of elders from the National Civil Rights Movement, stayed the course as news broadcasts and photographers recorded the senseless cruelty. Moreover, the incident at the Edmund Pettus Bridge on "Bloody Sunday" helped hasten the passage of the Voting Rights Act of 1965.[37]

Moving by a power greater than himself, Lewis left SNCC in 1966. He continued his relentless campaign for Civil Rights as an Associate Director of the Field Foundation. He actively participated in the Southern Regional Council's voter registration programs. John Lewis (a drum major for social justice and political justice) became the Director of the Voter Education Project (VEP); his efforts as a major voice for the disenfranchised transformed the nation's political climate by adding close to four million minorities to the voter rolls.

The devoted activism of the young up and coming leader soon began to attract national attention. In 1977 he was honorably summoned to the White House: President Jimmy Carter appointed John Lewis as the Director of a branch of the federal volunteer agency, ACTION, which consisted of more than 250,000 volunteers.[38] In 1981, serving as an elected Atlanta City Council member, Lewis became widely known as an advocate for ethics in government and neighborhood preservation. In 1986, he acquired a seat in Congress, where he became the Senior Chief Deputy Whip for the Democratic Party leadership in the House of Representatives. He was a member of the House Ways and Means Committee, the

Subcommittee on Income Security and Family Support and Chairman of the Subcommittee on Oversight.

John Lewis lives in Atlanta, Georgia, and is married to Lillian Miles. This holy union produced one son, John Miles. Notably, as a major voice representing the younger generation that refused to sit on the sidelines (while others stood on the frontline, risking their lives and limbs to advance their people) his name became synonymous with Civil Rights. John Lewis is the recipient of numerous awards from prominent national and international institutions. Lewis recognitions include:

> The Lincoln Medal from the historic Ford's Theatre, the Golden Plate Award given by the Academy of Excellence, the Preservation Hero Award given by the National Trust for Historic Preservation, the Capital Award of the National Council of La Raza, the Martin Luther King, Jr. Non-Violent Peace Prize, the President's Medal of Georgetown University, the NAACP Spingarn Medal, the National Education Association Martin Luther King Jr. Memorial Award, and the only John F. Kennedy "Profile in Courage Award" for Lifetime Achievement ever granted by the John F. Kennedy Library Foundation. The Timberland Company established the John Lewis Award and a separate John Lewis Scholarship Fund which honors the Congressman's noble commitment to humanitarian service by acknowledging members of society who perform outstanding humanitarian work.[39]

In permanently dismantling the Generational Laissez-Faire Entitlement Syndrome that presently plague the African American Village Community, we must revisit how several generations within the African American Village Community stood together in unconditional solidarity against the negative

122

forces and weapons of division (i.e., discrimination, bigotry, racism, marginalization and inequality). Their demand, under the auspices of unconditional entitlement, meant more than today's meager generational self-expression of Hip-Hop, Rap, Swag and the embarrassing public practice of pants hanging down from the rear-end of the body. Respect for elders was non-negotiable; this innate respect became synonymous with Black Pride and Black Power for themselves and their people.

The Beloved Community and Cultural Utilitarianism (similar to unconditional respect for the elders of the Village Community) became the order of the day. For example, after reading Dr. Martin L. King's book, *Stride Toward Freedom*, a small group of prideful Black students decided to take action themselves. On February 1, 1960, David Richmond, Joseph McNeal, Ezell Blair and Franklin McCain staged a sit-in at the restaurant of their local Woolworth store (Greensboro, North Carolina); this store strictly enforced the policy of not serving African Americans. Soon the torch igniting Empirical Hope became visible as other African American students joined the protest. In the course of time all seats in the establishment were completely occupied by the protestors. The students were continuously physically assaulted, but adhering to Dr. King's philosophy of nonviolent protest, they did not retaliate. The torch was strategically passed on to 40 college students later that month, in Nashville, Tennessee, who similarly staged a sit-in at a Woolworth's lunch counter. Through sheer numbers and zero retaliatory incidents, coupled with hundreds of arrests, the lunch counters began to desegregate in May of 1960. Most importantly, this nonviolent strategy, a form of effective and intellectual Black Psychological Warfare, was adopted by African American students all over the Deep South:

> Within six months these sit-ins had ended public restaurant and lunch-counter segregation in twenty-six

123

southern cities. Student sit-ins were also successful against segregation in public parks, swimming pools, theaters, churches, libraries, museums and beaches.[40]

The torch of Empirical Hope and the spirit of Civil Rights found its way to every major college campus in the country. With the assistance of SNCC (Student Nonviolent Coordinating Committee, John Lewis) and CORE (Congress of Racial Equality, James Farmer), organizers implemented a controversial plan entitled D Day. D Day would later be called the Children's Crusade by *Newsweek Magazine*.[41] The D Day Campaign called for students from Birmingham elementary schools and high schools (Miles College as well) to participate in the scheduled nonviolent protests. In retrospect, Dr. King hesitated to approve the use of children. Be that as it may, the bond between the two generations in the struggle for Civil Rights had been sealed as younger children witnessed and personally suffered through the daily degradation of their parents, loved ones, extended family, friends and other innocent victims of their generation.[42]

Later that same year, the children would once again stand side by side with the Village Community in a show of unconditional solidarity. The 16th Street Baptist Church was a rallying point for Civil Rights activities during the spring of 1963. On September 15, 1963, the indigenous terrorist group known as the Klu Klux Klan (KKK) bombed the 16th Street Baptist Church, killing four girls.[43] Be that as it may, this tragedy served as another cultural wake-up call: a call to arms (nonviolent protest, if you will) that promoted generational unity in the African American Village Community. The Civil Rights Movement once again became all inclusive as it was quite clear that no one could afford to straddle the fence. Similar to the preternatural occurrence of Ground Zero aboard the Mothership, the descendants of Africa were merging into one people. We were indeed at war for our right to exist as human beings and a Village Community, a community created by God. (We will elaborate further on both the D Day Children's Crusade and the bombing of the 16th Street Baptist Church in Chapter 6 when we revisit the historical Civil Rights Movement and the strategic promotion of Cultural Utilitarianism and the Beloved Community).

Out of the ashes of the 16th Street Baptist Church bombing a unified people emerged: a people empowered by a call that would move the masses. The once scattered Village Community became more unified. The all-inclusive concept that we are our brother's and sister's keepers and what affects one of us affects all of us, reached a utopian level after this unspeakable premeditated human tragedy. Instead of *I'ism*, *me'ism* or *individualism*, unconditional collective cultural entitlement became synonymous with the words *African American*. Most importantly, the critical message of solidarity, unification reached far beyond the city limits of Birmingham and into the minds, hearts and souls of the African American Village Communities throughout this great nation.

From the ashes of this tragedy arose an indigenous communal dedication to collectively implement and promote the Inter-Related Structure of Black Reality, a Communal Initiative, Empirical Hope, the Village Concept, Historical Discipline, Cultural Utilitarianism, the African American Experience and Communal Healing. The Black Alpha Male Constructionist wholeheartedly and eagerly assumed his God-assigned role as the 2 P's (Providers and Protectors) of the African American Village Community. Instead of retaliatory physical violence, African Americans employed the Ethic of Care coupled with the strength of character found in Black Psychological Warfare. From an African American liberation perspective, the Ethic of Care can be defined as the need to nurture and support each other, the oppressed inhabitants of the Village community, as we struggle for racial equality. By embracing the Ethic of Care we became wounded healers.

In closing, it is well to note that the Civil Rights generation was acutely aware of the continuous nature of the struggle for African American liberation. The generational leaders of the Civil Rights Movement may have won battles at various lunch counters, interstate bus systems, the Edmund Pettus Bridge, voting booths and other significant victories, but the war against oppression and marginalization wages on. The struggle is not confined to one particular generation by any stretch of the imagination. The vanguards of the Civil Rights Movement have passed the torch of Empirical Hope to the next generation of Civil Rights leaders and participants who will continue to struggle for our inalienable rights. Those who instinctively take the torch of Empirical Hope (by any and all means necessary) have the distinguished duty, a rite of passage, if you will, to keep the dream alive, and a dream conceived in truth can never die. It is well to note that the Black Alpha Male Constructionist of the Civil Rights Era instinctively knew (collectively as a people) that we admirably possessed the intellectual prowess to implement the strategy of nonviolent resistance. The leaders of the movement were well aware that all out physical confrontations with the evils of the day would cause more suffering to a people who historically endured unspeakable, inhumane atrocities.

Black Psychological Warfare (weapons of nonviolent resistance and nonviolent protest) soon became a force to be reckoned with. This new phase of the Civil Rights Movement would be launched by intellectual Black Alpha Males whose prime directive and sole purpose was the promotion of self-empowerment. In the spirit of *A House Divided...No More*, we will now examine the great historical and contemporary philosophies of the following notable scholars: David Walker, Maulana Karenga and Dr. Jawanza Kunjufu.

CHAPTER FIVE

Empowerment: The Village Concept

The Village Concept is the creation of indigenous self-reliant systems designed to address the unfinished task of emancipation in the African American Village Community. In the arena of Black Psychological Warfare, David Walker unequivocally believed that African Americans should be preoccupied with the unfinished task of emancipation. Walker was an audaciously outspoken Black American activist who demanded the immediate end of slavery in the nation. This courageous drum major for social justice served as a Boston agent and staff writer for the short-lived but influential *Freedom's Journal*, a weekly abolitionist newspaper published in New York. According to notable historians, this weekly journal was the first newspaper published by African Americans in the United States.[1]

The activism of David Walker stands over and against today's Laissez-Faire Entitlement Syndrome embraced by Generation E. In contrast to this present day cultural insult, emancipation, upward mobility, unconditional respect for African Americans and empowerment became the nucleus and primary focus of his life. Furthermore, to strengthen his position in the war against the oppression of his people, "Walker joined with those [activists] who repeatedly petitioned the Commonwealth for equal rights for all. He courageously spoke publicly against slavery and categorized racism as immoral."[2]

Aligned with the Prince Hall Freemasons, a respected Black human rights organization in the city of Boston, Walker utilized this allegiance and took seriously the tenets of Freemasonry. Walker, who was vested in emancipation, utilized these tenets to demand unconditional equality and respect for the inhabitants of the African American Village

Community. In addition, he embraced Black cosmopolitanism. This liberation ideology embodied remnants of African traditions, the common experiences of slavery, and promoted survivor's advocacy in a discriminatory and hostile world. The Meeting House, which is still standing on the north slope of Beacon Hill, was a center for communal empowerment that promoted the Communal Initiative of first-class citizenship. The Massachusetts General Colored Association (which utilized the African Meeting House) opposed colonization and was the first abolitionist organization in Boston committed to freeing all African Americans from the shackles of chattel slavery.[3]

Walker unapologetically took the potent weapon of Black Psychological Warfare to new levels as he fought against the oppression of his people. He began by publicly demanding the unconditional and long overdue emancipation of African Americans; in fact, he urged African Americans to break their own physical and psychological chains. In an early form of Black Empowerment, Black Power, Black Pride and the Ethic of Care Walker posited that African Americans had to assume immediate responsibility not only for themselves as individuals, but for each other as well (*A House Divided...No More*, if you will).

In his public proclamations, Walker used the Village Concept to stand toe-to-toe, face-to-face with institutional racism. He encouraged those who were educated to read the message in the pamphlets to those who could not read. The pamphlets Walker spoke of (published in1829) became widely known as *David Walker's Appeal to the Coloured Citizens of the World*. Dr. James Turner, Africana Research Center, Cornell University, writes:

> The publication can and should be marked as an event of major importance. The *Appeal* is the most seminal

expression of African American political thought to come forth during the early 19th century. The *Appeal* is fundamentally a treatise on the necessity of and moral justification to slavery as the most despicable form of oppression"[4]

The writing presents the very first sustained critique of slavery and racism by an African person in the United States. Most importantly, the African American Village Community was empowered by the writer of this treatise because the *Appeal:*

> Evidenced a level of writing craft, multidimensional analysis, and command of principles of religious and natural philosophy that dramatically belied, the conventional notion, at the time that Africans (African Americans) were incapable of complex reasoning, rational differentiation, and fluent conversation in the lingua franca, i.e., English."[5]

Few writers had the gift to adequately demonstrate knowledge of more than one discipline of thought. European writers considered this phenomenal feat unusual and virtually unfathomable for the son of a former slave.[6] *Walker's Appeal*, an intellectual work, provides a theoretical foundation for Black Nationalism and Pan-Africanism. In addition, the *Appeal* eloquently addresses the following ten major themes:

1. The profound degradation of African people, especially those in the United States, as a result of the racism and avarice that supported and shaped the system of slavery. (Walker was perhaps the first writer to combine an attack on White racism and White economic exploitation in a deliberate and critical way).

2. The unavoidable judgment a just God would bring upon the White American nation unless it repented and gave up its evil ways of injustice and oppression.

3. The imperative for Black people to face their own complicity in their oppression, and the need for them to end that complicity through resistance in every possible way, including the path of armed struggle.

4. The need for Black people to develop a far greater sense of solidarity, especially between the "free" and the captive populations within the United States and between the children of Africa here and Africans in the rest of the world. (This was the first clear depiction and widely publicized call for Pan-African solidarity).

5. The need to resist (by any means necessary) the attempts of the American Colonization Society to rid the country of its free Black population.

6. The need to gain as much education as possible as a weapon in the struggle.

7. The possibility that a new society of peace and justice could come into being if White America were able to give up its malevolent ways, especially its racism and avarice.

8. The need for an essentially Protestant Christian Religious undergirding for the Black struggle for justice.

9. The likelihood that he, Walker, would be imprisoned or assassinated as a result of the *Appeal.*

10. The repeated statement of his own essential sense of solidarity with his brothers and sisters in slavery.[7]

The 10 themes align with the terminology used in this exegesis. Theme one supports the implementation and promotion of Cultural Utilitarianism. Theme two parallels the Glass Ceiling in America and warns of God's impending judgment. Theme three supports the creation and sustaining of a Communal Initiative within the African American Village Community. Theme four summons the spirit of solidarity and further defines the Crystallization of Cause & Effect. Theme five states the urgent need for Communal Healing in the face of mass deportation and/or mass genocide. Theme six supports the impending urgency to *Get That Knowledge...* and the empowerment of Empirical Hope. Theme seven addresses the need for the formation of the Beloved Community. Theme eight references the proper use of Historical Discipline and how other oppressed people in biblical times were grounded in their faith during the struggle for liberation and social justice. Theme nine, similar to Dr. Martin L. King, speaks of Walker's impending date with imprisonment and/or assassination while simultaneously explaining his unconditional commitment to the embracing of the Inescapable Mutuality Paradigm. Theme ten revisits the need for unity and the concept of *A House Divided...No More* through the communal empowerment of the African American Experience.

Walker, in a most unapologetic manner, became an advocate for the human rights of African Americans and other people of African descent as well. However, due to his strategic vantage point of being free, the *Appeal* is structured from an indigenous-based Black perspective (the African American Experience, if you will) and eloquently argues the need for a collective conscious awareness among the people of color who are oppressed in the nation. Although his vision for total Black liberation extended far beyond his immediate surroundings (encompassing a world view), Walker was born and compelled to live his life in the confines of White America. This world view (according to Walker) consists of five indigenous necessary (unconditional) correctives in the continuous struggle for African American liberation, global liberation for people of color, and human equality: conscious awareness, the essentiality of unity, responsibility for self-determination, mutual cooperation to reinforce solidarity and last but equally important, the imperative need for political organization.[8]

The courageous Walker organized the *Appeal* into a preamble and four distinct articles. The first (1st) Article, "Our Wretchedness in Consequence of Slavery," forcefully condemns the atrocities and brutalities of slavery.[9] David Walker poignantly calls on the cruel White slaveholders to immediately reduce the use of Africans as slaves, who were relegated to the most abject position in society and the world.

Walker affirmed that all oppressed people of color should resort to self-reliance and self-determination. Likewise, he unequivocally believed that the immediate implementation of intellectual initiatives was non-negotiable and an important, necessary corrective in the struggle for political parity:

> Walker was adamant that African people should raise their voices (without fear) in defense of their own interest and assume responsibility for speaking on behalf of their freedom to rebuke their critics and enemies.[10]

The second (2nd) Article, "Our Wretchedness in Consequence of Ignorance," references facts about the beginning of civilization and develops an eloquent discourse on the historic role of Africa.[11] Similar to Carter G. Woodson's exegesis *The Mis-Education of the Negro*, Walker summarizes and elaborates on the two primary weapons of mass human destruction: ignorance and mis-education. He insists that ignorance blinds the mind and blocks the vision of freedom. In support of Black Psychological Warfare he surmises, "What we do for ourselves depends on what we know of ourselves and what we accept about ourselves."[12] Clearly, it is well to note that he was rebuking any and all aspects of today's Laissez-Faire Entitlement Syndrome.

In the third (3rd) Article, "Our Wretchedness in Consequence of the Preachers of the Religion of Jesus Christ," Walker boldly excoriates the blatant use of religious hypocrisy especially that which intentionally condones slavery while simultaneously proclaiming the practice and blessings of Christianity.[13] Walker meticulously deconstructs the moral virtue of Christians who promote Slavocracy. He cautiously warns of the impending judgment by God in stating, "Indeed the way in which religion was and is conducted by the Europeans and their descendants, one might believe it was a plan fabricated by themselves and the devil to oppress us."[14]

In addition to this religious analysis, Walker's moral philosophy posited the right to self-defense and the moral legitimacy of armed struggle to overthrow slavery. "He argued that freedom was the highest human right ordained by God, and that a slave was morally justified in taking the life of his master, if necessary, to command his freedom."[15] David Walker further declared that slaveholders forfeited any form of moral consideration through the unconscionable act of enslaving another human being.

In the fourth (4th) Article, "Our Wretchedness in Consequence of the Colonizing Plan," Walker addresses, in an eloquent manner, the prevalent immoral practice of American Colonization.[16] The activist insists that the true motive of the American Colonization Society was to secure slavery from the consistent disruption of Black abolitionists by luring away free Africans with devious schemes of lucrative settlements in Africa.

David Walker's stance against permanent ignorance illuminated the torch of Empirical Hope. The psychological planting of the seed of hope became a formidable weapon in Black Psychological Warfare. *David Walker's Appeal* was written and introduced during a time when national debates continuously focused on the moral dilemma on what to do about the confiscation of slave property: the enslaved.

Walker died under suspicious circumstances. He was found slumped in a doorway on the street. The cause of death is simply unknown. Many believed that it was poison as a result of large rewards offered by Southern slaveholders. Still others believed it could have been tuberculosis. Ironically, his son, Edwin G. Walker, was born a few months after his untimely mysterious death and in 1866 became the first Black elected to the Massachusetts legislature. In any event, the *Boston Evening Transcript* noted that the African American Village Community regarded the *Appeal* "as if it were a star in the East guiding them to freedom and emancipation."[17]

The roots and indigenous based dialect of modern day Black radicalism is unquestionably deeply embedded in David Walker's political philosophy and public debates. Through the writing and promotion of the *Appeal,* Walker is unequivocally the undisputed philosophical, intellectual and spiritual father of indigenous Black Psychological Warfare in America. Walker's psychological influence lit the torch of Empirical Hope. This torch was passed on to Marcus Garvey, Paul Robeson, Queen Mother Moore, Malcolm X, Ella Baker, H. Rap Brown, Kwame Toure, Fred Hampton, Rev. Henry Highland Garnet, Dr. W.E.B. Du Bois and the Rev. Dr. Martin L. King, Jr.[18]

David Walker's philosophy unequivocally supports the hypothesis that we must not, under any circumstances, be divided among ourselves. Moreover, as the struggle against oppression in America and abroad calls for solidarity, we must summon a preternatural power that can only come from an oppressed people who have decided that they are sick and tired of being sick and tired. In his public proclamation that we have an inherent right to claim our humanity, Walker boldly affirms:

> I call upon the professing Christians, I call upon the philanthropist, I call upon the very tyrant himself, to show me a page of history, either sacred or profane, on which a verse can be found, which maintains, that the Egyptians heaped the *insupportable insult* upon the children of Israel, by telling them that they were not of the human family. Can the Whites deny this charge? Have they not, after having reduced us to the deplorable condition of slaves under their feet, held us up as descending originally from the tribes of monkeys or orangutans? O! My God! I appeal to every man of feeling-is not this insupportable? Is it not heaping the most gross insult upon our miseries, because they have got us under their feet and we cannot help ourselves? Oh! pity us we pray thee, Lord Jesus, Master.[19]

In retrospect, the torch of Empirical Hope and the practice of engaging the oppressor as a unified community would be passed on to great leaders beyond Walker's lifetime. In his essay, "White Hopes and Other Coalitions" (Ebony, August 1966), the distinguished historian Lerone Bennett observes:

> We can clearly see that the history of the Black people in this country has been largely of a quest for reliable allies. Nobody in this country has tried harder and longer to cooperate with other people on a non-racial basis...I want to emphasize the point of *interest*

because so many people believe that building a coalition is a matter of love and friendship. Nothing could be further from the truth. *Large social groups do not have love affairs.*

The subjective and objective interest of White groups which contradict the objective and subjective interest of Black People, who are predominantly lower class and have material interests which cannot be satisfied without a structural transformation (social, political, educational, and economic) of American society- a structural transformation which threatens the interests of persons with large stakes in the status quo.[20]

In retrospect, another notable warrior and drum major for social justice who employed the necessary correctives of Black Psychological Warfare and the Village Concept in an effort to address the divided Village Community rose up and set a new standard of cultural pride and unity. Maulana Karenga (born Ronald McKinley Everett, also known as Roy Karenga or M. Ron Karenga) eloquently introduced a new necessary corrective to minister to our bruised humanity that was caused by the long night of slavery and the infamous Willie Lynch Syndrome. This specific corrective stressed a communitarian focus through the teachings and practice of Kawaida, promoted by the organization Us, which simply means "us Black people." The Us organization (in the interest of solidarity) respectively adopted the motto, "Anywhere we are, Us, is."[21]

Us has played a significant vanguard role in shaping Rites-of-Passage programs, the study of ancient Egyptian culture, the Black Arts Movement, Black Studies, the Black Student Union Movement, Afrocentricity, the founding of the Association for the Study of Classical African Civilizations, the independent school movement, African life-cycle ceremonies, the Simba Wachanga Youth Movement and Black theological and ethical discourse. Karenga has served on the executive and founding committees of the Black Power Conferences of the 1960's, the Black Leadership retreat, the Million Man March/Day of Absence, National Black United Front (NBUF) and the National African American Leadership Summit (NAALS).[22]

Karenga, along with other local and national leaders, created the National Association of Kawaida Organizations (NAKO). This cooperative based framework (consisting of numerous organizations) subscribes to the three basic tenets of the Kawaida philosophy: struggle, service and institution building. Furthermore, in addressing the divided African American Village Community, a core tenet of Kawaida affirms that culture is the fundamental source of a people's identity, purpose and direction.[23] This humanistic philosophy is derived from the hypothesis that all humans originated from Africa. The healing aspects of Kawaida for African Americans is that at the heart of this synthesis of African thought is the continuous quest to define ourselves and become the best of what it means to be both African and human in the fullest sense. This synthesis addresses the house divided and the aging psychological scars on the collective bruised humanity of the descendents of the African Diaspora. Healing through the effective use of Black Psychological Warfare involves an ongoing search for models of possibilities and excellence in every area of human life.

The gallant and formidable leader, Maulana Karenga, expands the ongoing search for possibility models to seven key core areas of culture: history, spirituality and ethics, social organization, political organization, economic organization, creative production (art, music, literature, dance) and ethos:[24]

It also involves creating a language and logic of liberation, one of opposition and affirmation, and a corresponding liberational practice to create a just and good society and pose an effective paradigm of mutually beneficial human relations and human possibility.[25]

In addressing the bruised humanity and healing in the divided house, Karenga's demands for reparations are a far cry from today's Generation E's faint demand for Laissez-Faire Entitlement. In the uncompromised demand and defense for reparations, Karenga affirms that *maagamizi*, the Swahili term for Holocaust, is more appropriate than *maafa*, which means calamity, accident, ill luck, disaster or damage. *Maagamizi* is derived from the verb *angamiza*, which specifically means to cause destruction, to utterly destroy. It carries with it a sense of profound intentionality. The "a" prefix strongly suggests an amplified destruction that speaks to the massive nature of the Holocaust.[26] In retrospect, the term "Holocaust," as it applies to the African Diaspora, refers to a morally monstrous act of genocide that is not only against the victims, but it is a crime against humanity. According to Karenga and other Black Alpha Male scholars, the Holocaust of African enslavement expresses itself in the following distinct ways:

- The morally monstrous destruction of human life.

- The morally monstrous destruction of human culture.

- The morally monstrous destruction of human possibility.[27]

In the *Husia*, the sacred text of ancient Egypt, we find a concept of restoration, healing and repairing the world. The word is *serudj*, and it is a part of a phrase *serudj-ta*, which means to repair and heal the world thereby making it more beautiful and beneficial than it was before.[28] This is an ongoing moral obligation in the Kawaida (Maatian) ethical tradition and is expressed as follows: 1) to raise up that which is in ruins; 2) to repair that which is damaged; 3) to rejoin that which is severed; 4) to replenish that which is depleted; 5) to strengthen that which is weakened; 6) to set right that which is wrong; and 7) to make flourish that which is insecure and undeveloped. An expansive and morally worthy concept of reparations as repair and healing requires more than monetary focus and payments.[29]

Dr Karenga, armed with the *Husia* supports the demands for reparations. The scholar affirms that there are five essential aspects within the parameters of this discourse and policy on reparations that unequivocally must be addressed. According to Karenga and other respected leaders, under no circumstances should these critical and vitally important aspects be excluded from any meaningful dialogue and moral approaches to reparations. The five unconditional aspects involve the following: 1) public admission; 2) public apology; 3) public recognition; 4) compensation; and 5) institutional preventive measures against the recurrence of the holocaust and other similar forms of massive destruction of human life, human culture and human possibility.[30]

Dr. Maulana Karenga pondered over the divided house of the African American Village Community, and in 1966, in an attempt to restore the Beloved Community (via the Village Concept), he created and established Kwanzaa, a cultural holiday and a Communal Initiative specifically designed to nurture and promote indigenous Communal Healing. This unique celebration is practiced by Africans of all religious faiths who come together based on the rich, ancient and varied common ground of their Africanness.[31] During the Black Freedom Movement, the embracing of Kwanzaa fulfilled an imperative need for an innate connection with our cultural groundedness in thought, practice, and self determination.

The African American branch of this festive (necessary corrective) celebration is rooted in ancient African history and culture. In its recreation and expansion of ancient tradition, Kwanzaa has developed as a flourishing branch of African American life and struggle. It is both an African American and Pan-African holiday, for it draws from the cultures of various African peoples, and it is celebrated by millions of Africans throughout the African world community. Kwanzaa speaks not only to African Americans in a special way, but in its emphasis on history, values, family, community and culture it similarly speaks to Africans as a whole.[32]

This celebration and communal embrace of family, community and culture begins on December 26 and ends on January 1st. The name Kwanzaa is derived from *"matunda ya kwanza,"* which means *first fruits* in Swahili, a Pan-African language (which historically and notably is the most widely spoken African language).[33] Furthermore, support for the communal aspects of this concept can be found in African history as far back as ancient Nubia and Egypt. This communal first fruits concept appears in ancient and modern times in other classical African civilizations (i.e., Yorubaland and Ashantiland). Similarly, this festive concept is also found in ancient and modern times among large societies and empires such as the Zulu or Swaziland or, and smaller societies and groups like the Matabele, Thonga and Lovedu, all of southeastern Africa.[34]

The five fundamental activities of Continental "first fruits" are as follow: ingathering, reverence, commemoration, recommitment and celebration. Kwanzaa consists of the following indigenous declarations and practices:

- Ingathering of the people to reaffirm the bonds between them;

- Special reverence for the Creator and creation in thanks and respect for the blessings, bountifulness and beauty of creation;

- Commemoration of the past in pursuit of its lessons and in honor of its models of human excellence (our ancestors);

- Recommitment to our highest cultural ideals in our ongoing effort to always bring forth the best of African cultural thought and practice; and

- Celebration of the Good—the good of life and of existence itself. The good of family, community and culture. The good of the awesome and the ordinary. In a word, the good of the divine, natural and social.[35]

Dr. Karenga introduced seven basic values of African culture that positively contribute to building and reinforcing family, community and culture among African Americans and Africans throughout the world. The *Nguzo Saba*, a Swahili term for "seven principles," includes the following:

- *Umoja*, unity (oo-MO-jah): To strive for and maintain unity in the family, community, nation and race.

- *Kujichagulia*, self-determination (koo-gee-cha-goo-LEE-yah): To define ourselves, name ourselves, create for ourselves and speak for ourselves.

- *Ujima*, collective work and responsibility (oo-GEE-mah): To build and maintain our community together

141

and to make our brothers' and sisters' problems our problems and to solve them together.

- *Ujamaa*, cooperative economics (oo-JAH-mah): To build and maintain our own stores, shops and other businesses and to profit from them together.

- *Nia*, purpose (nee-YAH): To make our collective vocation the building and developing of our community in order to restore our people to their traditional greatness.

- *Kuumba*, creativity (koo-OOM-bah): To do always as much as we can, in the way that we can, in order to leave our community more beautiful and beneficial than when we inherited it.

- *Imani*, faith (ee-MAH-nee): To believe with all our hearts in our parents, our teachers, our leaders, our people and the righteousness and victory of our struggle.[36]

Dr. Karenga introduced Kwanzaa to affirm and restore our rootedness in African culture. It is an expression of reconstruction and recovery of African culture. It is designed to serve as a regular communal celebration to reinforce the bonds (a celebratory Communal Healing, if you will) among us as a people.

At the nucleus of Dr. Maulana Karenga's passion to address the division of his people we find the Village Concept and Cultural Utilitarianism. Karenga was acutely aware of the Glass Ceiling and the evil tenets of capitalism in America. He unequivocally believed that we must reconnect with the lost traditions of communal living. By any means necessary, we as a people must reclaim the root of Africa that was intentionally stolen from the pluralistic tribes that were excavated from the Motherland. Capitalism in America has destroyed the ethics of the Village Concept that was once a way of life. This way of life embraces the extended family and the natural bonds among us as members of the human family. This way of life embraces the rituals of thanking God, the Creator and Unmoved Mover, showing unconditional respect for blessings received and acknowledging the beauty of creation. This way of life teaches the Village Community to respect and pay homage to our families, ancestors and to create, not destroy, the communities (Villages) in which we live. These African-based attributes, which directly stand against the greed promoted by capitalism, are ideas whose time has come.

Dr. Karenga ushered in an urgency to use a higher level of protest associated with the concept of Historical Discipline. In a most eloquent and unapologetic manner the scholar harnessed the power and importance of the African American Experience while simultaneously engaging in the task of empowering our minds. This drum major for social justice was historically aware of notable Black liberation leaders such as Nat Turner, Denmark Vesey and Gabriel Prosser, just to name a few, who stood toe-to-toe with the Goliaths of their eras by engaging the enemy through physical confrontations, including massive-coordinated slave revolts, insurrections, and last but not least, courageous one-on-one assaults. However, as time progressed and African Americans began to methodically reassemble themselves into distinct, smaller villages (the African American Village Community) the struggle for equality on American soil required a new more refined form of nonviolent resistance: the Black intellect. Black Psychological Warfare became a necessary corrective against the attractiveness and lure of the crumbs from the bountiful capitalistic table. This lure, as Dr. Karenga noticed, was slowly and methodically becoming a force to be reckoned with. Young, misguided African Americans—Generation E—

suffering from Historical Euthanasia began to buy into the hype and were poisoned and infected with greed. *I'ism* and *Me'ism* replaced the Civil Rights concepts of *we* as a people and united *we* stand. The torch of Empirical Hope was now being dropped, abandoned and left on the side of Freedom Road to simply die out. Generation E had consciously and unconsciously embraced the destructive forces of the Laissez-Faire Entitlement Syndrome.

It is well to note that when the torch of Empirical Hope passed from Dr. Karenga to the next generation of Civil Rights leaders (the Constructionist), the arrogant, vigilant, watchful and protective gatekeepers of capitalism decided to engage the enemy (the Black Alpha Males) at an earlier age to cut off the continuous supply and grooming of generational leaders. With the strong enticing lure of immediate materialistic gratification promoted through the tenets of capitalism, the creation and promotion of unethical and offensive Rap Music, billions of dollars of targeted investments into the Industrial Prison Complex (human corrals) and the underground promotion of crack-cocaine, the Black Alpha Male began to fall through the cracks of society. To add insult to injury, two new weapons were strategically introduced and implemented to counteract the stronghold of Black Psychological Warfare: the Fourth Grade Failure Syndrome and special education.

Dr. Jawanza Kunjufu, a widely known notable scholar who has dedicated years to the empowerment of his people through the promotion of the Village Concept, first noticed the subtle conspiracy, the Fourth Grade Failure Syndrome, as he toured public and private schools and colleges throughout this nation. As early as 1974, the inconspicuous deception had become clear. Moreover, as previously stated, the gatekeepers of this capitalistic society decided to launch a seek-and-destroy mission against Black Alpha Males during early infancy. The conspiracy went virtually unnoticed until Dr.

Kunjufu sounded the alarm and uncovered indisputable evidence of this weapon of mass human destruction. Dr. Kunjufu confirmed the intellectual observations of Harry Morgan in *How Schools Fail Black Children*. Morgan eloquently states:

> When Blacks enter first grade the stories they create express positive feelings about themselves in the schooling situation, but by the second grade students' stories express 'negative imagery of the teacher and school environment.' By the fifth grade the overall feeling expressed by students is that of cynicism. In other words, upon entering school in primary grades, Black children possess enthusiasm and eager interest; however, by the fifth grade the liveliness and interest are gone, replaced by passivity and apathy. Primary grades presented a more nurturing environment than intermediate and upper grades. In early childhood education much of the activity is child-teacher centered and child-child interactive. In primary grades, Blacks progress and thrive at the same rate as their counterparts until the third grade. I found after the third grade, the achievement rate of Blacks began a downward spiral which appeared to continue in the child's academic career. The classroom environment was routinely transformed from a socially interactive style to a competitive, individualistic, and minimally socially interactive style of learning.[37]

This poor transition (particularly between the primary and intermediate divisions) is appropriately called the Fourth Grade Failure Syndrome. This breach in transition specifically affects African American males. Essentially and noticeably, the move from a socially interactive style of learning to a more competitive, individualistic, minimally social style of learning became a formidable and effective weapon against young

Black Alpha Males; these particular males became intentional human targets (slated for certain failure) and were considered expendable human commodities. Furthermore, Dr. Kunjufu noticed in his travels that there was an apparent (planned) intentional absence of male teachers, particularly African American males. According to Dr. Jawanza Kunjufu, men were routinely the janitors of the building, physical education teachers or strategically found at high level administration positions. Therefore, most qualified males usually entered the picture in the upper grades well after the conspiracy already was under way. To add insult to injury, principals informed Kunjufu that they routinely and unapologetically placed their best qualified teachers, including men, in the upper grades. This routine strategy was used to contain and control the most undisciplined students. "This band-aid approach is part of the conspiracy."[38] Kunjufu contends that if educators and administrators addressed the problem in the primary division, the problem would not surface in the upper grades.

In my book entitled *ABSENT, The Assimilation of African American Males Into Nonbeing*, I also addressed the issue of the intentional shortage of African American male teachers. I asserted that the gatekeepers of wealth and the promoters of capitalism created this shortage based on their untrue assumption that African American males are expendable human commodities, not valuable human capital. They are routinely placed at the top of the bad list and at the bottom of the good list.[39]

The predominance of females and White teachers, specifically in African American Village Communities, is a primary psychological weapon of mass human destruction. Chapter 5 of the book *ABSENT* categorizes this phenomenon as *Territoriality in the Teaching Profession*.[40] This system is faltering miserably without the egalitarian aspect of a level playing field comprised of both male and female teachers.

Although the ratio of African American male teachers to White and African American females during the 1960's and 1970's were unbalanced, the valuable presence of the Black Alpha Male leveled the playing field. Due to his presence, students (males and females) had more respect for authority figures, and discipline was equitably distributed. This God-ordained egalitarian balance is now missing. Public education, which is a female dominated sector of society, is miserably failing at educating children, especially African American males, regardless of their social, economic or demographic background. There are some exceptional, gifted, talented and sincerely dedicated female teachers from both sides of the cultural spectrum, but until the egalitarian balance is restored, the system will continue to fail students. This system will continue to produce generations of dysfunctional, misplaced, angry African American males who will continuously rebel against the overwhelming, unnatural dominance of female (matriarchal) authority figures both at home and in the public school system.[41]

Notable scholars, including Dr. Jawanza Kunjufu, noticed that within the parameters of this failing system, students have been programmed and will not respond to conventional classroom instruction. They will not respond because this female-dominated scenario reminds them of the similar conditions they face at home. Due to the antics of anti-male government based interventions, most African American households throughout this nation are headed by women. The results can be categorized as a sociological catastrophe. Evidence of this social catastrophe is manifested through acts of random and unprovoked violence in schools. Violence has escalated to unprecedented levels. This rise in the epidemic of violence corresponds with the declining quality of education and grade averages. The absent moral value system correlates with the absent male, particularly the Alpha Male in the Village Community. Make no mistake, capitalistic society's

147

frail and foolish efforts to rewrite the natural laws of nature created by God have left the African American Village Community and the nation's public school system as a whole in a state of chaos. Violence, rebellion and all out defiance are apparently the order of the day.[42]

In the arena of Black Psychological Warfare, the missing link is quite apparent. African American students must have access to visible, authentic role models who look like them. They need teachers who can motivate and educate them to meet the difficult challenges of competing for a quality education, fair housing and job opportunities head on. In counteracting the Fourth Grade Failure Syndrome, the Black Alpha Male Constructionist will bring to the table of teaching a special knowledge, cultural sensitivity, excitement and encouragement. Since teaching is a lifelong commitment, it is important that African American students, especially the endangered and targeted males, learn from other successful Black Alpha Males. The Black Alpha Male Constructionist (teacher, par excellence) through God's all wise providence, projects a presence that instantly connects to the psyche of students. Since this particular Black male can intuitively identify with students' present, past and future struggles, there is an instant, preternatural homogeneous bonding process. This intangible presence warrants immediate, consistent and growing respect. This presence is comprised of a certain masculine stature and an innate authoritative voice tone. It is a natural, nurturing and correcting spirit emanating from a masculine perspective. It nurtures and effectively ministers to the immediate needs of students, and they begin to feel the cosmic balance of a more egalitarian distribution of male and female authority figures. It is a God-given quality that cannot, under any circumstances, be replaced, ignored, cast out, cast aside, underestimated, substituted or eliminated by the powers that be. It cannot be erased from the natural order, the natural cosmic balance of the universe, due to a few foolish, egotistic lawmakers whose primary purpose is to target and exterminate the Black Alpha Male during his early and vulnerable stages of educational, social and biological development.[43]

According to Kunjufu and other scholars, you cannot teach a child you do not love. You cannot teach a child you do not respect. You cannot teach a child you don't understand.[44] Within the parameters of Black Psychological Warfare, Dr. Kunjufu addresses the role of racism and fear in quite an eloquent manner. The scholar insists that:

> Many of our males have been taught that racism is a sign of insecurity, not inferiority. People that are secure are comfortable with differences. Only insecure people have to rationalize and dwell on the fact that they are different. If African people were inferior, there would be no need for discrimination. I argue that racists know more about the African American culture than we know about ourselves...Dr Kunjufu continues and states, during an empowerment session I will explain to the men how special they are and how afraid this country is of African American males reaching their full potential. This explains lynching and castration.[45]

Long ago, during the intentional destruction of the African villages and the stockpiling of slaves in slave ships, the White invaders could see determination in the eyes of the Black Alpha Male. In an unspoken gesture his eyes said, "We will rise again. Not only will we return from this abyss, but we will beyond a reasonable doubt restore, reconstruct, reclaim and rebuild the African Village Community." In retrospect, the determined Black Alpha Male historically became a silent psychological and physical threat due to his indomitable spirit of uncompromised resistance to the continuous inhumane abuses (both aboard the Mothership and on American soil), all out resistance to the Willie Lynch Indoctrination, resistance to segregation and resistance to the relentless campaign of unprovoked inhumane lynching. This innate resistance (a gift from God, the Creator and Unmoved Mover) became a force to be reckoned with; therefore, the government launched the War on Poverty, or rather, a war to promote the permanent poverty status of African American males, the Providers and Protectors of the Village Community. The promotion of the Great Society did not, by any stretch of the imagination, include the male child of African American women.

The real problem in America is the White man's instinctive fear of the potential uprising of Black Alpha Males. During the years following the Civil War, the powers that be masked the issue by calling it the Negro problem in America. The real problem, if I may interject, was what to do with the ex-male slaves after his usefulness as a major labor force in America was outlawed. The problem was compounded by the fact that the Black Alpha Male no longer could be beaten into submission. The Nathaniel Jones and Rodney King cases are vivid reminders of the wall of fear that shadows the Black Alpha Male. In defense of the brutal beatings, the White officers said they feared for their lives as the unarmed man (King) grunted like an animal.[46]

The general concept of mass genocide would draw too much attention. In retrospect, the brutal killing of the Black Panthers led by J. Edgar Hoover of the FBI, through the notorious seek and destroy (Anti-Alpha Black Male) program of counterintelligence appropriately entitled COINTELPRO drew public outrage. In Chicago on December 4, 1969 at 4:00 a.m., the Chicago Police stormed the Panthers' apartment and shot Fred Hampton twice in the head and once in the arm while he slept. During the raid, Mark Clark was also killed: 90 bullets were fired, and only one returned from the Panthers.[47]

Through the strategic process of elimination, coupled with strategic planning, this country determined that the Black Alpha Male had to be contained, controlled by any and all means necessary. A biological weapon previously used by the U.S. Government in the Tuskegee syphilis experiment had been exposed and similarly could not be used without drawing public attention and public outrage. Only a slow, methodical, deliberate strangulation would suffice. The system used had to render the Black Alpha Male useless and unnecessary to the survival and function of the family, extended family and the African American Village Community at large. As a result, various social policies were designed and implemented to assist African American women and children. This new form of genocidal assimilation promoted through welfare reform and the public school system was designed to methodically move the Black Alpha Male into a permanent state of invisibility or nonbeing, if you will. Most importantly, the powers that be decided to throw a one-two-three punch against males (ex-slaves) and any and all up-and-coming generational leaders: 1) the war to promote poverty on the Black Alpha Male, 2) the Fourth Grade Failure Syndrome and 3) the targeting of Black Alpha Males for special education.

The Fourth Grade Failure Syndrome and the placement of African American males in special education have become the norm. As was previously stated, Dr. Jawanza Kunjufu became aware of this weapon of mass human destruction and wrote the groundbreaking series, *Countering The Conspiracy to Destroy Black Boys*. The goals of Kunjufu's solution-driven initiatives are empowerment and the unapologetic promotion and sustaining of the Village Concept. The objective of the book is to specifically pinpoint why, when and how African American males are denied the skills necessary for manhood. Most importantly, Dr. Kunjufu's exegesis discusses proven strategies that can be developed to negate the conspiracy to destroy Black boys and enhance African American male development. Kunjufu unequivocally believes in the power of the extended family and the tradition of the Village Concept (the creation of indigenous self-reliant, self-sufficient systems within the parameters of the greater African American Village Community with the prime directive [initiative] of addressing the unfinished task of emancipation in America). Kunjufu's declaration for liberation involves the following mandate:

> Every concerned African American man should ask himself if he is providing some positive direction to at least one African American male child. Furthermore, concerned administrators, teachers, parents should solicit men to speak in the schools that solely lack a male presence.[48]

In a poem, Pledge on Black Manhood, Jawanza Kunjufu writes the following words of empowerment:

I am the Black man
Some know me as Imhotep, Ramses, Martin, or Malcolm
Others know me as the brother on the corner or in jail.

I am both, Detroit Red and Malcolm.
From this day forward, I pledge my life to the liberation of my people. I will put God first in my life.

Black women will feel safe when they see me. I will be a supportive, responsible, and loving husband. I will hug, talk and listen to, and educate my children. I will be involved in the Scouts, Role Model and Rites-of-Passage.

Why?
Because I am the Black man-the original man, the one and only. The one that other men are afraid of, because they know whenever I've seized the opportunity-I succeed.[49]

The critically acclaimed series, *Countering the Conspiracy to Destroy Black Boys,* promotes the paradigm of the Crystallization of Cause & Effect. The causes of the conspiracy include:

- White male supremacy/institutional racism
- A capital intensive economy
- Drugs
- The male socialization process
- Double child rearing standards among parents
- Parental apathy
- Low teacher expectations
- Lack of understanding of the male learning styles
- Negative peer pressure and gangs
- The lack of positive male role models.[50]

In order to correct the problems pertaining to the divisive weapons used, the solutions have to address the causes. Dr. Kunjufu recommends implementing the following solution-oriented strategies:

- *Racism.* We must understand and resist racism and empower our community to reach its full potential.

- *High Tech Economy.* We must lobby for a high tech economy that would include a federal jobs bill, a reduction in the defense budget, more money allocated for education and training, a reduction in foreign imports and Black economic development.

- *Drugs.* We must patrol our borders, enhance self-esteem, prevent stores from selling drug paraphernalia, use the money from drug busts for community programs, allocate more money for treatment and increase community watch groups.

- *Male Socialization Process.* We must increase Rites-of-Passage programs and produce programs for electronic media to portray Black males' strengths, mental and spiritual.

- *Parental Double Standards.* We must have workshops and books that inform parents of the necessity to teach their sons and daughters to be equally responsible and self-sufficient.

- *Parental Apathy.* We must market the PTA to attract parents, increase the number of families receiving services from Chapter One and Head Start, and provide more workshops.

- *Lower Teacher Expectations.* We must have mandatory in-service trainings on expectations from Africentric educational scholars.

- *Learning Styles.* We must have mandatory in-service trainings using books that explain the race sensitive differences of boys, girls maturation rates and learning styles. A moratorium on special education placement of Black boys, a Black male classroom and seminars on how to effectively attract more Black male teachers to the classroom.

- *Negative Peer Pressure and Gangs.* We must have programs that teach boys the distinction between battles and wars, conflict management and peer group monitoring.

- *Lack of Male Role Models.* We must have a media campaign showing Cub Scouts, classroom teachers and other role models all being female and its dire consequences for Black male development.[51]

In his solution-oriented paradigm, Dr. Kunjufu cites two distinct programs that are effectively intervening at the right time with the proper strategies to minimize the impact of the conspiracy. The programs are located in Waterloo, Iowa, and Houston, Texas. In Waterloo, 50 to 75 at-risk Black boys in fourth grade are matched to Black male role models; these carefully chosen men spend four to six hours a week interacting with the children. In-service training is provided for parents, mentors and teachers. The Houston initiative is entitled, "The Fifth Ward Enrichment Program." Role models go into the schools to provide counseling and tutoring during the school day and recreational and informational sessions during the evenings and weekends. In 1985, the ideology and psychological use of empowerment was made by Dr. Kunjufu to a private school in Newark, New Jersey. In 1989, at the National Association of Black School Education's Conference (NABSE) in Portland, Oregon, he suggested the use of a Black male classroom to counter the conspiracy. The sixteen major components of the classroom include:

- Black male teachers
- 20 to 24 students
- Cooperative learning
- SETCLAE Curriculum
- Physical education
- Nutritious daily meals
- Science labs
- Martial arts training
- Phonics
- Musical instruments
- Whole-brain lesson plans and tests
- Math word problems

- Junior Business League
- Corporate sponsors for summer employment
- Academic contests and assemblies
- Monthly parent meetings.[52]

In support of this innovative strategy, Kunjufu's SETCLAE initiative (Self-Esteem Through Culture Leads to Academic Excellence) promotes the power of cooperative learning and high teacher expectations that would best socialize the endangered human species, Black boys. This drum major for social and educational justice contends that this type of classroom would correct the problem of Black boys not being taught by an African American male teacher. The high energy that boys naturally have would be channeled into daily physical education and martial arts. Boys' competence in handling objects and artifacts would be used in the science lab. Music would be used to teach mathematics. This classroom would teach critical thinking skills. It would use word problems and establish a Junior Business League, which would show the relevance of the classroom to the street. "It should be amazing to everyone that the same boy who failed math is able to measure kilos and grams for drugs and to convert it to dollars and cents on the street".[53] Kunjufu wholeheartedly and unequivocally believes that the African American Village Community should take indigenous (sole) responsibility to counter the conspiracy by using Rites-of-Passage programs. Indigenous Rites-of-Passage programs throughout the African American Village Community will feature positive adult male role models, skills development, Black culture and a male socialization process that will inevitably lead to manhood. The conspiracy can be addressed through a creditable Rites-of-Passage program. Kunjufu recommends implementing such programs as follows:

1. Organize a group of Black men willing to participate in the program.
2. Develop study sessions with this group, discussing Black history and male development.
3. Identify a facility and decide the frequency and length of the proposed meetings with the young brothers. (Age is discretionary.)
4. The program should provide skills development, Black history, male socialization, recreation and a "Big Brother".
5. Recommended frequency of meetings is weekly, with one week allocated to a field trip, the study of Black history, the development of skills and Rites-of-Passage (male socialization).
6. Field trips should include prisons, drug abuse centers, teenage pregnancy centers, public hospital emergency rooms on Saturday evenings, best high school honors classes, the stock market, camping and computer oriented businesses.
7. The nine minimal national standards that all programs should include are as follows: African history, economics, politics, career development, community involvement, family responsibility, physical development, spirituality and values (e.g., Nguzo Saba and Maat).[54]

Authentic Communal Healing through a Communal Initiative can take place, according to Dr. Kunjufu, when we teach Black boys the distinction between a battle and a war. This generation of males must learn that it may be better to keep their mouths shut and lose the battle in order to be available to fight the continuous war of liberation for African Americans.[55] The present generation, Generation E, must dismiss the misplaced negative ideologies of the Laissez-Faire Entitlement Syndrome and begin to study and adhere to the teachings and philosophies of Elijah Muhammad and Marcus Garvey. These two great Black Alpha Males had a track record of turning Reds into Malcolms without government grants or doctorates in clinical psychology. Through the psychological planting of the seed of hard work, knowledge of history and a belief in God, the Creator, these noble leaders empowered the African American Village Community to use two additional (potent) weapons available to an oppressed people: self-love and self-respect. The scholar Nathan Hare shares that tradition in the writing, "I Am A Black Man."

> The evidence of anthropology now suggests that I, the Black man, am the original man, the first man to walk this vast imponderable earth. I, the Black man, am an African, the exotic single quintessence of a universal Blackness. I have lost, by force, my land, my language, in essence, my life. I will seize it back so help me.

> Toward that end, if necessary, I will crush the corners of the earth, and this world will surely tremble. Until, I, the Black man, the first and original man can arm in arm with my woman, erect among the peoples of the universe a new society, humane to its cultural core, out of which at long last will emerge, as night move into day, the first truly human being that the world has ever known.[56]

We will now revisit and examine the effective use of Black Psychological Warfare during the historic Civil Rights Movement in America. The embracing of the ideologies of Cultural Utilitarianism and the Beloved Community will be explored. Through the research, expertise and perspective of Julian Bond we will revisit the documentary, *A Time for Justice* and the PBS series, *Eyes on the Prize: America's Civil Rights Years*. This thorough in-depth analysis and cultural investigation will include reports on Medgar Evers, Jimmie L. Jackson, the Edmund Pettus Bridge, Project C, D Day (the controversial Children's Crusade) and Emmett Till.

CHAPTER SIX

Revisiting the Spirit of Civil Rights

In promoting Cultural Utilitarianism (the greatest good for the greatest number of people) and ushering in the Beloved Community (a global vision in which all people can share in the wealth of the earth via the unconditional, all-inclusive spirit of sisterhood and brotherhood), we must revisit the spirit of Civil Rights. Within the parameters of this historical movement, the belief and indigenous public support of the Village Concept took center stage. Notably, a drum major for social justice, Julian Bond, took the time to preserve and document the nonviolent weapon of Black Psychological Warfare used by an oppressed people (African Americans) in their collective struggle for equality in America.

Bond's historical chronologies capture firsthand the souls of Black folks empowered by the unique preternatural force and innate power of the African American Experience (a unique historical experience derived from the pluralistic tribes of Africa who were forced to merge into one people during the long night of slavery to become African Americans) and the binding cultural ties of the Inter-Related Structure of Black Reality: a collective consciousness (the cultural bridge if you will) connecting the Inescapable Mutuality paradigm and the African American Experience.

Bond, who routinely and throughout his career has been on the cutting edge of leadership and social change, was a former Chairman of the NAACP and the first Black Vice Presidential nominee. During the historical Civil Rights Movement, Bond continued to deliver a powerful message for equality, freedom and justice with a renewed sense of relevance. In an examination of Julian Bond's *modus operandi* (MO) we find that as the founder of SNCC (the Student Nonviolent Coordinating Committee), he organized sit-ins and

159

voter registration drives to further the cause of Civil Rights for his people. Bond effectively used the media to promote the cause of social justice and equality. This drum major for social justice appeared on "America's Black Forum," the oldest Black-owned show in television syndication.[1]

This elite graduate of Morehouse College helped found a literary magazine called *The Pegasus*; he was also an intern at *Time Magazine*.[2] While still a student, Bond founded the Committee on Appeal for Human Rights (COAHR) in 1960, an Atlanta University Center student rights organization. This indigenous based Civil Rights organization implemented three years of successful nonviolent, anti-segregation protests that won integration at the city's movie theaters, lunch counters and parks.

Through the power of the media, the skillful up and coming leader promoted his Civil Rights agenda: serving as the group's communications director, Bond tactfully and in an expeditious manner headed SNCC's publicity and printing department, and he edited the organization's newsletter. In 1961, this Civil Rights activist joined the staff of a new protest newspaper, *The Atlanta Inquirer*; he later became the paper's managing editor.

In 1965, Bond was elected to a one-year term to the Georgia House of Representatives (in a special election) but was not seated due to his outspoken opposition to the Vietnam War.[3] During the second election in 1966, he won again but was again similarly barred from membership. Finally, he successfully won the seat a third time for a two-year term and was seated in November of 1966 due to a Supreme Court ruling that the Georgia House violated his Civil Rights.

From 1966 to 1975, Bond served four terms as a Democrat in the Georgia House. He organized the Georgia legislative Black Caucus. Not surprisingly, he served six consecutive successful terms in the Georgia Senate (1975–1986). Moreover, with unconditional Civil Rights as his focus, Julian Bond was elected Chairman of the National Association for the Advancement of Colored People (NAACP). After the organization celebrated its 100 year anniversary in 2009, he quietly stepped down when Roslyn M. Brock became his successor in February of 2010.[4]

In revisiting the spirit of the Civil Rights Era it is well to note that Bond not only personally fought for Civil Rights but also took the time to create and narrate groundbreaking documentaries on the collective and individual power derived from the African American Experience. The documentaries eloquently depict the engagement of Black Psychological Warfare during the continuous struggle for Civil Rights. The award winning documentaries, *A Time for Justice* and *Eyes on the Prize*, preserved history. In them viewers witnessed:

> A first-hand eyewitness to many watershed moments in the history of the Civil Rights Movement, Bond delivers powerful speeches on the century's long struggle of African-Americans for equality, diversity in the shaping of laws, and Civil Rights moving into the future, as well as keynotes on African American's impact on music, national affairs, and leadership.[5]

A Time for Justice depicts the battle cry for Civil Rights from a foot soldier's perspective. Produced in 1994 by Charles Guggenheim, a three-time Academy Award winner, the documentary recalls the crises in Montgomery, Little Rock, Birmingham and Selma. It reveals the heroism of common people overlooked by history who risked their lives for the cause of freedom, justice and equality.

The film opens at the cemetery grave site of Jimmie Lee Jackson, an African American who was killed by state troopers while trying to protect his mother during a voting rights demonstration in Marion, Alabama. It was only fitting and proper to stand at Jimmie Lee Jackson's grave because, "Jimmie was a symbol of something that guns and bullets cannot destroy; guns and bullets cannot destroy ideas."[6] This extraordinary documentary won a distinguished Academy Award in 1995 for Documentary Short Subject. In accurately depicting the actual, blatant oppression of African Americans, the narrator goes on to say:

> Imagine being unable to eat or sleep in most restaurants and hotels; being unable to sit where you wanted in a movie theater; having to sit in the back when you boarded a bus, even an empty one; being forced to attend an inferior school; and even being forbidden to drink from certain water fountains. These were the facts of everyday life for all Black people in the Southern part of the United States as recently as 1960. They were citizens of a country founded on the principle that all people were created equal. Yet, they were treated unequally, and declared unequal by the law. In the middle of the 1950s, a movement of ordinary men and women arose to challenge this way of life. Using boycotts, marches, and other forms of protest, they ultimately forced the South to end its peculiar system of so called legalized segregation. They succeeded because, in a democracy, when the people speak the government must listen.[7]

Julian Bond also narrated the critically acclaimed *Eyes on the Prize*, a 14-hour documentary series about the African-American Civil Rights Movement. The series was produced in two stages. Broadcast in 1987 on PBS, the first *Eyes on the Prize: America's Civil Rights Years 1954–1965* consists of the first six episodes and covers the time period between the *Brown v. Board of Education of Topeka* decision and the Selma-to-Montgomery marches. The remaining eight episodes—*Eyes on the Prize II: America at the Racial Crossroads 1965–1985*—were broadcast on PBS in 1990. The series was also shown in the United Kingdom on BBC2. Created and produced by Henry Hampton at Blackside, Inc., the award-winning series used primary sources, including archival footage and interviews with persons involved in the mentioned events, to record the growth of the Civil Rights Movement in the United States. Special attention was given to the ordinary people who effected the change. "It wasn't no Civil War, wasn't no world war. Just people in the same country, fighting each other."[8] The documentary depicts unsung heroes and foot soldiers who stood their ground until they won their freedom. Notably, Claybourne Carson, a Stanford University history professor and editor of the published papers of Martin Luther King, Jr., cited the series as more than just a historical document. According to this distinguished professor:

> It was the principal film account of the most important American social justice movement of the 20th century…Because of its extensive use of primary sources and in-depth coverage of the material; it has been adopted as a key reference and record of the Civil Rights Movement.[9]

Eyes on the Prize: America's Civil Rights Years aired in the following sequence:

1 – "Awakenings" (1954–1956)
- Murder of Emmett Till
- Montgomery Bus Boycott

2 – "Fighting Back" (1957–1962)

- Central High School and the Little Rock Nine
- James Meredith and the University of Mississippi

3 – "Ain't Scared of Your Jails" (1960–1961)
- Nashville Sit-ins and Boycotts
- Freedom Riders

4 – "No Easy Walk" (1961–1963)
Martin Luther King, Jr. and . . .
- Albany, Georgia
- Birmingham, Alabama
- The March on Washington

5 – "Mississippi: Is This America?" (1962–1964)
- Medgar Evers
- Murder of Goodman, Chaney, and Schwerner
- Mississippi Freedom Democratic Party

6 – "Bridge to Freedom" (1965)
- Voting rights movement in Selma, Alabama[10]

Eyes on the Prize: America at the Crossroads similarly aired in the following sequence:

1 – "The Time Has Come" (1964–1966)
- Malcolm X
- Lowndes County Freedom Organization
- The March Against Fear

2 – "Two Societies" (1965–1968)
- Martin Luther King and Chicago
- Detroit Riot of 1967

3 – "Power!" (1967–1968)
- Election of Carl Stokes as Cleveland Mayor

- Birth of the Black Panther Party
- Community control of the Ocean Hill-Brownsville school district in Brooklyn

4 – "The Promised Land" (1967–1968)
- The final years of Martin Luther King, Jr.
- The Poor People's Campaign and Resurrection City

5 – "Ain't Gonna Shuffle No More" (1964–1972)
- Muhammad Ali
- The movement at Howard University
- National Black Political Convention

6 – "A Nation of Law?" (1968–1971)
- Fred Hampton and the Black Panther Party in Chicago
- Attica Prison rebellion

7 – "The Keys to the Kingdom" (1974–1980)
- Busing and the Boston public school system
- Maynard Jackson and the city of Atlanta
- Allan Bakke and affirmative action

8 – "Back to the Movement" (1979–1983)
- Miami Riot of 1980 and preceding events
- Election of Harold Washington as Chicago Mayor and preceding events
- Overview of the movement and its effect upon the nation and the world[11]

During this in-depth imperative, historical visitation, the narrator, Julian Bond, showcased the indomitable fortitude of an oppressed people (inclusive of individuals, events and collective group activities) who proclaimed that *now is the time* to let justice, judgment, and righteousness run as a mighty river. The implementation and effective use of Black

Psychological Warfare rode the wave of Civil Rights. Its positive effects surfaced in the hearts, minds, souls, and the collective consciousness of a people who boldly proclaimed that the house was not divided but unified in its efforts to achieve unconditional parity: unconditional inalienable parity at every level of human intercourse in America. In segment five of *America's Civil Rights Years*, Medgar Evers became a symbol of the power embedded in one Black Alpha Male Constructionist. He was a force to be reckoned with.

Medgar Evers was born July 2, 1925, in Decatur, Mississippi. The third of five children, he was the son of James Evers, a sawmill worker and owner of a small farm. This drum major for social justice was listed in *Who's Who in American Colleges* while at Alcorn College (now Alcorn State University) in 1948, where he pursued a degree in business administration. Evers served as president of his junior class, sang in the school choir, played football, ran track and most importantly, was a distinguished member of the debate team.[12] Evers, wise to the assault on African Americans, engaged in Black Psychological Warfare in a place where blatant discrimination and racism were the orders of the day, a place in America where African Americans dared not speak of Civil Rights, much less actively and publicly campaign for their elusive human rights. In his courageous quest to sit at the table of humanity, Evers recalls the tragedy of the times in which African Americans lived:

> I was born in Decatur here in Mississippi, and when we were walking to school in the first grade White kids in their school buses would throw things at us and yell filthy things, the Civil Rights leader recollected. This was a mild start. If you're a kid in Mississippi this is the elementary course. I graduated pretty quickly. When I was eleven or twelve a close friend of the family got lynched. I guess he was about forty years

old, married, and we routinely played with his kids. I remember the Saturday night a bunch of White men beat him to death (while he was hanging) at the Decatur fairgrounds because he sassed back a White woman. They just left him dead on the ground. Everyone in town knew it but never [said] a word in public. I went down and saw his bloody clothes. They left those clothes on a fence for about a year. Every Negro in town was supposed to get the message from those clothes and I can see those clothes now in my mind's eye.... But nothing was said in public. No sermons in church. No news. No protest. It was as though this man just dissolved except for the bloody clothes.... Just before I went into the Army I began wondering how long I could stand it. I used to watch the Saturday night sport of white men trying to run down a Negro with their car, or white gangs coming through town to beat up a Negro.[13]

After courageously serving in the Army during World War II, Evers decided, after witnessing other people fight for freedom and equality, to return to America and fight on his own shores for the freedom of his people. Evers and his brother Charlie, who also fought in the war, decided to vote in the next election. They were threatened, along with their father, and were physically blocked by an armed crowd of White Mississippians, two hundred strong. The brothers did not vote in the election that day. However, they joined the National Association for the Advancement of Colored People (NAACP) and became active in the ranks.

It was on one historical night while his father was dying in the deteriorating Negro ward (the basement of the hospital) that he witnessed another attempted lynching of an African American outside who was simply trying to defend himself from a White mob. The mob gathered outside the hospital to finish him off. Evers intensified his efforts with the NAACP and was named the state field secretary. He became one of the most vocal, recognized and feared NAACP members in the state of Mississippi. He boldly spoke of the collective need to overcome hatred and promoted equality and understanding between the races. A few weeks prior to his untimely assassination death, someone threw a bomb at his house. In response, Evers intensified his voter registration drive to increase the number of African Americans on the voters roll. His days were filled with meetings, economic boycotts, marches, prayer vigils, picket lines and bailing out demonstrators arrested by an all-White police force.[14]

On June 12, 1963, President Kennedy publicly called White resistance to Civil Rights for African Americans "a moral crisis" and unequivocally pledged his support.[15] That same night, just after midnight, Evers, carrying a handful of t-shirts that read "Jim Crow Must Go," was shot in the back in front of his home.[16] Evers was one of the first martyrs of the Civil Rights Movement. Medgar Evers' tragic and senseless death prompted President John F. Kennedy to ask Congress to support an uncompromising, comprehensive Civil Rights Bill. President Lyndon B. Johnson signed the bill into law the following year.[17]

Notably, the indomitable spirit of Civil Rights ignited to a preternatural level. The death of Medgar Evers was a milestone in the hard-fought integration war that rocked America in the 1950s and 1960s. While the assassination of such a prominent Black figure foreshadowed the violence to come, it also spurred other prominent Civil Rights leaders, themselves targets of White supremacists, to new fervor. They, in turn, were able to infuse their followers, both Black and White, with a new and expanded sense of purpose. They ignited a new spirit of Civil Rights that would never die and a spirit of unification, one that replaced human apprehension and skepticism with the discipline of nonviolent protest and courage. *Esquire* contributor Maryanne Vollers wrote:

> People who lived through those days will tell you that something shifted in their hearts after Medgar Evers died, something that put them beyond fear... At that point a new motto was born: After Medgar, no more fear.[18]

Courage began to resonate in the hearts, minds and spirits of African Americans, who collectively responded to years of oppression and the killing of Jimmie Lee Jackson (who was defending his mother from a White state trooper's nightstick). Following Jackson's death, close to 600 Civil Rights marchers set out on March 7, 1965, to petition the state capital in Montgomery for their inherent Civil Rights, specifically voting rights. Six blocks into the march, local and state lawmen drove the peaceful marchers back with unnecessary and inhumane force, using tear gas and billy clubs. This historic confrontation became known as "Bloody Sunday".[19] Julian Bond's *Eyes on the Prize* revisited the stand at the Edmund Pettus Bridge and the voting rights movement in Selma, Alabama, in segment 6, "Bridge to Freedom" (1965).

The second march took place on March 9. Only the third march, which began on March 21 and lasted five days, made it to Montgomery, 51 miles (82 km) away. The marchers averaged 10 miles (16 km) a day along U.S. Route 80, known in Alabama as the "Jefferson Davis Highway."[20] Protected by 2,000 soldiers from the U.S. Army, 1,900 troops from the Alabama National Guard under Federal command and many FBI agents and Federal Marshals, the marchers arrived in Montgomery on March 24, and at the Alabama Capitol building on March 25.[21]

This courageous campaign, along with the courageous efforts of the drum major for social justice Medgar Evers, grew out of the voting rights movement in Selma, Alabama. This strategic segment of the movement was launched by the determination of the Dallas County Voters League (DCVL) and the Student Nonviolent Coordinating Committee (SNCC). In addition to these two indigenous coalitions another force to be reckoned with joined the Civil Rights Movement in a show of solidarity. When entrenched White resistance to Black voter registration proved to be formidable and intractable: the Southern Christian leadership Conference (SCLC) joined the struggle for voting rights equality.

In response to the Jimmie Lee Jackson murder, James Bevel strategically and methodically initiated the plan to march peacefully to Montgomery. Through this nonviolent protest, the marchers hoped to gain media attention regarding the blatant violations of their God inherited Civil Rights. Dr. King agreed with the peaceful methods of Bevel's plan to march from Selma to Montgomery and to ask Governor Wallace to protect African Americans registrants. King organized the second march after Bloody Sunday; it was set for March 9, 1965. The noble and wise leader led 2,500 marchers to the Edmund Pettus Bridge, held a short prayer session and surprisingly turned the marchers around, obeying the court order preventing them from marching all the way to Montgomery.

On March 21, close to 8,000 people assembled at Brown Chapel for the third and final march. On the morning of the 24th, the march crossed into Montgomery County and the highway widened again to four lanes. All day, as the march approached the city, additional marchers were ferried by bus and car to join the protestors. By evening, several thousand marchers had successfully reached the final campsite at the City of St. Jude, a Catholic complex on the outskirts of

Montgomery. That night, on a makeshift stage, a "Stars for Freedom" rally was held, with singers Harry Belafonte, Tony Bennett, Frankie Laine, Peter, Paul and Mary, Sammy Davis, Jr. and Nina Simone all performing. On Thursday, March 25, 25,000 people marched from St. Jude to the steps of the State Capitol Building where King delivered the speech, "How Long, Not Long."

> The end we seek, King told the crowd, is a society at peace with itself, a society that can live with its conscience...I know you are asking today, How long will it take? I come to say to you this afternoon however difficult the moment, however frustrating the hour, it will not be long.[22]

Notably, the torch of Empirical Hope illuminating the demands for Civil Rights caught the attention of the presiding President of the United States. Embedded in this hope was the belief that a people united shall never be defeated. President Lyndon B. Johnson quoted Dr. King in the following manner:

> Even if we pass this bill, the battle will not be over. What happened in Selma is part of a far larger movement which reaches into every section and state of America. It is the effort of American Negroes to secure for themselves the full blessings of American life. Their cause must be our cause, too, because it is not just Negroes but really it is all of us who must overcome the crippling legacy of bigotry and injustice. And we shall overcome.[23]

Julian Bond, the narrator of the award winning series, revisited the historical Birmingham Campaign during segment 4, "No Easy Walk (1961–1963)." In the early 1960's, the city of Birmingham embraced the distinction of being one of the most racially divided cities (second to none) in the United

States. African Americans routinely faced insurmountable legal and economic disparities as well as unprovoked violence at any given moment without any evidence of probable cause. Peaceful protests using Black Psychological Warfare were organized to address the continuous intentional inequalities in employment and to end segregation in the public sector.

SCLC organizers Fred Shuttlesworth, a native of Birmingham and Wyatt Tee Walker, developed a strategy entitled Project C. Project C consisted of a series of sit-ins and marches that were intended to provoke mass arrests. The goal was to address White business owners' blatant and arrogant resistance to the African American Village Community's attempt to peacefully negotiate a truce. Walker, one of SCLC's founders and the executive director from 1960–1964, planned and supported the peaceful strategy. He counted on the Commissioner of Public Safety Bull Conner overreacting to the demonstration; that was his *modus operandi* (MO).

> My theory was that, if we (the African American Village Community) mounted a strong nonviolent movement, the opposition would surely do something to attract the media, and in turn induce national sympathy and attention to the everyday segregated circumstances of a person living in the Deep South.[24]

The plan was to use a variety of nonviolent methods of confrontation, including sit-ins at libraries and lunch counters, kneel-ins by Black visitors at White churches and a march to the county building to mark the beginning of a voter registration drive. SCLC's goal was to fill the jails with protestors to force a negotiation with city government as the demonstrations continued. However, not enough people were arrested to affect the functioning of the city. Furthermore, Bull Connor successfully obtained an injunction barring the protest and raised bail bond for those arrested from $300 to $1,200.

When the movement organizers ran out of money, Dr. King, Ralph Abernathy and 50 Birmingham residents ranging from 15 to 81 years of age were arrested on Good Friday, April 12, 1963.[25]

While in jail on April 16, King released his "Letter from Birmingham Jail," written on the narrow margins of a newspaper, scraps of paper given to him by a janitor and later a legal pad given to him by his SCLC attorneys. The letter responded to eight politically moderate White clergymen who accused King of agitating local residents and not giving the incoming Mayor a chance to make any changes. The essay was a culmination of many of King's ideas that he had touched on in earlier writings. King's arrest attracted national attention, including the corporate officers of retail chains who had stores in downtown Birmingham. After King's arrest, the chains' profits began to erode. National business owners pressed the Kennedy administration to intervene. King was released on April 20, 1963.[26] To reenergize the campaign, SCLC organizers devised a plan called D Day.

The historical D Day Campaign would appropriately be called the Children's Crusade by *Newsweek Magazine*.[27] This nonviolent campaign recruited the help of students from Birmingham's elementary and high schools as well as Miles College. James Bevel, the drum major for Civil Rights and equality (SCLC's Director of Direct Action and Nonviolent Education), initiated the idea; Bevel also carefully organized and thoroughly educated the students in nonviolent tactics and philosophies. Noting that Dr. King was seriously hesitant about using children, James Bevel organized workshops to help students overcome their fear of jails and police dogs. The organizers showed film footage of the 1960's Nashville sit-ins at lunch counters. Birmingham's Black radio station, WENN, supported the new plan by telling students to arrive at the demonstration meeting place with a toothbrush to be used in jail. Thousands of flyers were distributed in Black schools and neighborhoods that said, "Fight for freedom first then go to school" and "It's up to you to free our teachers, our parents, yourself, and our country."[28]

On May 2, 1963, more than 1,000 students skipped school to participate; they gathered at the 16th Street Baptist Church. The young demonstrators (some who eluded the Parker High School principal who attempted to lock the gates of the school) were given specific instructions to march to the downtown area. The group was instructed to integrate preselected building sites and to peacefully petition for a meeting with the Mayor. Marching in disciplined ranks, they were instructed to leave in carefully organized small groups and continue on their course until they were arrested. More than 600 students were arrested; the youngest was eight years old. However, the children's spirit and thirst for Civil Rights were heard as they left the church singing designated hymns and freedom songs such as "We Shall Overcome."[29] The authorities assembled paddy wagons and school buses to take the children to jail. Be that as it may, when no squad cars were left to block the streets, Connor, whose authority extended to the local fire department, employed the use of their trucks. The total number of jailed protesters increased to 1,200; the Birmingham jail capacity was 900. The cramped conditions in the jails were similar to the inhumane conditions aboard the Mothership; its capacity was 600, yet the human cargo was 1,000 during any given voyage.

When Connor realized that the Birmingham jails were full, on May 3, he changed police tactics to keep protesters out of the downtown business area. Another thousand students gathered at the church and left to walk across Kelly Ingram Park. Black parents and adults who were observing cheered the marching students. As the demonstrators left the church, police warned them to stop and turn back, "or you'll get wet."[30] When they continued, Connor ordered the city's fire hoses, set at a level that would peel bark off a tree or separate bricks from mortar, to be turned on the children. Boys' shirts were ripped off, and young women were pushed over the tops of cars by the force of the water. When the students crouched or fell, the blasts of water rolled them down the asphalt streets and concrete sidewalks. In addition, Connor allowed angry White spectators to aggressively push forward toward the innocent protestors; in immediate retaliation numerous bystanders (African Americans) began to throw rocks and bottles at the police. To disperse the peaceful protestors, Connor ordered police to use German shepherd dogs to keep them in line. During a kind of truce, protesters went home. Police removed the barricades and re-opened the streets to traffic. That evening King told worried parents in a crowd of a thousand, "Don't worry about your children who are in jail. The eyes of the world are on Birmingham. We're going on in spite of dogs and fire hoses. We've gone too far to turn back."[31]

As planned, the initiative to use children drew the attention the organizers wanted. Connor's angry response to a nonviolent protest consisting of innocent children turned public sentiment toward the cause of Civil Rights. White reporters who covered the vicious attack on unarmed children were appalled and ashamed of the blatant, arrogant display of White superiority. This overriding sentiment was captured in the following manner:

> A battle-hardened Huntley-Brinkley reporter later said that no military action he had witnessed (while serving in combat duty) had ever frightened or disturbed him as much as what he saw in the city of Birmingham, Alabama. Two out-of-town photographers covering the Children's Crusade that day were Charles Moore (*Life Magazine*) and Bill Hudson (*Associated Press*). Moore

was a Marine combat photographer who was "jarred" and "sickened" by the use of children and what the Birmingham police and fire departments did to them. Moore was hit in the ankle by a brick meant for the police. He took several photos that were printed in *Life Magazine*. The first photo Moore shot that day showed three teenagers being hit by a water jet from a high-pressure fire hose. It was titled "They Fight a Fire That Won't Go Out."[32]

Television cameras broadcast to the nation the scenes of fire hoses knocking down school children and police dogs attacking unprotected children demonstrators. Such coverage, especially Bill Hudson's image of Parker High School student Walter Gadsden being attacked by dogs (published in the *New York Times* on May 4, 1963), shifted international support to the protestors, making Bull Connor, "the villain of the era."[33] President Kennedy, at a White House press conference, told the *New York Times* that the photo "made him sick."[34] Most importantly, after decades of indigenous disagreements among African American leaders, when the photos were released, the African American Village Community, moved by the power of God, instantaneously unified behind Dr. King. In addition to this paradigm shift, White reporters continued their public disapproval of the methods used against the protestors. A *New York Times* special editorial called the behavior of the Birmingham City Police "a national disgrace."[35] In agreement with the *New York Times*, the *Washington Post* editorialized:

> The spectacle in Birmingham ... must excite the sympathy of the rest of the country for the decent, just, and reasonable citizens of the community, who have recently demonstrated at the polls their lack of support for the very policies (unethical) that have produced the Birmingham riots. The authorities who tried, by these brutal means, to stop the freedom marchers do not

speak or act in the name of the enlightened people of the city.[36]

The situation reached a crisis on May 7, when 70 members of the Birmingham Chamber of Commerce pleaded, sincerely and candidly, with the protestors and organizers to call off the protests. Breakfast in the jails literally took four hours to distribute. The NAACP sent out an appeal to sympathizers to picket in more than 100 cities.

News of the mass arrest of the children reached the Soviet Union and Europe. No business of any kind was being conducted in or around downtown Birmingham. The entire civil infrastructure had completely collapsed. In a well planned strategic move, while organizers and participants flooded the downtown area and businesses, groups of children approached the police and announced, "We want to go to jail."[37] Six hundred picketers flooded downtown as large groups of protesters sat in stores singing freedom songs. Streets, sidewalks, stores and buildings were virtually overwhelmed with 3,000 protestors. On May 8 at 4 a.m., White business leaders agreed to most of the protestors' demands. On May 10, Fred Shuttlesworth and Dr. King informed reporters that the leaders of the movement reached an agreement with the city of Birmingham to desegregate all of the city's rest rooms, lunch counters, fitting rooms and drinking fountains within 90 days. In addition, the agreement encompassed the hiring of African Americans as salesmen and clerks. Protestors, who were jailed during the demonstrations, including the children, would be released on bond and/or released on their own recognizance.

President Kennedy publicly supported the efforts of the United Auto Workers, National Maritime Union, United Steel Workers and the American Federation of Labor and Congress of Industrial Organizations (AFL-CIO) to raise $237,000 in bail money to free demonstrators. After the campaign, President Kennedy's administration drafted a Civil Rights Act Bill. Diehard Southerners in Congress held up the passage of the bill for 75 days. It was passed into law in 1964. The Civil Rights Act of 1964 applied to the whole nation. It prohibited racial discrimination in employment and in accessing public places. It is well to note that organizer Wyatt Tee Walker called the Birmingham campaign and the Selma marches "Siamese twins" joining to "kill segregation...and bury the body."[38]

In closing out Part II (Black Psychological Warfare) of this imperative historical exegesis, we will inevitably find a clear distinction between the present day African American Village Community and the Village Community of the Civil Rights Era. It is clear to see that in the latter community there is a noticeable absence of Historical Euthanasia and most importantly, the self-destructive social tenets of capitalism and Generational Laissez-faire Entitlement. When collectively called upon, the younger generation stepped up to the table of humanity and in solidarity repeated the Civil Rights demands of their parents, the elders of the African American Village Community. They did not passively watch and observe the struggle for racial equality and Civil Rights, but they took the weapon of Black Psychological Warfare (nonviolent protest) and walked hand-in-hand with their elders and generational leaders of the Village Community. Likewise, when Emmett Till was murdered in August 28, 1955, the leaders of the Village Community stood hand-in-hand throughout this great nation and declared to those who promote White superiority and racism that the killing of innocent African American children would not be tolerated.

Emmett Louis "Bobo" Till, featured in the *Eyes on the Prize* segment entitled "Awakenings (1954–1956)," was born July 25, 1941. This 14 year old African American boy was murdered in Money, Mississippi (Delta region) because he innocently spoke to 21 year old Carolyn Bryant, a White woman and the married proprietor of a small grocery store. In retaliation, Roy Bryant, and J.W. Milam forcibly took Emmett Till from his great uncle's house and shot him in the head. They wrapped a 70-pound cotton gin fan around his neck with barbed wire and then disposed of his body in the Tallahatchie River. His body was retrieved three days later.[39]

Till's mother, Mamie Till Bradley, insisted on an open casket at the public funeral for her son in Chicago where he was raised. She wanted the casket opened so that the world could see the brutality of the unprovoked killing of an innocent child. It was estimated that more than 10,000 mourners attended the funeral, and images of his mutilated body were made public as two Black magazines and numerous newspapers across the country weighed in on the tragedy. Most importantly, the tide turned when a picture of Till smiling was strategically placed in print next to his disfigured body. As a result, the White community expressed shame at the people who caused Till's death. One article read, "Now is the time for every citizen who loves the state of Mississippi to stand up and be counted before hoodlum White trash brings us to destruction."[40] The letter went on to state that Negroes were not the downfall of Mississippi society but Whites like those in White Citizens' Councils who condoned violence.

Similar to the Children's Crusade and Emmitt Till's death the 16th Street Baptist Church bombing on September 15, 1963, that killed four, young, innocent African American girls empowered the African American Village Community as never before. The church bombing was featured in the *Eyes on the Prize* segment, "No Easy Walk (1961–1963)."

Addie Mae Collins (aged 14), Denise McNair (aged 11), Carole Robertson (aged 14) and Cynthia Wesley (aged 14) were killed in the attack, and 22 additional people were injured, one of whom was Addie's younger sister, Sarah. Close to 8,000 mourners, including 800 clergies representing all races, attended the two services (one family requested a separate service).[41]

The enemy had sent a necessary corrective message to stir the consciousness of the children. The children learned that they were not, by any stretch of the imagination, exempt from the war of hatred, strife, racism, classism, bigotry and division in America. The message was quite clear: all the inhabitants of the African American Village Community were considered fair game for random acts of violence, annihilation, assimilation and segregation. This fate was non-negotiable and binding and there were no exceptions to the rule.

The African American Village Community was united and divided...no more. The children of the historic Civil Rights Era received and properly digested the message sent by White America. However, be that as it may, the African American Village Community sent their own collective and straightforward message: A people united can never be defeated. We are all in this together. One for all and all for one. ..And we shall overcome!

The system of Slavocracy (a weapon of mass human destruction) came face to face with the indomitable ancestral and contemporary power of the African American Experience and Empirical Hope. Delivering a message from the holds of the slave ship, the indigenous power of unity (unconditional unity) became a force to be reckoned with. The preternatural unity of the pluralistic tribes of Africa once again stunned White America. The message was embedded in the hypothesis that Truth crushed to the ground shall rise again.

Collectively, we declared that we will not go silently into the night. We will not go silently into the abyss of second-class citizenship and political disenfranchisement. We will not go silently into the night and abyss of permanent inequality and daily humiliation and degradation. We will not go silently into the night and abyss of lack of purpose and serving others as a permanent beast of burden. On the contrary, through the preternatural power of Historical Discipline and the effective implementation of Black Psychological Warfare, African Americans shocked the promoters, believers and supporters of White supremacy. The Village Concept which is the creation of indigenous self-reliant systems within the greater African American Village Community: its prime directive and sole purpose—addressing the unfinished task of emancipation in America—had come full circle. In tracing our historical footsteps (the inhabitants of the Village Community) it is well to note that during the climatic years of the Black Power and Civil Rights Movement, we were a people with a purpose, and unity of the masses became the order of the day.

In the final chapter of this historical exegesis on the African American Experience we will examine the imperative need for authentic indigenous Communal Healing; a special healing that becomes a necessary corrective for an oppressed people as they move from the abyss of historical darkness into the marvelous light of liberation. Moreover, let the record reflect that only God, the Creator and Unmoved Mover, can deliver this cultural based healing to an oppressed people; a people who were extracted unwillingly from their Motherland. A people who were resurrected from the abyss of the inhuman system of Slavocracy, from the certain predetermined fate of destitution, destruction, and genocidal extermination due to the saving grace of God; a peculiar people formed from the pluralistic tribes of mother Africa and specifically selected by God, to unapologetically represent the dreams and the hopes of the slaves.

181

Part III:

Divided...No More

Human progress is neither automatic nor inevitable...every step towards the goal of justice requires sacrifice, suffering, and struggle; the tireless exertions and passionate concern of dedicated individuals...[1]

Dr. Martin L. King, Jr.

Chapter Seven

NAACP
Carter G. Woodson – ASALH
Tim King – Urban Prep Academies
Taki S. Raton – Blyden Delany Academy
Gloria Ann Jones – Fathers Who Care
Alicia Archer – CLEAN Kids
Mary Moore & Barbara Sanders – Deborah Movement

CHAPTER SEVEN

The Indigenous Healing Process

This final chapter will focus on solutions and best practices that have been consciously initiated by individuals and organizations to address the schism that is presently plaguing the African American Village Community. At the extreme core of this solutions-based initiative are the Mission Statement, vision statement and six main objectives of the National Association for the Advancement of Colored People (NAACP). The directives are as follows:

Our Mission:
The mission of the National Association for the Advancement of Colored People is to ensure the political, educational, social, and economic equality of rights of all persons and to eliminate race-based discrimination.

Vision Statement:
The vision of the National Association for the Advancement of Colored People is to ensure a society in which all individuals have equal rights without discrimination based on race.

Objectives:
The following statement of objectives is found on the first page of the NAACP Constitution. The principal objectives of the Association shall be:

- To ensure the political, educational, social, and economic equality of all citizens.

- To achieve equality of rights and eliminate race prejudice among the citizens of the United States.

- To remove all barriers of racial discrimination through democratic processes.

- To seek enactment and enforcement of federal, state, and local laws securing Civil Rights.

- To inform the public of the adverse effects of racial discrimination and to seek its elimination.

- To educate persons as to their constitutional rights and to take all lawful action to secure the exercise thereof, and to take any other lawful action in furtherance of these objectives, consistent with the NAACP's Articles of Incorporation and this Constitution. [1]

To make the six principle objectives of the NAACP's Constitution even clearer, I have extracted key words from each objective and elaborated on them below. I am thoroughly and personally convinced that *A House Divided...No More* is dedicated to the proposition that collectively and through the empowerment of the African American Experience we will:

Ensure (economic equality), achieve (the equality of rights), remove (all barriers), seek (to secure Civil Rights), inform (the public) and educate (persons as to their inalienable constitutional rights) so that authentic indigenous Communal Healing can continuously occur in the African American Village Community. In juxtaposition to this present day communal agenda we will promote (the preternatural planting of fertile seeds of self-advocacy and self-empowerment), empower (through the unapologetic and continuous promotion of unconditional solidarity) and implement (the binding communal ties of a Cultural Utilitarianism initiative throughout the greater African American Village Community, which stands over and against the historic and present day plague of division, the Laissez-Faire Entitlement Syndrome and Historical Euthanasia among the descendants of the African Diaspora).[2]

The activism, communal dedication and communal commitment of Carter G. Woodson exemplifies *A House Divided...No More*. Woodson, an African American historian, author, journalist and founder of the Association for the Study of Negro Life and History (ASNLH), now the Association for the Study of African American Life and History (ASALH), was among the early scholars to study and value Black History. This noble and consistent drum major for social justice recognized the imperative need and acted upon the importance of a people having awareness and knowledge of their impressive legacy and contributions to humanity.[3] Today, Woodson is known as the Father of Black History and was the founder of the *Journal of Negro History*.

The story of Black History Month begins in Chicago, Illinois during the summer of 1915. Woodson traveled from Washington, DC, to participate in a national celebration of the 50th anniversary of emancipation sponsored by the State of Illinois. The scholar had recently received a doctorate from Harvard three years earlier and was inspired by the three-week celebration and decided to form an organization to specifically promote the scientific study of Black life and history.

On September 9, 1915, Woodson met with A.L. Jackson and three others at the Wabash YMCA and formed the ASNLH. During a lecture at Hampton Institute, he proudly told the audience, "We are going back to that beautiful history and it is going to inspire us to greater achievements."[4]

Woodson further believed that publishing a scientific history would transform race relations by the dispelling of widespread falsehoods about Africans and people of African descent. He hoped that others would popularize the findings that he and other Black intellectuals would publish in the *Journal of Negro History*, which he established in 1916. As early as 1920, Woodson urged the nation's Black civic organizations to unapologetically promote the achievements of African Americans that researchers were consistently uncovering. A graduate member of Omega Psi Phi, he urged his fraternity brothers to take up the work. In 1924, they responded with the creation of Negro History and Literature Week, which they renamed Negro Achievement Week. Their outreach was extraordinarily significant, but the tenacious Woodson desired a greater impact.[5]

Eager for more notoriety and expansion of his concept, Carter G. Woodson decided (in 1925) to have the ASNLH spearhead and shoulder this noble gesture and responsibility. He sent out a press release in February 1926 announcing Negro History Week. Woodson targeted February for reasons of tradition and reform. Two great Americans who played a prominent role in shaping Black History had birthdays during the month of February: Abraham Lincoln (February 12) and Frederick Douglass (February 14).[6] The vision nurtured by Woodson encompassed the study and celebration of the Negro as a race. During his critical analysis the researcher discovered evidence of the preternatural power of the African American Experience. It was the Union Army, and most importantly, thousands of Black soldiers and sailors who achieved the monumental task of securing victory against the supporters of Slavocracy with their blood, sweat and tears. Rather than focus on two men who were part of a greater movement, Woodson believed that the focus should be on the countless sacrifices of courageous, noble Black men and women who unselfishly contributed to the advancement of their people.

Carter G. Woodson, in an adventurous move, wrote a historical letter publicly proclaiming the intent of the ASNLH to research and share their findings on Negro contributions and achievements through a house (home) study department. The following are excerpts from the October 1, 1927, letter addressed to Mr. Thomas H. Barnes, 311 W. State Street, Oleans, New York:

> The association is trying to bring before the world the whole truth that the truth may make men free. To do this it has decided not only to publish informing books but offer by mail instruction in Negro life and history. The newly established Home Study Department has, therefore, been established for the special benefit of those who would like to study the aspects of African civilization which were neglected in the schools in which they were trained.[7]

The house would be divided...no more. During the 1960's, the study and celebration of Black History began to shift from the original weeklong celebration to the concept of a month long Communal Initiative. Finally, in 1976, 50 years after the first celebration, ASALH (originally known as ASNLH) was successful in formally institutionalizing the shift from a single week to a month long initiative. Dr. Carter G. Woodson, an intellectual innovator who was once ostracized by some of his contemporaries for defining a category of history in terms of ethnic culture and race, soon became a household name. It is only proper and fitting that we examine the following timeline to commemorate his accomplishments:

1926
Woodson launches first Negro History Week.

1933
Woodson publishes *The Mis-Education of the Negro.*

1950
Woodson passes away on April 3rd. Prof. Rayford Logan of Howard University becomes Executive Director of the Association.

1970
Carter G. Woodson Building, headquarters of the Association, opens in Washington, DC.

1972
ASNLH changes its name to the Association for the Study of Afro-American Life and History (ASALH).

1976
Association changes Negro History Week celebration to Black History Month. Woodson Home designated a National Historic Landmark.

2003
Congress passes legislation authorizing the Woodson Home to be established as a National Historic Site within the National Park System. Sylvia Cyrus becomes ASALH Executive Director.

2006
On February 27, the National Parks Service adds the Woodson Home Site as the 389th site in their inventory. ASALH office moves to the Howard University campus.

2008
Carter G. Woodson's Appeal is published. Written in 1921 but lost for 80 years, ASALH publishes the book as a limited leather-bound edition.[8]

    This historical and contemporary investigation to find evidence of authentic indigenous Communal Healing reveals another exemplary model (a necessary corrective if you will) in the healing process. The activism and communal dedication of a group of African American civic, business, educational leaders and a drum major for social justice have become a force to be reckoned with. In the tradition of *A House Divided...No More*, former Hales Franciscan High School President Tim King has quietly and successfully spearheaded the establishment of new high schools in Chicago that focus on providing strong college preparatory options specifically for minority boys in the underserved African American Village Community.[9]

Tim King and others (as previously mentioned) were disturbed by the epidemic of violence and the escalating drop out rate for males in the Village Community. In addition, a 2006 University of Chicago study reported that only one in forty African American males in Chicago Public Schools graduate from a four-year university. In 2005, the Chicago Board of Education approved a charter application for Urban Prep Academies Charter Schools. The first school, Urban Prep Charter Academy for Young Men [Englewood Campus] (Chicago, Illinois) officially opened its doors the subsequent September: specifically extending an olive branch (if you will) for endangered and underserved minorities (targeting the endangered human species-African American males).[10]

Urban Prep is the first charter high school for boys in the country. This innovative school located in Chicago, Illinois, successfully enrolled 550 students in grades 9 through 12. A second Urban Prep School opened in 2009 in the East Garfield Park Community, recruiting only 9th graders. The third campus, following the same creed and mission of the first two schools, opened in the fall of 2010 in the South Shore community. Leaders plan to open six schools in the Chicago area. Approximately 85 percent of the students enrolled are low-income African Americans. Admission to Urban Prep is non-selective and determined by a non-biased lottery system.

The spirit of unity is nurtured daily and is embedded in the creed of Urban Prep. The following creed is recited in unison by students during mandatory morning assemblies at each campus:

> We believe. We are the young men of Urban Prep. We are college bound. We are exceptional not because we say it, but because we work hard at it. We will not falter in the face of any obstacle placed before us. We are dedicated, committed and focused. We will never succumb to mediocrity, uncertainty or fear. We never fail because we never give up.

> We make no excuses. We choose to live honestly, nonviolently, and honorably. We respect ourselves and, in doing so, respect all people. We have a future for which we are accountable.

> We have a responsibility to our families, community, and world. We are our brothers' keepers. We believe in ourselves. We believe in each other. We believe in Urban Prep. We believe.[11]

In 2010, Urban Prep Charter Academy for Young Men made national headlines when 100 percent of students in the first graduating class in its history were admitted to accredited four-year colleges or universities. The mission statement of the school was fulfilled to its fullest potential: the purpose of the school is to provide a high-quality college preparatory education to young men that results in graduates succeeding into an accredited college.[12] Prior to this historic monumental accomplishment, during the Presidential Inauguration in 2009, Urban Prep students traveled to Washington, DC. They were admirably referred to as "little Obamas."[13] In addition to this distinguished honor they were recognized by Oprah Winfrey and Mayor Richard M. Daley of Chicago. Diane Sawyer, ABC World News Tonight anchor, profiled the school (all campuses) in its "Person of the Week" segment.[14] The news segment revealed that Urban Prep Programs (launched in 2005) implemented the core curriculum on mentoring by recruiting recent college graduates from around the nation to work as mentors, leaders and educators for one year. These carefully screened Fellows are matched with a Pride (about 20 students) and provide academic support and social guidance in one course.

The focus of technology is strong in the schools, and each student receives access to a laptop computer. Students must adhere to a clearly communicated set of rules; for example, they must wear khaki pants, a white collared dress shirt, a solid red necktie and a black two-button blazer that features an embroidered school crest. During summer programs, students participate in academic, professional and service programs at distinguished universities both in the United States and abroad. The participating universities include Northwestern University, Georgetown University, Oxford University and Cambridge University in the UK. In athletics, students compete with one another and other public schools in Chicago. The sports options include wrestling, track and field, cross country, golf, football, bowling, basketball and baseball.[15]

Urban Prep structures its educational approach through the following four curricular and extracurricular arcs:

- The Academic Arc: a rigorous college prep curriculum with added focus on reading, writing and public speaking skills.

191

- The Service Arc: a focus on deepening the students' sense of responsibility and identification of community needs by completing volunteer programs throughout the area.
- The Activity Arc: a focus on increasing students' confidence, interpersonal skills and leadership qualities by participating in at least two school-sponsored activities per year (sports, clubs, etc.).

- The Professional Arc: a focus on providing students with valuable experience in a professional setting by requiring them to spend one day a week within such a setting. This serves to positively reinforce character and leadership development in students, as well as providing for them a means of work experience.[16]

In retrospect, Carter G. Woodson, who wrote the groundbreaking exegesis, *The Mis-Education of the Negro,* set the stage for the indigenous Communal Healing of the Negro's (today's African Americans) inadequate education status in America. Parity at every level of human intercourse requires a Communal Initiative empowered by the African American Experience. It is well to note that history teaches us about the powerlessness of uneducated people. Prior to the United Negro College Fund's theme, "A mind is a terrible thing to waste," Woodson used these particular words to address the blatant inequalities in the educational arena.[17] The torch initially lit by Carter G. Woodson would stand the test of time as future leaders of the Civil Rights struggle fanned the flames of empowerment through education. We will now examine the commendable efforts of a leader who unapologetically and skillfully promotes an Afrocentric curriculum.

Similar to the unification efforts of Carter G. Woodson and Mr. Tim King (Urban Prep Academies), the activism and communal dedication of Taki S. Raton, a drum major for social justice, has become exemplary in not only uniting the Village Community but also raising a positive awareness of the rich heritage of contributions derived from Black culture.

Raton received his B.A. in Art with a concentration in Sculpture from the College of Artesia (New Mexico) and his M.A. in Inner City Studies Education from Northeastern Illinois University (Chicago, Illinois). Mr. Taki Raton (a Black Alpha Male intellectual) is the founder and principal of the educational institution Blyden Delany Academy (Milwaukee, Wisconsin). This distinct educational institution specifically adheres to a student-centered and instructional developmental model in addition to an African-centered curriculum. T. Raton (personal communication, September 12, 2010)

From 1998 to 2008, Blyden Delany Academy was a private school that served students in kindergarten through eighth grade. However, during the 2008-09 academic years the academy faced increased operational cost combined with a noted decrease in per pupil funding allocation under the auspice of the Milwaukee Parental Choice Program (MPCP). Rather than diminish the qualitative mission and vision of Blyden the principal and Board selected not to open for the fall. Taki Raton is currently serving as Adjunct Professor at Springfield College in Milwaukee, Wisconsin. He is presently (as of 2011) promoting plans for the continuation of the Washington Bouchet Saturday School Model (WBSSM) for African American students first grade through twelfth grade.

Be that as it may, under his direct leadership Raton successfully raised the standard of excellence in education. This drum major for educational equity and parity was invited by 100 Black Men of Chicago to bring 13 select students from Milwaukee, Wisconsin to the October 16, 2009, 100 Black Men Invitational Honor Student Reception at the Merchandise

Mart (Chicago, Illinois). Raton's group joined more than 250 students from the Chicago area to explore open enrollment admission and scholarship opportunities with 41 college and university representatives from around the country. Raton graciously accepted an invitation from the 100 Black Men of Chicago to participate in the 2010 selection process. The selection criteria included a 3.3 minimum GPA and a 23 or above cumulative score on the ACT. T. Raton (personal communication, September, 12, 2010)

Taki Raton, a wise educator and scholar in his own right, developed and successfully implemented academic strategies employing the Washington Bouchet Education and Development Initiative (WBEDI). This unique combination consisting of an elementary and secondary instructional and social development model includes ten academic incubators specifically designed to accurately document past research, attract existing scholarships and help inspire active material enrichment in the cultivation of baseline instructional texts and teaching strategies in noted disciplines of study. Named after prominent African American achievers, the incubators used support the continuous development and cultivation of:

- Accelerated academic competency
- Secondary level education preparedness
- Critical thinking skills incorporation
- Acceptable positive peer and elder interaction
- A vision and commitment to college admission
- A commendable moral character and presence
- Future career mobility orientation
- Community service and accountability. T. Raton (personal communication, September 12, 2010)

As an educational consultant to the distinguished Mary McLeod Bethune Saturday School (Chicago), Raton fused the

Nannie Helen Burroughs School of Ethical Studies and Humanistic Values to inspire elementary and secondary level students. Raton defined the obtainable level of achievement in the following manner: self-respect, respect for others, respect for the law, respect for elders, appropriate classroom behavior, appropriate public behavior, concepts of pluralistic civility, preparation for responsible societal membership and the importance of literacy and proper decorum.

Taki Raton, the first Black professional to be employed at the distinguished Art Institute of Chicago in 1973 in the Department of Museum Education, engaged in specialized training at the Institute before focusing on his teaching career. Raton refined his artistic skills in exhibit preparation, visual structural designs and the sensitive placement of two and three dimensional works of art in a hall or full room setting. This acquired and refined skill was woven into the visual imaging of Blyden Delany The founder wanted students to see mirror reflections of their own beauty and glory as they walked the halls and sat in their classrooms. Raton unequivocally believed it was the responsibility of adults, schools such as Blyden, the community and other Black institutions to rescue, reclaim, reinterpret, reconstruct, resurrect, restore and redeem for our children our rightful (inherent) place on the world stage of time and achievement. It is the contention of Blyden Delany Academy that if the pristine higher order models of history and culture are presented and taught to the children, the desired character molding will eventually occur and lead to the expectation and will of competitive academic achievement.

Walking into Blyden Delany Academy was nearly like walking into a museum. When entering Blyden, guests were greeted with a life-sized, free standing paper Mache statue of a Kemetic (Egyptian) King that was made by students as an art project. Students also made the pillars adorned with breath taking African designs and were responsible for the synthetic floral arrangements on small tables covered with red African fabric. The students showcased a small display case featuring mounted color pictures of the Pyramids of Giza, the world's first calendar in 4236 B.C.E., the African Imhotep, the world's first medical doctor of record and the young boy King Tutankhamen. Therewith, additional items on display includes framed pictures of Queen Hatshepsut's temple, the Glider of Saqqara (noting that the ancient Africans had knowledge of heavier-than-air flight technology during the fourth or third century B.C.E.), the Olmec Head (proving that Africans were in this part of the world nearly 2000 years before Columbus), the circular zodiac in the ceiling of a room in the Egyptian Temple of Dendera (a room believed to have been used as an observatory by the ancient Kemites), Harriet Tubman leading runaway slaves to freedom, oil paintings of Malcolm X and a depiction of the 1995 Million Man March are highlighted. The inventors section includes a bronze framed print of Garrett A. Morgan (who invented the three-way automatic stop sign - successfully receiving a patent on November 20, 1923) and other Black inventors such as George Washington Carver, Lewis Latimer, Grandville T. Woods and Dr. Charles Drew.

Blyden Academy corridors also proudly and purposely featured notably pictures of prominent African Americans who contributed to the fields of science and technology. A framed photograph of Dr. Lloyd Albert Quarterman was mounted on a wall. Dr. Quarteman was included in Ivan Van Sertima's work, *Blacks in Science – Ancient and Modern*. In the late 1970's, Quarterman was awarded a distinguished certificate of appreciation by the U.S. Secretary of War for work essential to the production of the Atomic Bomb, thereby contributing to the successful conclusion of World War II.

Numerous mounted foam boards featuring prominent historical and accurate facts were clearly visible. The Ebers Papyrus supports the hypothesis that more than 4,000 years ago, around 1500 B.C.E., ancient Africans had medical knowledge of the cardiovascular system, dermatology, tumors, burns, fractures and intestinal disorders. In addition, historical quotes from Edward Burns and Phillip Ralph's *World Civilizations* supported the hypothesis that the arts and sciences in Egypt had reached unparalleled heights in both of these areas as early as 3000 B.C.E. when the rest of the world was steeped in ignorance. Quotes, photos, and prints from leaders such as Marcus Garvey, Edward Wilmot Blyden, Haki R. Madhubuti, Booker T. Washington, Elijah Muhammad, Martin R. Delany, Sojourner Truth and Ida B. Wells were presented for viewing. The Kemetic goddess Auset and her son Heru (sitting on her lap), the Egyptian scarab and collages of famous African American historical figures were meticulously displayed. Additional life-sized paper Mache statues of Chaka Zulu and Hannibal on his elephant, all student projects, were displayed in the school's visitor waiting area. Many of the two and three dimensional works of art were proudly shown at the September 2006 R.A.W. Art Exhibit at the Parkway Ballroom (Chicago) and in an art tribute to Emmett Louis Till at the African American Women's Center in Milwaukee, Wisconsin. T. Raton (personal communication, September 12, 2010)

In the tradition of *A House Divided...No More*, Raton unapologetically promoted an African-centered curriculum to assist in the healing process. The African-centered curriculum used in such a structured learning climate underscored the school's operative philosophy that the culture of the school must be stronger than the culture the children bring into the building. Blyden's culture and vision were strong enough to offset and redirect all of the negative and dysfunctional experiences and tendencies that our children face in their world. The principal (Taki Raton) affirmed that we have to tell our children the truth about our history (African American history) and our unique accomplishments and gifts.

At the core of the indigenous Communal Healing process at Blyden was the following mission statement:

Blyden Delany's mission is to structure an academic and social developmental program that is ethically anchored, moral principled and accomplishment driven towards student ascension to notable heights of ethical prominence, cultural integrity, creative accomplishment and academic achievement as modeled by classical, historical, and present day higher order African American and African world exemplars.

Inspired and guided in the mission by preeminent African and African American exemplars, the school's vision is to employ the highest examples inherent in the African centered curriculum model towards the attainment of the maximum social, moral, ethical and intellectual development of the Blyden Delany students. The Core Values were:

- To develop a love for self through knowledge of self.

- To assist students to reach and maintain at level of accelerated and highly competitive performances on traditional cross subject area academic competency indicators and district required standardized standard testing instruments.

- To center the students as an active participant in the learning process.

- To stimulate a love for and appreciation of African World History and Culture.

- To structure a positive learning and developmental environment reflecting moral and ethical family values and responsible community contributory participation.

- To rescue, reclaim, reconstruct, cultivate, and effectively employ old school African American modeled social and ethical behavioral norms and African World ethical wisdom teachings towards the instruction and cultivation of learning readiness, self respect, acceptable moral character, positive peer group interaction, respect for elders, respect for and support of family membership, and a dedication to contributory community accountability and growth.

- To explore the history of African Americans in business and in current entrepreneurial models as a foundation to the instruction of business development and financial literacy necessary for success in local, regional, national and global free enterprise market arenas.

- To equip the Khepera Saturday School students with an obtainable personal future vision that would inspire self motivational academic success in secondary and higher education learning agendas.

- To impart the necessary foundational attitudes, skills, appearance and values necessary to successfully access careers and professional mobility in today's diverse national, international and global societies. T. Raton (personal communication, September 12, 2010)

In addition to promoting educational excellence, Blyden also promoted character education and cultural pride. The academy's success in behavioral discipline produced a record of no suspensions between 2001 and 2005. In addition, students successfully reached at norm reading and math levels according to prescribed standardized testing. A former Blyden eighth grader, Kumasi Allen, was included in the 2007–2008 listing of *Who's Who* of American Elementary and Middle School Students. In 2002, then Blyden seventh grader Vida Bridges (12 years old) won the citywide Annual Martin Luther King Essay Contest in January. Sponsored by UPN Channel 24 and Playmakers apparel outlets, her essay theme, according to published reports, focused on the following question: "Why Dr. Martin Luther King, Jr. Inspired Me?"

Tamara Horton, a prominent 2002 Blyden graduate, was nominated in 2003 (while attending North Division High School in Milwaukee) to be a National Scholar representing the state of Wisconsin at the National Young Leaders Conference (NYLC) held in Washington, DC. As cited in her notification letter, Horton was selected because she is an outstanding focused and determined individual who achieved academic excellence and consistently displays evidence of strong leadership potential. The following year while a junior at North High School, Horton (16 years old) was honorably appointed to the Milwaukee County Youth Commission. Youth Commissioners are chosen (by a distinguished group of leaders) from area high schools to participate over a two-year period in weekly afterschool meetings (on Wednesdays) at the County Court House. The selected student members discuss and debate issues related to county government and assist in developing initiatives aimed at promoting and cultivating interest in political agendas among young people. Applicants were specifically selected from submitted essays detailing why a student would desire to be a Youth Commissioner and what they can individually contribute to the ongoing advancement of the Milwaukee County Youth Commission. In a January 26, 2004, *Milwaukee Community Journal* article on Horton, she says that the emphasis on Black History and Black Culture at Blyden Academy gave her the background and confidence to pursue membership in this youth-centered program. T. Raton (personal communication, September 12, 2010)

This seed of Empirical Hope based on the power of the African American Experience was embedded in the Blyden Academy Pledge that Raton created. Each morning over the PA system a student recited the following pledge with pride:

> We the students of the Blyden Delany Academy pledge to work in the best interest of our social, moral and academic development. We additionally pledge to respect our fellow classmates as we all join together for the continued growth and highest good of our school.

The pledge was then followed by the student-led Blyden Delany Academy Affirmation:

> I love myself. I love my beautiful image. I am in the image of my Creator. My Creator blessed me to be the best. I will excel in school. I will work. I will study. I will create. And I will build. I am the perfect design of success. I am just simply, magnificently fabulous! T. Raton (personal communication, September 12, 2010)

Raton, a leader par excellence, addressed the hunger for self-affirmation by focusing on the spirit of Black Pride that was once alive and thriving during the Civil Rights Movement and the Black Power, Black Pride Era of our rich history. Blyden Delany Academy, Milwaukee's only all-Black private, African-centered elementary school serving students from kindergarten (age four) through eighth grade, had an extremely memorable and successful, community-applauded 10-year operation from 1998 to 2008. In the midst of historical ignorance, Historical Euthanasia and the waywardness of Generation E, Taki Raton stood on the shoulders of great Black Alpha Males (intellectual Constructionist) who faced the Goliaths of oppression. Taki promoted an awareness of the Mis-*Education of the Negro* and policies that were designed to permanently keep Negros in the abyss of ignorance. Similar to Carter G. Woodson, this brave scholar researched, compiled and assembled data that White America believed was buried and long forgotten—out of sight, out of mind and into the abyss, the sea of forgetfulness.

Taki S. Raton courageously submerged into the sea of historical bountifulness and emerged with an Afrocentric curriculum, an approach that he unequivocally believed would be a healing balm for his people. He believed that there is a balm (cultural deliverance) in Gilead. This drum major for social, educational, economic and political justice continues to fight the good fight. He will finish his course, and he will keep the faith for years to come as he participates in the return of *A House Divided...No More.*

The activism and communal dedication of Mrs. Gloria Ann Jones, wife of Walter A. Jones, founder of Fathers Who Care (FWC), exemplifies the preternatural power of the union between a man and his wife: moving by the power of God, the Unmoved Mover the couple strives for the eloquent utopia of *A House Divided...No More.* Mrs. Jones, the Austin High School sweetheart of Walter Jones, grew up in Chicago. It was at this particular school and on the West Side of this particular city that she met her lifelong mate. In 1950, Mrs. Jones's mother, Mary Trull, travelled to Chicago, Illinois during the Great Migration. Richard Powell, her father, similarly moved from Mount Bayou, Mississippi. Trull would eventually be forced to raise her children as a single mother due to the oppressive practice of forcing African American males from the household, thereby systemically excluding them from the table of humanity. Gloria Jones became personally and culturally aware of the sociological, political, educational, economic and psychological forces working against the structure of the African American family at a young age.

Moved by a Power greater than herself, Mrs. Jones began to embrace the ideology of the Beloved Community. She experienced an uncompromised devotion from her soul (similar to Ida B. Wells during the Yellow Fever epidemic that took the lives of her parents and infant brother) to keep her family together by any means necessary. As she witnessed the division catapulted by the long night of slavery and the divisive social and political policies that followed (which purposely separated African American men and women), she was determined to stand toe-to-toe against the Goliaths of separation, divorce and male bashing (of former husbands or significant other) that were continuously plaguing the African American Village Community, particularly the Black family. The concepts of the Beloved Community and the indigenous healing process meant that the union of husband and wife must unequivocally become an uncompromised way of life if we are to restore the African American Village Community to a state that is pleasing to God, the Creator and Unmoved Mover. Mrs. Gloria Jones believes that the family structure will and can stand over and against anything that separates us. She affirms that healing must begin with the family unit; when the family is strong and unified, the African American Village Community (one family at a time as well as collectively) will similarly become strong and unified. G. Jones (personal communication, November 12, 2010)

Gloria Jones, similar to Michelle Obama, acquired the *First Lady* seat when her husband, moved by the power of God, organized the Fathers Who Care initiative in 1998. FWC is a Chicago-based, not-for-profit, father and family friendly initiative that was birthed out of Congressman Danny K. Davis' Fathers, Families and Public Policy Task Force in July 1998. The prime directive of the initiative is to provide a warm, supportive and nurturing environment for fathers who are not from traditional family settings.

FWC advocates on behalf of indigent fathers and their families in the areas of responsible fatherhood, involvement and healthy relationships, re-entry opportunities, spirituality, men's health and wellness, social justice, and community empowerment. The prime directive of FWC is to actively support programs that dispel negative myths about African American men in the lives of their children. In addition, mentoring and empowering future leaders one student at a time has become a major focus of this grassroots organization. The Fathers Who Care Mission Statement is as follows:

> Fathers Who Care (FWC) is a comprehensive, parental involvement, social service initiative, that was created to provide a nurturing and educational environment for non and custodial fathers who may or may not be indigent, but are interested in building positive parental involvement and social skills, while also maintaining a positive and successful relationship with their children and significant others...[18]

The FWC program goal is as follows:

To gather and dispense information while networking with other fathers and concerned citizens on how we as fathers can best serve our families, communities and children, while also networking with other creditable local and state agencies, schools, churches, and elected officials, etc., on building needed resources to assist in the empowerment of fathers and their families throughout the State of Illinois.

The FWC program provides an ongoing array of services for fathers. The objectives are as follows:

- Recruit fathers who are in need of supportive services.
- Assess each father's current needs.

- Personally design and implement a service plan to address those needs.
- Provide monthly Fatherhood Empowerment Groups to strengthen fathers in areas that need immediate intervention.
- Provide individual counseling and intervention to fathers on a weekly basis.
- Teach appropriate life skills where necessary.
- Provide referrals and immediate placement as needed.
- Monitor and evaluate agencies that provide services to fathers and their significant others.
- When applicable, advocate and provide men's health and wellness opportunities. G. Jones (personal communication, November 12, 2010)

God divinely assigned Mrs. Gloria Ann Jones to stand side-by-side with her husband; no matter what may come, they would stay together. The quiet drum major for social justice affirms that prayer is the key. She serves as a model for the healing process between the Black Alpha Male and his mate. She quietly, yet firmly, supports her husband and listens for times when he (Mr. Walter Jones) needs advice in making vital decisions concerning FWC. Furthermore, she trusts that her husband is being led by the spirit of the living God and walks stride-for-stride with him both in their public and their private lives. Notably and admirably, she works hard behind the scenes at all sponsored events such as *The Expo For Today's Man* (10 years and running), feeding the homeless at May School in Chicago (5 years and running) and mentoring programs for elementary and middle school students.

FWC is supported by public officials, dignitaries and notable organizations throughout Illinois. Congressman Danny Davis is an honorary executive board member of FWC and supports all events and community initiatives. In addition,

FWC supports and stands in solidarity with the following organizations:

- Illinois Council on Responsible Fatherhood
- National Fatherhood Initiative
- Fatherhood Educational Institute
- Leaders Network
- Mountain Men, Men of Trinity, Mission Men and Men on a Mission.

Mrs. Gloria Jones unequivocally believes that we can achieve Dr. King's dream if we come together and support and love each other, especially within the parameters of the family as a whole and specifically within the dynamics between husband and wife. Mrs. Jones is gravely concerned about the absence of strong Black male leaders and the need for supportive mates. She believes that leaders have not surfaced because of high rates of incarceration among Black Alpha Males. In the abyss of incarceration, their hope dissipates; this dissipation dilutes the potential for unlimited unity within the African American Village Community. G. Jones (personal communication November 12, 2010)

The enemy targets Black Alpha Males—the Malcolms, Martins and Obamas—because the collective enemies of the African American Village Community instinctively fears a sudden unexpected increase (a positive surge) in exceptional generational leadership throughout this great nation. Mrs. Gloria Jones believes that a strong, supportive Black woman can help offset the weapons of mass human destruction. The call to participate in the indigenous healing process is a call for unity. According to Mrs. Jones, this call for unity supports the hypothesis that a true woman of God who supports her mate/husband and positively contributes to the indigenous Communal Healing *process* in the African American Village

Community will not interfere with the move of the Creator. Furthermore, she affirms that God wisely chooses a mate for exceptional leadership for such a time as this. Leadership is important in that it is a necessary corrective and driving force in the struggle for parity at every level of human intercourse. G. Jones (personal communication November 12, 2010)

Mrs. Jones does not shy away from the philosophy of loving yourself first. She believes this first love enables and empowers you to love others. With this preternatural love, the sky is the limit. Finally, in addressing the schism between Generation E and the generation that continues to struggle for equality and liberation in America, Mrs. Jones believes we should revisit and create an ongoing Communal Initiative, similar to the philosophy of Carter G. Woodson that teaches the present and future generations Black History. This history will not only anchor us (African Americans) in the present but will ground us together and become a categorical imperative (a force to be reckoned with if you will) in the indigenous healing process.

In juxtaposition to this drum major for social and educational justice the activism and communal dedication of sister Alicia Archer, founder of CLEANkids, a not-for-profit organization on the South West Side of Chicago, serves as a reminder that everyday heroes are stepping up to the table of humanity. Archer stands in the tradition of Mrs. Gloria Ann Jones of Fathers Who Care, Taki S. Raton of Blyden Delany Academy, Tim King of Urban Prep Schools and Carter G. Woodson of ASALH. These unsung heroes are taking their rightful seat (at the table of humanity) in a most humble and unapologetic manner while simultaneously claiming their Civil Rights. They are unapologetically asserting their God-inherent right to develop, sustain and promote the ideologies of the Beloved Community.

Archer's paternal grandparents, Otto and Clara Archer, came to Chicago from Vicksburg, Mississippi in 1916. They no longer wanted to work as sharecroppers, so they came to Chicago, seeking employment opportunities. They wanted a better life for their children as well as themselves. During quiet talks with her dad (Wilbert Archer) she discovered there was a lynching of an African American every three days. This was a major factor in the couple's decision to relocate. Otto and Clara were faithful, active members of Progressive Baptist Church under the leadership of Rev. T. E. Brown. Otto joined the male choir and eventually recorded a hit album entitled *The Progressive Church*. The Archers later joined the Antioch Missionary Baptist Church under the spiritual leadership of Rev. Wilbur Nathaniel Daniel.

Alicia Archer's maternal grandparents, Bernice and Edward Vanorsby (born in Tangipahoa Parish, Louisiana), similarly decided to migrate North. Edward Vanorsby came to Chicago to complete his education at Wendell Phillips High School and then returned to Louisiana where he met her grandmother. The couple was joined in holy matrimony. They moved to Chicago around 1936 and eventually purchased a gas station and an apartment building. Alicia's father, Wilbert Archer, Sr., and mother, Erma Lee, was 16 and 13 years of age, respectively, when they met. They both attended Doolittle Elementary School and Wendell Phillips High School in Chicago. They were joined in holy matrimony on August 20, 1949, and were married for 55 years before her mother went on to be with the Lord. In 1962, the couple moved to the Englewood neighborhood on the South Side of Chicago; at that time it was a beautiful area. They had the distinct honor of being the second African American family to move on the block. Archer's mother was a member of the PTA, and both of her parents were on the block club committee.

Alicia Archer was born in Chicago and was the youngest of five children. This drum major for social justice always possessed a great undying, unconditional love for her people (African Americans). In examining her *modus operandi* (MO), she can best be described as a person who is always willing to lend a hand. She accepted Jesus Christ as her personal Savior at an early age. After the passing of her mother, the move of God intensified in her, and the desire to bring indigenous Communal Healing to the African American Village Community overwhelmed her being. A. Archer (personal communication, December 6, 2010)

Moved by the power of God, Alicia Archer wanted to make a difference in this world and in the lives of the people God placed in her path. In 2008, the Lord spoke to her. He placed a special (divinely inspired) mission in her soul for the protection and nurturing of children. As she pondered her spiritual experience, the word CLEANKids began to resonate in her mind again and again. Finally, it became clear that He was pronouncing her calling and was giving her an option to choose her proclamation. Two distinct names continuously surfaced: the first was "Christ Lives *Eternally* and 'Nternally" or "Christ Lives *Externally* and 'Nternally." Archer reports that the Holy Ghost gave her the names before the assignment. With His divine assistance, she chose Christ Lives Eternally And 'Nternally, which ultimately became the free Christian Saturday summer outreach program appropriately called CLEANkids. A. Archer (personal communication, December 6. 2010)

Archer is honored to be a part of something that helps to mold local youth into strong, productive young men and women of which we can be proud. The answer to God's summoning has been a wonderful journey and labor of love. Most importantly, in 2010, the summer program expanded into a year-long program (however, only certain aspects of the program will be implemented during non-summer months).

CLEANkids offers mentoring, fun educational trips, discussions, block cleanups, daily devotion, light exercise, breakfast, lunch and more. The participants have taken trips to New York, WKKC Radio Station (Chicago), The Oriental Museum, Brookfield Zoo, Millennium Park, Haunted Trails Amusement Park and Kiddie Land, just to name a few.

Archer believes there are several reasons why division, violence and despair plague the African American Village Community. First and foremost, we as a community and as individuals here and abroad do not reverence God the way our ancestors did. Most of us have the *I* syndrome instead of the *we* mindset. Alicia Archer unequivocally believes that when we collectively put God and His teachings first in our lives, we will learn how to love his Son, Jesus Christ, ourselves and one another. This will ultimately eliminate the division among our people. It will also make us think twice about harming or killing another human being (part of God's Creation). A. Archer (personal communication, December 6, 2010)

Secondly, Archer believes we need to seriously hold each other accountable. It is not fair nor is it productive for the majority of people (in the Village Community) to sit back and complain about their situation and what is happening in their community or in the world while the minority becomes exhausted because they are doing most, if not all, of the work. A wise African proverb tells us, "It takes a *village*."[19]

Thirdly, Alicia Archer believes in engaging the destructive spirit of self-annihilation by being proactive. Take some time to think about what you can do *now,* not later, to make your community a better and safer place. This is Dr. King's vision of the Beloved Community. Archer encourages other activists to regularly attend the Chicago Alternative Policing Strategy meetings (CAPS), work with and be friendlier with police officers, speak out against crime, get to know your neighbors and watch out for them. Furthermore, become a block club committee member, have block club parties, be an active PTA member and most importantly vote!

Last but not least, pray for your community! Prayer destroys all the works of the enemy (the Prince of Darkness) including violence (domestic and Black on Black), drug abuse, inadequate healthcare, biological and psychological diseases, alcoholism, joblessness (unemployment & underemployment), foreclosures, child abuse (physical & mental), homelessness, poverty and despair—that plague our community! A. Archer (personal communication, December 6, 2010)

The CLEANkids organization is in alliance with Syron Smith, the distinguished and respected founder of the Block Club Union Charities (BCUC). CLEANkids' mission is to empower and inspire youth with fun and educational programs while introducing them to Jesus Christ. The organizers of the free, innovative program require that parents volunteer at least twice for their kids to be a part of the CLEANkids program. This hands on approach enables parents to actually see and be a part of what their children are doing; in turn, the founder receives the assistance she needs to maintain discipline and structure. A. Archer (personal communication, December 6, 2010)

Archer's personal prayer is that each and every child will ultimately become caring, responsible, morally sound, productive citizens who have a personal relationship with God through Jesus Christ. Furthermore, she unequivocally believes that the love and quality time the organizers give the kids will follow them into their adult lives. Hopefully, the lessons from the program will give the participants a foundation and a desire to continuously strive for greatness. This preternatural nurturing will enable them to be better parents themselves and will encourage them to be actively involved in their community and in the world. In addition, Alicia Archer offers a message to the women of the African American Village Community: "And the LORD God said, It is not good that the man should be alone; I will make him a *help mate* for him" (Genesis 2:18). Alicia Archer affirms that the role of women is to be a helpmate to their husbands and significant others and to be all that God created them to be. Archer embraces the power that comes from having faith in God and stands firm in what is right: loving yourself enough to do whatever is takes to stay on the right path and not be led astray by other people, places and things. The healing process, indigenous Communal Healing, can begin when we collectively exercise our faith. Archer's faith-based hypothesis is rooted in *agape* love.

In addition to agape love, it is a categorical imperative that women of color surround themselves with positive role models, especially other positive women that they can emulate so that our youth and the entire African American Village Community can benefit. Collectively, women of color should strive for Godliness and excellence in their lives. Not surprisingly, Alicia Archer aspires to follow the historical footprints of great women such as Sojourner Truth. Sojourner Truth stands out to Archer for several reasons: first, her name, Sojourner Truth (especially *Truth,* which speaks for itself), encompasses powerful, positive connotations. In a famous, powerful, historical and soul moving speech entitled *Ain't I a Woman?* Sojourner emphasized the strength and power of women.[20] This specific historical speech stood out to Archer because she unequivocally believes that all women, including women of color, are powerful and have a God-given right and mandate to speak the truth.

Secondly, Alicia Archer discovered through intensive research, that Sojourner also initiated programs in Chicago. Sojourner married a Chicago newspaperman, organized many civic and self-help clubs in Chicago and became chairman of the Chicago Equal Rights League (CERL). Archer graciously acknowledges that the opportunity she has today to make a difference is directly linked to great women like Sojourner Truth who paved the way. She was a trailblazer, and all modern day trailblazers (especially women of color) can similarly become empowered when they stand and demand equality in the African American Village Community.

Walking in the fullness of her vocation, Alicia Archer is living a life full of purpose, love, joy, peace and prosperity. After her human assignment is over and she meets the Lord, He will undoubtedly say, *well done, Alicia Archer, thou good and faithful servant.* Archer's life is a purpose driven life. When the dust clears and future generations of African American leaders rise up to face the Goliaths of their eras, Alicia Archer will be remembered as a humble, loving and obedient servant who answered the call of God, the Creator. In a quiet and unassuming manner, she is keeping the dream alive. Most importantly, because of her unselfish and tireless efforts to bring about authentic, indigenous Communal Healing in the African American Village Community, the future participants of CLEANkids will define and write a new vision that will nurture, support and sustain the Beloved Community. A. Archer (personal communication, December 6, 2010)

The activism and communal dedication of Mary Moore and Barbara Sanders of the Chicago Deborah Movement (a newly formed national movement of empowered spirit-filled women under the direct umbrella of the Black Alpha Male Constructionist Phillip Jackson's Black Star Project) are exemplary human models of *A House Divided...No More.*

213

Mary Moore's soul became sick and tired of the random unprovoked violence plaguing the inner city youth of the greater African American Village Community. When she repeatedly witnessed the epidemic of Black on Black violence Mary Moore began to ask herself and the Village Community at large, Where is the outrage from the pillars and leaders of the community? While watching the nine o'clock news (Chicago) she received her divine answer as she witnessed a special determined group of African American women calling themselves the Deborahs. This group of Christian believers collectively decided that they could no longer stand in silence and watch the genocidal forces of destruction ravage their Village Community. The bold women marched to the Chicago Police Department Headquarters and challenged those in authority who had sworn under oath to serve and protect. That very night, Moore made a call to connect with those drum majors for social justice; while attending the next meeting, she became a member. Barbara Sanders, moved by a Power greater than herself, attended the same meeting. Sanders was inspired by the passion and commitment of the group as well as the plan of action (and not just talk). Both women individually and collectively decided to become part of the solution: a Communal Initiative, if you will.

The I Am Deborah Movement mission statement is as follows: Our mission is to revitalize the Black Community (the African American Village) through spiritual development and cultural awareness by actively utilizing diverse methods of engagement. We are spiritually driven women moving in action to improve the Black Community and the world.[21] Walking stride-for-stride and mirroring the Old Testament biblical figure Deborah, the *modus operandi* (MO) of the participants of this new movement can best be described in the following manner:

Deborah leaders are rare. They accomplish great amounts of work without direct involvement because they know how to work through other people. They are able to see the big picture, which often escapes those directly involved, so they make good mediators, advisors, and planners. Deborah fits this description perfectly. She had all these leadership skills and she had a remarkable relationship with God. The insight and confidence God gave Deborah placed her in a unique position in the Old Testament. Deborah is among the outstanding women of history. Her story shows that she was not power hungry. She wanted to serve God. Whenever praise came her way, she gave God the credit. She didn't deny or resist her position in the culture as a woman and wife, but she never allowed herself to be hindered by it either. Her story shows how God can accomplish great things through people who are willing to be led by Him. Deborah's life challenges us in several ways. She reminds us of the need to be available both to God and to others. She encourages us to spend our efforts on what we can do rather than on worrying about what we can't do. Deborah [A drum major for social justice] challenges us to be wise leaders. She eloquently demonstrates what a person can accomplish when we are moved by the power of God, the Unmoved Mover. M. Moore (personal communication, January 10, 2011)

According eyewitness accounts in the Holy Bible, Deborah's presence among the people commanded respect. As she led her people into a successful battle, she went beyond the battle and became a model of how to live for God once the battle was over. Her leadership style drew people together and served as a vivid reminder that a wise leader should never forget about the spiritual condition of the people being led. A true leader continuously promotes and nurtures a genuine concern for people, not just personal success. The power of a leader comes from his or her innate ability to promote and sustain unity among people who are oppressed due to marginalization and disenfranchisement.

The leaders of the Deborah Movement seek to restore unity (including self-love and self-respect) in the African American Village Community. In her effort to become a healing balm to her people, Barbara Sanders believes that a committed group of people, whether a block club, a school or a social service group, can positively transform the lives of people they interact with through quality connections. The ability to communicate with love becomes paramount to building unity in the world community. Sanders unequivocally believe in the Village Concept that constitutes embracing everyone and not just your own (the extended-fictive family, if you will). This drum major for social justice further affirms that modeling is paramount in the movement to restore the Village Community. People will forget what you say, but they will never forget what you did or how you made them feel. Therefore, the indigenous work of the Deborah Movement must be from the heart.

Mary Moore perceives unity as the state of being one; this special oneness is something that is complete within itself. Community is a special place where there is an abundance of love, respect, sharing and caring. When transformed by love, community looks like heaven. It is a place of natural beauty with clean streets and manicured green lawns. Elders are appreciated, protected, respected, honored, loved and cared for unconditionally. It is a place where people can sit on their front porches in total peace and watch the children freely play. It is Mary Moore's desire and goal to transform our Village Community into a place where men are men and women are women, where all schools unapologetically teach Black Pride and thoroughly educate our children about their rich history.

Most importantly, it is a place where the 2 P's (Providers and Protectors) of the African American Village Community can fulfill their God-assigned roles. Moore embraces the songs "Home" by Ms. Stephanie Mills and the remix of "Wake Up Everybody" by Mr. John Legend as well as my own Black History CD Soundtrack of a historical speech I (Dr. Michael James) recorded entitled *Black Freedom.* It is well to note that Mary Moore consistently promotes the CD Soundtrack throughout the Village Community. The Black History CD Soundtrack consist of the following speeches supported by powerful musical scores created by Daniel Wilson Studios-Track 1: *We As The People*; Track 2: *Now Is the Time*; Track 3: *Black Freedom*; Track 4: *A Message From the Mountain Top.* M. Moore (personal communication, January 10. 2011)

Barbara Sanders harbors an uncompromising desire to work closely with other positive Black Alpha Males who fearlessly go into the trenches of the Village Community to bring about indigenous Communal Healing. In working with males from all sectors of the city to restore the Village Community, it is important to have open communication. Dismissing her role as the traditional cook and seamstress, Sanders affirms that we must redefine the role of women in order to cooperatively brainstorm solutions and strategies. A woman's instincts and intuition are valuable assets and cannot, by any stretch of the imagination, be replaced or replicated. In the tradition of the Beloved Community, we need for the men of the Village Community to embrace what women can bring to the table of humanity. Sanders insist that she and others are willing to work with strong Black men because there is nothing like the awesome power of a Black man working to promote positive change in the community: she considers it is a pleasure to witness the movement of God through positive Black Alpha Males as they continuously labor to restore the Village Community to a level of respectability. B. Sanders (personal communication, January 10, 2011)

Similarly, Mary Moore unequivocally believes that her efforts with the Deborah Movement are not, by any stretch of the imagination, designed to override the efforts of positive, dedicated Black Alpha Males. On the contrary, she loves, appreciates, adores and respects her male counterparts. This supportive sister admits that when she sees Black Alpha Males doing good in the hood it represent the natural order of the Creator. She cherishes her rightful place beside them as a queen, chosen by God, and has learned how to be supportive and less aggressive. Furthermore, when we as a people come together to do what God has collectively called us to do (rise up from a past rooted in pain), we destroy the plan of the White man—the gatekeepers of wealth, the capitalists—to divide and destroy us. Her mission, which is to be obedient and do God's will, takes precedence over any lingering effects of the Willie Lynch Syndrome. In essence, God's has called on woman, the completion of man and creation, to be the way of reconciliation and redemption for the world.

The respected and highly visible dedicated women of the I Am Deborah Movement exemplify the philosophy and theme of this exegesis: *A House Divided...No More.* Barbara Sanders supports and endorse the collective efforts of the African American Village Community as we confront and defeat the spirit of division. This Deborah warrior affirms that *divided...no more* means we must stop the divisiveness across color lines, demographics, education and economic status. We must stop the non-contributory ego monster from preventing organizations from working with each other. Finally, we must immediately stop embracing the crab-in-a-barrel syndrome from sabotaging the efforts of positive people in the group. This spirit of division serves no purpose and is self defeating. We must, once and for all, dissolve the mental chains of the Willie Lynch syndrome, including the infamous and notorious six chains of oppression discussed earlier in Chapter 3.

Mary Moore's personal philosophy of *divided...no more* is based on atonement, reconciliation and responsibility. If given the proper human fertilization, this special unity can permanently occupy our hearts, minds, bodies and souls. On October 16, 1995, one million plus Black Alpha Males stood together. They collectively stood up and made a solemn pledge to be divided...no more. Sixteen years later (2011), Moore stands side-by-side with those who faithfully continue to serve as positive role models in the African American Village Community.

The I Am Deborah Movement is proclaiming with a loud voice that it was the innate creativity of the Black woman that inspired her to season food the White man considered trash. It was with God's help (the Unmoved Mover) that she skillfully and inconspicuously nourished a dying generation of children and Black men back to health. It was her innate strength that endured the consistent and repeated inhumane acts of rape both aboard the Mothership and on the slave plantations; this feat was accomplished while she was required to nurse and nurture her biological offspring and the non-biological offspring of the slave master's wife (and his other sexual partners). She accomplished these insurmountable tasks while looking into the eyes of the White slave masters who repeatedly abused her people. Let it be known this day as she watches over the Village Community that it will be her innate strength once again that will nurse, nurture and restore an oppressed people back from the brink of intentional genocidal destruction (including political, psychological, economic, social and educational strangulation and marginalization). It will be through her tireless and uncompromised devotion that the dream will inevitably become a reality. Barbara Sanders, Mary Moore and the other unsung heroes of the Beloved Community and the Deborah Movement will be able to collectively say that the African American Village Community is now, as of this day, *A House Divided...No More.*

In closing out this innate cultural dialogue is well to note that authentic historical healing (Communal Healing) takes time. The psychological scars caused by the long night of slavery, institutional racism and marginalization require a special healing process in lieu of one law (e.g., the Thirteenth Amendment) or, and band-aid approach (Affirmative Action). However, those who actively participate in the healing process will find a sense of fulfillment (personally, collectively and spiritually) when the healing process unfolds into a mass movement and the Village Community is restored to a level of respectability. This in-depth, unique imperative investigation, *A House Divided...No More*, reminds us specifically that numerous courageous people, both on the front lines (who receive media recognition) and behind the scene drum majors for social justice (people who never make the local or national news) are fighting for our liberation. They are fighting for our collective and individual parity and equality at every level of human intercourse. I humbly salute and acknowledge the noble efforts of Michelle Obama, Mae Jemison, Rosa Parks, Coretta Scott King, Ida B. Wells, Dorothy Tillman, Lyn Hughes, Margaret Burroughs, Yvette Moyo-Gillard, Adam Clayton Powell, Sr., Adam Clayton Powell, Jr., John Lewis, James Farmer, David Walker, Dr. Maulana Karenga, Dr. Jawanza Kunjufu, Julian Bond, Medgar Evers, Jimmie Lee Jackson, the participants of Bloody Sunday at the Edmund Pettus Bridge, the participants of D Day (Children's Crusade), Emmett Till, the NAACP and Carter G. Woodson, Tim King, Taki S. Raton, Gloria Ann Jones, Alicia Archer, Barbara Sanders and Mary Moore. Because of your individual and collective responses to a greater Power (God, the Unmoved Mover), the Beloved Community is an idea whose time has come. Most importantly, *A House Divided...No More* can become a reality in this day. Because of you, it is *Time for Indigenous Communal Healing.*

Epilogue

A People United Can Never Be Defeated

The CeaseFire initiative is a categorical imperative in our quest for unity in the African American Village Community. Dr. Gary Slutkin (the executive director) and the Chicago Project's 8 Point Plan represent a grassroots effort to stop the violence. The plan is as follows:

- Identify and notify high risk persons that using guns is not tolerated, and emphasize that alternative means of resolving conflicts need to be found.

- Street-based outreach programs are developed to help at-risk persons successfully access a GED, jobs, safety, literacy programs, individual counseling, and provide individualized alternatives.

- Conflicts are prevented and mediated.

- Safe havens and local after school programs are made available.

- Materials are distributed throughout the community, notifying and (most importantly) constantly reminding high risk individuals and groups of alternatives and risks.

- Pressure against illegal gun possession and use is increased within the community, and norms are changed about gun use.

- All shootings within the community are countered with rapid, coordinated and sustained responses by the residents, clergies and police.

221

- If needed, prosecutions and sentencing are ensured by the State Attorney's Office and the U.S. Attorney's Office. [1]

Without further ado, let it be known this day that Black-on-Black violence must stop! We must, by any and all means necessary and with all resources available to us, send a unified, uncompromised mandate that random and unprovoked violence, which has historically and continuously plagued, embarrassed and strangled the African American Village Community, will not, by any stretch of the imagination, be tolerated or accepted. In order to create, sustain and nurture the Beloved Community, we must unite with a prime directive to make those who continue to perpetuate the evil activities of Black-on-Black violence totally uncomfortable and out of place in the Village Community. Through the power of the African American Experience, Cultural Discipline, Empirical Hope, Cultural Utilitarianism, Communal Healing, the Inter-Related Structure of Black Reality, the Village Concept and Ethic of Care, we must call upon an indigenous preternatural empowerment derived from Ground Zero to participate in a Communal Healing process. Therefore, moving by a Power greater than ourselves, we will collectively engage the enemy disguised as the Glass Ceiling, the Rule of Containment, the Rule of Selective Engagement, the Rule of Annihilation, the Socialization of Division and most importantly, the Laissez-Faire Entitlement Syndrome.

The Beloved Community is obtainable. Let it be known this day that through our own collective efforts derived from the power of our Blackness, we will, we must and shall overcome by any means necessary. Let it be known that as of this day, the day that God has made, we will collectively embrace the uncompromised philosophy that a people united shall never be defeated.

Let it be known that as of this day, a house divided against itself cannot stand. We as a people have been ordained by God with a purpose: to evolve from the huts of history's shame and a past that's rooted in pain to unequivocally become *A House Divided...No More.*

To: My loyal and faithful readers
From... *The Desk of* Dr. Michael James

It is with great pride (Black Pride) and pleasure that I will present to the Village Community the next level of intellectual (Black Psychological Warfare) empowerment entitled:

RISE...

The African American Experience
(A movement of the people, for the people, and by the people)

African American Firsts

The Honorable Lorraine H. Morton, first African American female and African American Mayor of Evanston, Illinois. Elected in 1993 and re-elected in 1997 and 2001. Morton also served on the Evanston's City Council as the 5th Ward Alderman for nine years. The Honorable Morton began as an educator in Evanston at Foster School and continued as a distinguished middle school teacher at Nichols and Chute (also in Evanston). Notably, the Evanston Civic Center was renamed in her honor in November 2009. The Lorraine H. Morton Civic Center stands as a testament to the indomitable spirit and power of the African American Experience.

African American *Firsts* of the 21st century include:

- Colin Powell: Secretary of State
- Robert L. Johnson: Founder of Black Entertainment Television [BET]
- Shelia Johnson: Female billionaire
- Halle Berry: Received Academy Award for Best Actress (Monster's Ball, 2001)
- Beyonce Knowles: ASCAP Pop Music Songwriter of the Year Award (first woman)
- Captain Vernice Armour (USMC): Combat pilot in the U.S. Armed Services (first female)
- Serena Williams: Career Grand Slam in tennis
- Condoleezza Rice: Secretary of State (first woman)
- Jeanine Menze: U.S. Coast Guard Aviator (first woman)
- Shani Davis: Winter Olympic Gold Medal Winner 1,000 Meter Speed Skating
- Tony Dungy (Indianapolis Colts) and Lovie Smith (Chicago Bears): Super Bowl XLI, NFL Head Coaches

- Barbara Hillary: Reached the North Pole (first African American woman)
- Sophia Danenberg: Successfully reached the Peak of Mount Everest
- Tyler Perry: Entrepreneur, owns a movie and television studio
- Tiana: Disney Princess (first woman of color portrayed)
- Duke Ellington: Portrait appeared (by himself) on Circulating U.S. Coin
- Ursula Burns: CEO of Xerox Corporation, an S&P 100 Company
- Charles F. Bolden, Jr.: Administrator of National Aeronautics and Space Administration
- Desiree Rogers: White House Social Secretary
- Lisa P. Jackson: Administrator of the Environmental Protection Agency
- Eric Holder: United States Attorney General
- Deval Patrick: Governor of Massachusetts
- Phylicia Rashad: Broadway Theatre's Tony Award for Best Actress in a Play[2]

Footnotes-Introduction

[1] John Donne Quotes.
<http://www.goodreads.com/author/quotes/77318.John_Donne>.
Retrieved August 9, 2010.
[2] Brainy Quote.
<http://www.brainyquote.com/quotes/authors/m/martin_luther_king
_jr_6.html>. Retrieved April 3, 2011.
[3] You've been had. Been took! Hoodwinked. Bamboozled! Led
astray...
<http://foreclosureblues.wordpress.com/2011/02/28/you%E2%80%
99v...>. Retrieved April 20, 2011.
[4] Kwanzaa. A Celebration of Family, Community, and Culture. The
Founder's Message 2000.
<http://www.officialkwanzaawebsite.org/origins1.shtml>.
Retrieved July 7, 2010.

Footnotes Part I *Page*- Unity Is the Key

[1] Brainy Quote.
<http://www.brainyquote.com/quotes/authors/m/martin_luther_king
_jr_6.htm>l. Retrieved April 3, 2011.

Footnotes-Part I
Chapter 1

[1] Still I Rise by Maya Angelou.
<http://www.poets.org/viewmedia.php/prmMID/15623>. Retrieved
August 9, 2010.
[2] The White House Historical Association/White House
History/Timelines.
<http://www.whitehousehistory.org/whha_timelines/timelines_
africanamericans-04.html>.Retrieved August 4, 2010.
[3] Ibid.
[4] Ibid.
[5] Ibid.
[6] Ibid.
[7] Ibid.

[8] Ibid.

[9] The White House Historical Association/White House History/Timelines.
<http://www.whitehousehistory.org/whha_timelines/timelines_african-americans-03.html>. Retrieved August 4, 2010.

[10] Ibid.

[11] Ibid.

[12] Ibid.

[13] Ibid.

[14] The White House Historical Association/White House History/Timelines.
<http://www.whitehousehistory.org/whha_timelines/timlines_african-americans-04.html>. Retrieved August 4, 2010.

[15] Ibid.

[16] Ibid.

[17] Ibid.

[18] Ibid.

[19] Ibid.

[20] A Family's Journey between White Houses: Michelle Obama's Family tree has roots in a Carolina slave plantation.
<http://quickproxy4.chipublib.org/YVDgO147/url=http://proquest.umi.com/pqdweb?index=3...>. Retrieved August 3, 2010.

[21] Ibid.

[22] Ibid.

[23] Ibid.

[24] It's Time to Take One Giant Step for Womankind; [Northwest, FNW Edition].
<http://quickproxy4.chipublib.org/YVDgO147/url=http://proquest.umi.com/pqdweb?index=1>. Retrieved August 3, 2010.

[25] Ibid.

[26] Ibid.

[27] Catherine Reef, Black Explorers (American Profiles). pp. 86-87.

[28] Mae Jemison. < http://www. notablebiographies.com/Ho-Jo/Jemison-Mae.html>. Retrieved July 30, 2010.

[29] Mae Jemison phones home while in orbit. Science students talk to astronaut.
<http://quickproxy4.chipublib.org/YVDgO147/url=http://proquest.umi.com/pqdweb?index=3>. Retrieved August 3, 2010.

[30] Reef, p. 107.

[31] Ibid.

[32] Dr. Mae Jemison.
<http://quest.nasa.gov/women/TODTWD/Jemison.bio.html>.
Retrieved July 2, 2010.
[33] Ibid.
[34] Ibid.
[35] Reef, pp. 86-87.
[36] Ibid.
[37] Ibid.
[38] Dr. Mae Jemison.
<http://quest.nasa.gov/women/TODTWD/Jemison.bio.html>.
Retrieved July 2, 2010.
[39] Mae Jemison Quotes.
<http://womenshistory.about.com/od/quotes/a/mae_jemison.htm>.
Retrieved July 30, 2010.
[40] Explorer Hero: Mae Jemison by Christian Walsh.
<http://myhero.com/go/hero.asp?hero=M_jemison>. Retrieved July
30, 2010.
[41] Mae Jemison, "I recall looking at the stars, knowing I'd go up
there some day.
<http://quickproxy4.chipublib.org/YVDgO147/url=http://proquest.
umi.com/pqdweb?index=3...>. Retrieved August 3, 2010.
[42] John Donne Quotes.
<http://www.goodreads.com/author/quotes/77318.John_Donne>.
Retrieved August 9, 2010.
[43] Rosa Parks. < http://www.africanonline.com/rosa_parks.htm >.
Retrieved July 30, 2010.
[44] Ibid.
[45] Women of the Hall. National Women's Hall of Fame.
<http://www.greatwomen.org/women.php?action=viewone&id=117
>. Retrieved July 30, 2010.
[46] Rosa Parks-Black History Month.
<http://ww.gale.cengage.com/free_resources/bhm/bio/parks_r.htm>.
Retrieved July 30, 2010.
[47] Civil Rights Timeline. Black American History, a history of black
people in the United States.
<http://www.africanonline.com/civil_rights_timeline.htm>.
Retrieved July 30, 2010.
[48] Rosa Parks-Black History Month.
<http://www.gale.cengage.com/free_resources/bhm/bio/parks_r.ht>.
Retrieved July 30, 2010.
[49] Ibid.

[50] Ibid.

[51] Ibid.

[52] Civil Rights Timeline. Milestones in the modern civil rights movement. <http://www.infoplease.com/spot/civilrightstimeline1.html>. Retrieved August 9, 2010.

[53] Rosa Louise Parks Biography. <http://www.rosaparks.org/bio.html>. Retrieved July 30, 2010.

[54] Ibid.

[55] Ibid.

Footnotes-Part I
Chapter 2

[1] Coretta Scott King Quotes. <http://www.brainyquote.com/quotes/authors/c/coretta_scott_king.html>. Retrieved August 10, 2010.

[2] Ibid.

[3] Ibid.

[4] The King Center. The Beloved Community of Martin Luther King, Jr. <.http://www.thekingcenter.org/ProgServices/Default.aspx>. Retrieved August 10, 2010.

[5] Ibid.

[6] Coretta Scott King (American Activist). Famous Quotes by Coretta Scott King. <http://quotesdaddy.com/author/Coretta+Scott=King >. Retrieved August 10, 2010.

[7] Coretta Scott King. New World Encyclopedia. < http://www newworldencyclopedia.org/entry/Coretta_Scott_King>. Retrieved August 10, 2010.

[8] Coretta Scott King (American Activist). Famous Quotes by Coretta Scott King. <http://quotesdaddy.com/author/Coretta+Scott=King>. Retrieved August 10, 2010.

[9] The King Center. The Beloved Community of Martin Luther King, Jr. <.http://www.thekingcenter.org/ProgServices/Default.aspx>. Retrieved August 10, 2010.

[10] Coretta Scott King. New World Encyclopedia. < http://www newworldencyclopedia.org/entry/Coretta_Scott_King >. Retrieved August 10, 2010.

[11] Ibid.

[12] Ibid.

[13] Ibid.

[14] Ibid.

[15] Ibid.

[16] Ibid.

[17] Ibid.

[18] Ibid. Ida B Wells. Wikipedia, the free encyclopedia. <http://en.wikipedia.org/wiki/Ida_B._Wells >. Retrieved July 2, 2010.

[19] Ibid.

[20] Ibid.

[21] Ibid.

[22] Ibid.

[23] Dauntless crusader; A moving biography of civil rights and anti-lynching activist Ida B. Wells. <http://quickproxy4.chipublib.org/YVDg0147/url=http://proquest. umi.com/pqdweb? index=0...>. Retrieved August 3, 2010.

[24] The Memphis Diary of Ida B. Wells. Miriam Decosta-Willis. p. 1.

[25] Ibid.

[26] Ida B Wells. Wikipedia the free encyclopedia. <http://en.wikipedia.or/wiki/Ida_B._Wells>. Retrieved July 2, 2010

[27] Dauntless crusader; a moving biography of civil rights and anti-lynching activist Ida B. Wells. <http://quickproxy4.chipublib.org/YVDg0147/url=http://proquest. umi.com/pqdweb? index=0...>. Retrieved August 3, 2010.

[28] Ibid.

[29] Ida B Wells. Wikipedia, the free encyclopedia. <http://en.wikipedia.or/wiki/Ida_B._Wells >. Retrieved July 2, 2010.

[30] Ibid.

[31] Ibid.

[32] Ibid.

[33] Ibid.

[34] The Memphis Diary of Ida B. Wells. p. 178.

[35] Ibid. p. 179.

[36] Ida B Wells. Wikipedia, the free encyclopedia. <http://en.wikipedia.or/wiki/Ida_B._Wells>. Retrieved July 2, 2010.

[37] Ibid.

[38] Ibid.

[39] Dorothy Tillman. Wikipedia, the free encyclopedia. <http://en.wikipedia.org/wiki/Dorthy_Tillman>. Retrieved August 23, 2010.
[40] Ibid.
[41] Ibid.
[42] Ibid.
[43] Ibid.
[44] Ibid.
[45] My Space-Dorothy Wright Tillman. <http://www.mysapce.com/dorothytillman>. Retrieved August 23, 2010.
[46] Ibid.
[47] Dorothy Tillman. WVON. Coffee, Tea & Conversation with Dorothy Tillman. <http://www.wvon.com/personalities/dorothy-tillman.html>. Retrieved August 23, 2010.
[48] The Final Call. Reparations resolution passed in Chicago. <http://www.finalcall.com/national/reparations5-30-2000.htm>. Retrieved August 23, 2010.
[49] Ibid.
[50] Ibid.
[51] Ibid.
[52] Ibid.
[53] Front Page Magazine. Obama's World, Part II. <http://97.74.65.51/readArticle.aspx?ARTID=30896>. Retrieved August 23, 2010.
[54] Ibid.
[55] Ibid.
[56] 10 Reasons Why Congress Should Back a Reparations Commission. <http://news.newamericamedia.org/news/view_article.html?article_id=74afaa2bd8a36dc137...>. Retrieved August 30, 2010.

Footnotes-Part I
Chapter 3

[1] Lyn Hughes, An Anthology of Respect: The Pullman Porters National Historic Registry of African American Railroad Employees, p. 1.
[2] Ibid. p. 2.
[3] Ibid.

[4] Ibid.
[5] Ibid.
[6] Ibid. p. 3.
[7] Ibid.
[8] Ibid.
[9] Ibid. p. 8.
[10] Ibid. p. 9.
[11] Brotherhood of sleeping Car Porters. Wikipedia, the free encyclopedia. < http://en.wikipedia.org.wiki/Brotherhood_of-Sleeping_Car_Porters>. Retrieved August 14, 2010.
[12] Pullman Porters Helped Build Black Middle Class. <http://www.npr.org/templates/story.php?storyId=103880184>. Retrieved August 14, 2010.
[13] Lyn Hughes, an Anthology of Respect. p. 9.
[14] Ibid., p. 10.
[15] Ibid., p. 12.
[16] Ibid., p. 61.
[17] Ibid., pp. 56-57.
[18] Ibid., pp. 53-55.
[19] Ibid.
[20] A. Philip Randolph Porter Museum. <http://www.aphiliprandolphmuseum.org/general_info.html>. Retrieved August 14, 2010.
[21] DuSable Museum of African American History. Wikipedia, the free encyclopedia. <http://en.wikipedia.org/wiki/DuSable_Museum_of_African_American_Hsitory>. Retrieved July 2, 2010.
[22] Eugene Pieter Feldman, The birth and the Building of the DuSable Museum. p. 61.
[23] Ibid. p. 87.
[24] DuSable Museum of African American History. From Wikipedia, the free encyclopedia. <http://en.wikipedia.orgwiki/DuSable_Museum_of_African_American_Hsitory>. Retrieved July 2, 2010.
[25] Ibid. p. 2.
[26] Ibid.
[27] Ibid., p. 3.
[28] Ibid.
[29] Margaret Taylor Burroughs: Biography from Answers.com. <http://www.answers.com/topic/margaret-taylor-burroughs>. Retrieved August 14, 2010.

[30] The History Makers. Margaret Burroughs Biography.<http://www.the historymakers.com/biography/biography.asp?bioindex=39>. Retrieved July 2, 2010.

[31] Margaret Taylor Burroughs: Biography from Answers.com. <http://www.answers.com/topic/margaret-taylor-burroughs>. Retrieved August 14, 2010.

[32] Ibid.

[33] Ibid.

[34] Real Men Cook. <http://www.realmencook.com/History.html>. Retrieved August 18, 2010.

[35] Ibid.

[36] Ibid.

[37] Real Men Cook .Mission Statement. <http://www.realmencook.com/Mission.html>. Retrieved August 18, 2010.

[38] Knowledge Is The Key. (WAK)

[39] Still I Rise by Maya Angelou. <http://www.poets.org/viewmedia.php/prmMID/15623>. Retrieved August 9, 2010.

[40] Ibid.

[41] Yvette Moyo Gillard. <http://www.linkedin.com/in/marketinginnovatoryyvettemoyo1>. Retrieved August 21, 2010.

[42] Real Men Cook-Chicago Event Page. <http://www.realmencook.com/Chicago.html>. Retrieved August 18, 2010.

[43] Real Men Cook. Gimme Five. <http://www.realmencook.com/Gimme5.html>. Retrieved August 18, 2010.

[44] Real Men Cook. Real Men Charities Presents Real Men Cook in Multiple Cities Across the Country. <http://www.realmencook.com/RMCharities.html>. Retrieved August 18, 2010.

[45] Michael James, Brother to Brother (A Message of Hope), p. 9.

[46] Ibid., pp. 9-10.

[47] Ibid., p. 9.

Footnotes-Part II
Chapter 4

[1] I Have A Dream. < http://www.mklonline.net/dream.html>.Retrieved April 4, 2011.

[2] The Silent Protest: Parade organized by Harlem religious and civicleaders and the NAACP, 1917. <http://www2.si.umich.edu/chico/harlem/text/silentprotest.html>. Retrieved September 5, 2010.

[3] Ibid.

[4] Ibid.

[5] Adam Clayton Powell, Sr. Wikipedia, the free encyclopedia. <http://en.wikipedia.org/wiki/Adam_clayton_Powell, _Sr.>. Retrieved September 5, 2010.

[6] Adam Clayton Powell, Sr. (1865-1953). <http://www2.si.umich.edu/chico/Harlem/text/acpowell.html>. Retrieved August 23, 2010.

[7] Glory Days: Adam Clayton Powell, Sr. <http://www2.scholastic.com/browse/article.jsp?id=4790>. Retrieved September 5, 2010.

[8] Powell, Adam Clayton, Sr. (1865-1953). The Black Past: Remembered and Reclaimed. <http://www.blackpast.org/? q=aah/powell-sr-adam-clayton-1865-1953.>. Retrieved September 5, 2010.

[9] Adam Clayton Powell, Jr.-Wikipedia, the free encyclopedia. <http://en.wikipedia.org/wiki/Adam_Clayton_Powell, _Jr.>. Retrieved August 23, 2010.

[10] Ibid.

[11] Ibid.

[12] Ibid.

[13] Ibid.

[14] Ibid.

[15] Ibid.

[16] Ibid.

[17] Adam Clayton Powell, Jr. Black Power Between Heaven and Hell. < http://www.black-collegian.com/african/adam.shtml>. Retrieved August 23, 2010.

[18] Ibid.

[19] March on Washington. All about the march on Washington, August 28, 1963. <http://www.infoplease.com/spot/marchonwashington.html>. Retrieved September 3, 2010.

[20] Ibid.

[21] Ibid.

[22] Ibid.

[23] Ibid.

[24] James Farmer Project. < http://jamesfarmer.umwblogs.org/>. Retrieved August 24, 2010.

[25] James Farmer, Civil Rights Giant in the 50's and 60's. <http://www.interchange.org/jfarmer.html>. Retrieved August 24, 2010.

[26] Ibid.

[27] Ibid.

[28] Ibid.

[29] Ibid.

[30] Ibid.

[31] Ibid.

[32] When in the Course of Human Event. Thomas Jefferson. <http://www.humanevents.com/article.php?id=21399>. Retrieved September 5, 2010.

[33] American Experience. Eyes on the Prize. Primary Sources. Patience is a Dirty and Nasty Word. <http://www.pbs.org/wgbh/amex/eyesontheprize/sources/ps_washington.html>. Retrieved September 3, 2010.

[34] Biography of John Lewis. <http://jhnlewis.house.gov/index.php?option=com_content&task=view&id=17&irem=31>. Retrieved September 3, 2010.

[35] Ibid.

[36] Ibid.

[37] Ibid.

[38] Ibid.

[39] Ibid.

[40] Segregated Lunch Counters. <http://www.spartacus.schoolnet.co.uk/USAsitin.htm>. Retrieved September 6, 2010.

[41] Birmingham Campaign. <http://en.wikipedia.org/wiki/Birmingham_campaign>. Retrieved September 6, 2010.

[42] Ibid.

[43] 16th Street Baptist Church Bombing. Wikipedia, the free encyclopedia. <http://en.wikipedia.org/wiki/16th_Street_Baptist_Chruch_bombing>. Retrieved September 6, 2010.

[1] David Walker (abolitionist). Wikipedia, the free encyclopedia. <http://en.wikipedia.org/wiki/David_Walker_ (abolitionist)>. Retrieved September 8, 2010.

[2] Ibid.

[3] Ibid.

[4] David Walker's Appeal, p. 9.

[5] Ibid., p. 10

[6] Ibid.

[7] Ibid., p. 15.

[8] Ibid., p. 18.

[9] Ibid., p. 16.

[10] Ibid., p. 16.

[11] Ibid., 17.

[12] Ibid.

[13] Ibid.

[14] Ibid.

[15] Ibid.

[16] Ibid.

[17] David Walker (abolitionist). Wikipedia, the free encyclopedia. <http://en.wikipedia.org/wiki/David_Walker_ (abolitionist)>. Retrieved September 8, 2010.

[18] Ibid.

[19] David Walker's Appeal. Excerpts from the Appeal. <http://www.pbs.org/wgbh//aia/part4/4h2931t.html>. Retrieved September 8, 2010.

[20] David Walker's Appeal, p. 19.

[21] Ibid.

[22] Dr. Maulana Karenga's Bio. <http://www.africawithin.com/karenga/karenga_bio.htm>. Retrieved September 8, 2010.

[23] African Philosophy. Wikipedia, the free encyclopedia. <http://en.wikipedia.org/wiki/African_philosophy>. Retrieved September 17, 2010.

[24] Ibid.

[25] Ibid.

[26] The Ethics of Reparation: Engaging the Holocaust of Enslavement. < http://www.africawithin.com/karenga/ethics.htm>. Retrieved September 8, 2010.

[27] Ibid.

[28] Ibid.

[29] Ibid.

[30] Ibid.

[31] Kwanzaa. A Celebration of Family, Community, and Culture. The Founder's Message 2000. <http://www.officialkwanzaawebsite.org/origins1.shtml>. Retrieved July 7, 2010.

[32] Ibid.

[33] Ibid.

[34] Ibid.

[35] Ibid.

[36] Ibid.

[37] Dr. Jawanza Kunjufu, Countering the Conspiracy to Destroy Black Boys, p. 32.

[38] Ibid., p. 39.

[39] Dr. Michael James, ABSENT, The Assimilation of African American Males into Nonbeing, p. 89.

[40] Ibid., p. 79.

[41] Ibid., p. 94.

[42] Ibid., p. 97.

[43] Ibid., pp. 98-99.

[44] Dr. Jawanza Kunjufu, Countering the Conspiracy to Destroy Black Boys, p, 184.

[45] Ibid., p. 190.

[46] ABSENT, p. 11

[47] Ibid., p. 19.

[48] Kunjufu, p. 185.

[49] Ibid., p. 205.

[50] Ibid., p. 193.

[51] Kunjufu, pp. 193-194.

[52] Ibid., p. 50.

[53] Ibid., p. 51.

[54] Ibid., p. 149.

[55] Ibid., p. 136.

[56] Ibid., p. 148.

Footnotes-Part II
Chapter 6

[1] Julian Bond: Official Biography. < http://a-s.clayton.edu/mlking/Julian%20Bond%20official%20biography.htm >. Retrieved October 1, 2010.

[2] Ibid.

[3] Ibid., p. 2.

[4] Ibid.

[5] Julian Bond. Speaker Profile and Speaking Topics. <http://www.apbspeakers.com/speaker/julian-bond>. Retrieved October 1, 2010.

[6] A Time for Justice: America's Civil Rights Movement. <http://osulibrary.oregonstate.edu/video/hist171.html>. Retrieved October 1, 2010.

[7] A Time for Justice. <http://www.uen.org/Lessonplan/preview.cgi?LPid=565>. Retrieved October 1, 2010.

[8] Eyes on the Prize. Wikipedia, the free encyclopedia. <http://en.wikipedia.org/wiki/Eyes on the prize>. Retrieved October 1, 2010.

[9] Ibid., p. 2.

[10] Ibid.

[11] Ibid.

[12] Medgar Evers. Wikipedia, the free encyclopedia. <http://en.wikipedia.org/wiki/Medgar_Evers>. Retrieved October 14, 2010.

[13] Medgar Evers. <http://www.africanwithin.com.bios.medgar_evers.htm>. Retrieved October 14, 2010.

[14] Ibid., p. 4.

[15] Ibid.

[16] Ibid.

[17] Ibid.

[18] Ibid., p. 2.

[19] The Selma to Montgomery March: The Struggle for Voting Rights. <http://www.byways.org/stories/73679>. Retrieved October 14, 2010.

[20] Ibid.

[21] Selma to Montgomery Marches. Wikipedia, the free encyclopedia. <http://en.wikipedia.org/wiki/Selma_to_Montgomery_marches>. Retrieved October 14, 2010.

[22] Ibid., p. 9.

[23] Ibid., p. 7.

[24] Birmingham campaign. Wikipedia, the free encyclopedia. <http://en.wikipedia.org/wiki/Birmingham_campaign>. Retrieved September 6, 2010.

[25] Ibid., p. 6.

[26] Ibid., p. 7.

[27] Ibid.

[28] Ibid.

[29] Ibid., p. 8.

[30] Ibid.

[31] Ibid., pp. 8-9.

[32] Ibid., p. 9.

[33] Ibid.

[34] Ibid., p. 10.

[35] Ibid.

[36] Ibid.

[37] Ibid., p. 11.

[38] Ibid., p. 13.

[39] Murder of Emmett Till- <Wikipedia.org/.../Murder_of_Emmett...>. Retrieved January 10, 2011.

[40] Ibid., p. 3.

[41] 16th Street Baptist Church bombing. Wikipedia, the free encyclopedia. < http://en.wikipedia.org/wiki/16th_Street-Baptist_Church_bombing>. Retrieved September 6, 2010.

Footnotes-Part III
Chapter 7

[1] NAACP. Our Mission. < http://www.naacp.org/pages/our-misssion>. Retrieved July 29, 2010.

[2] Ibid.

[3] Carter G. Woodson. Wikipedia, the free encyclopedia. <http://en.wikipedia.org/wiki/Carter_G._Woodson>. Retrieved October 21, 2010.

[4] The History of Black History Month. <http://www.asalh.org/blackhistorymonthorigins.html>. Retrieved October 21, 2010.

[5] Ibid.

[6] Ibid.,p, 2,

[7] Dr. Carter G. Woodson. Founder of Black History Month.
<http://www.freemaininstitute.com/woodson.htm>. Retrieved July 29, 2010.
[8] ASALH timeline. < http://www.asalh.org/asalhtimeline.html>.
Retrieved October 21, 2010.
[9] Urban Prep Academies. Wikipedia, the free encyclopedia.
<http://en.wikipedia.org/wiki/Urban_Prep_Charter_Academy-for -Young_Men>. Retrieved October 18, 2010.
[10] Ibid., p. 2.
[11] Ibid.
[12] Ibid., p. 3-4.
[13] Ibid.
[14] Ibid., p. 3.
[15] Ibid., p. 3-4.
[16] Ibid., p. 3.
[17] UNCF Breaks Ground in D.C. on New National Headquarters.
<http://www.diverseeducation.com/article/14730/>. Retrieved April 22, 2011.
[18] Mission Statement: Fathers Who Care.
<http://www.volunteermatch.org/search/org96466.jsp>. Retrieved August 10, 2010.
[19] It Takes a Village-Wikipedia, the free encyclopedia.
<http://www.en.wikipedia.org/wiki/It_Takes_a_Village>.
Retrieved May 5, 2011.
[20] Ain't I A Woman? Wikipedia, the free encyclopedia.
<http://www.en.wikipedia.org/wiki/Aint'_I_a_Woman%3F>.
Retrieved May 5, 2011.
[21] Deborah Sisters on a mission to save our communities.
<http://www.articles. chicagotribune.com/2010-12-20/news/ct-met-deborah-move>. Retrieved January 10, 2011.

Footnotes-Epilogue & African American Firsts

[1] CeaseFire illinois.og.
<http://www.ceasefirechicgo.org/main_pages/infointro.html>.
Retrieved October 21, 2010.
[2] List of African American firsts.
<http://en.wikipedia.org/wiki/List_of_African-American_firsts>.
Retrieved November 6. 2010.

Bibliography

Adam Clayton Powell, Jr. Black Power Between Heaven and Hell.
      < http://www.black-collegian.com/african/adam.shtml1>.
      Retrieved August 23, 2010.

Adam Clayton Powell, Jr.-Wikipedia, the free encyclopedia.
      <http://en.wikipedia.org/wiki/Adam_Clayton_Powell, _Jr.>.
      Retrieved August 23, 2010.

Adam Clayton Powell Sr. (1865-1953). The Black Past:
      Remembered and Reclaimed. <http://www.blackpast.org/
      ?q=aah/powell-sr-adam-clayton-1865-1953>. Retrieved
      September 5, 2010.

Adam Clayton Powell, Sr. (1865-1953). <http://www2.si.umich.
      edu/chico/Harlem/text/acpowell.html1>. Retrieved August
      23, 2010.

Adam Clayton Powell, Sr. Wikipedia, the free encyclopedia.
      <http://en.wikipedia.org/wiki/Adam_Clayton_Powell,
_Sr.>. Retrieved September 5, 2010.

A Family's Journey between White Houses; Michelle Obama's
      Family Tree Has Roots In A Carolina Slave Plantation.
      <http://quickproxy4.chipublib.org/YVDgO147/url=http://pr
      oquest.umi.com/pbdweb?index=3...> Retrieved August 3,
      2010.

African Philosophy. Wikipedia, the free encyclopedia. <http://en
      wikipedia.org/wiki/African_philosophy>. Retrieved
      September 17, 2010.

Ain't I A Woman? Wikipedia, the free encyclopedia.
      http://www.en.wikipedia.org/wiki/Aint'_I_a_Woman%3F>
      .Retrieved May 5, 2011.

American Experience. Eyes on the Prize. Primary Sources. Patience
      is a Dirty and Nasty Word.<http://www.pbs.org/wgbh/amex

/eyesontheprize/sources/ps_washington.html>. Retrieved September 3, 2010.

A. Philip Randolph Pullman Porter Museum. <http://www.aphilip randolphmuseum.org/general_info.html>. Retrieved August 14, 2010.

ASALH Timeline. <http://www.asalh.org/asalhtimeline.html>. Retrieved October 21, 2010.

A Time for Justice. <http://www.uen.org/Lessonplan/preview/cgi? LPid=565>. Retrieved October 1, 2010.

A Time for Justice: America's Civil Rights Movement. <http : //osulibrary.oregonstate.edu/video/hist171.html>. Retrieved October 1, 2010.

Biography of John Lewis. <http://johhnlewis.house.gov/index. php?option=com_content&task=view&id=17&Item=31>. Retrieved September 3, 2010.

Birmingham Campaign. <http://en.wikipedia.org/wiki/ Birmingham_campaign>. Retrieved September 6, 2010.

Brainy Quote. <http://www. brainyquote.com/quotes/authors/m/martin_ luther_king_jr_6.html>. Retrieved April 3, 2011.

Brainy Quote. <http://www. brainyquote.com/quotes/authors/m/martin luth103526.html>. Retrieved April 3, 2011.

Brotherhood of Sleeping Car Porters. Wikipedia, the free encyclopedia. <http://en.wikipedia.org.wiki? Brotherhood_of-Sleeping_Car_Porters>. Retrieved August 14, 2010.

Carter G. Woodson. Wikipedia, the free encyclopedia. <http://en. wikipedia.org/wiki/Carter_G._Woodson>. Retrieved October 21, 2010.

Coretta Scott King Quotes. <http://www.brainyquote.com/quotes/authors/c/coretta_scott_king.html>. Retrieved August 10, 2010.

Civil Rights Timeline. Black American History, A History of Black People in the United States. <http://www.africanonline.com/civil_rights_timeline.htm>. Retrieved July 30, 2010.

Civil Rights Timeline. Milestones in the Modern Civil Rights Movement. <http://www.infoplease.com/spot/civilrightstimeline1.html>. Retrieved August 9, 2010

Coretta Scott King. New World Encyclopedia. <http://www newworldencyclopedia.org/entry/Coretta_Scott_King>. Retrieved August 10, 2010.

Coretta Scott King (American Activist). Famous Quotes by Coretta Scott King.<http://quotesdaddy.com/ author/Coretta+Scott King>. Retrieved August 10, 2010.

David Walker (abolitionist). From Wikipedia, the free encyclopedia. <http://en.wikipedia.org/wiki/David_Walker._ (abolitionist)>. Retrieved September 8, 2010.

David Walker's Appeal. Excerpts from the Appeal. <http:// www.pbs.org/wgbh//aia/part4/4h2931t.html>. Retrieved September 8, 2010.

Dauntless Crusader; a Moving Biography of Civil Rights and Anti-Lynching Activist Ida B. Wells. <http://quickproxy4 chipublib.org/YVDgO147/url=http://proquest.umi.com/pqd web?index=0...>. Retrieved August 3, 2010.

Deborah Sisters on a mission to save our communities. <http://www.articles. chicagotribune.com/2010-12-20/news/ct-met-deborah-move>. Retrieved January 10, 2011.

Dorothy Tillman. Wikipedia, the free encyclopedia. <http://en.wikipedia.org/wiki/Dorthy_Tillman>. Retrieved August 23, 2010.

Dorothy Tillman. WVON. Coffee, Tea & Conversation with Dorothy Tillman. <http://www.wvon.com/ personalities/ dorothy-tillman.html>. Retrieved August 23, 2010.

Dr. Carter G. Woodson. Founder of Black History Month. <http: //www.freemaininstitute.com/woodson.htm>. Retrieved July 29, 2010.

Dr. Mae Jemison. <http://quest.nasa.gov/women/TODTWD /jemison.bio.html>. Retrieved July 2, 2010.

Dr. Martin Luther King, Jr. I Have A Dream Speech.<http://www. mklonline.net/dream.html>.Retrieved April 4, 2011.

Dr. Maulana Karenga's Bio. <http://www.africawithin.com/ karenga/karenga_bio.htm.>. Retrieved September 8, 2010.

DuSable Museum of African American History. Wikipedia, the free encyclopedia. <http://en.wikipedia.org/wiki/DuSable_ Museum_of_African_American_History>. Retrieved July 2, 2010.

Explorer Hero: Mae Jemison by Christian Walsh. <http://myhero. com/go/hero.asp?hero=M_jemison>. Retrieved July 30, 2010.

Eyes on the Prize. Wikipedia, the free encyclopedia. <http://en. wikipedia.org/wiki/Eyes on the prize>. Retrieved October 1, 2010.

Front Page Magazine. Obama's World, Part II. <http://97.74.65.51/ readArticle.aspx?ARTID=30896>. Retrieved August 23, 2010.

Glory Days: Adam Clayton Powell, Sr. < http://www2.scholastic. com/browse/article.jsp?id=4790>. Retrieved September 5, 2010.

Ida B Wells. Wikipedia, the free encyclopedia. <http://en.wikipedia

org/wiki/Ida_B._Wells>. Retrieved July 2, 2010.It Takes a Village-Wikipedia, the free encyclopedia. <http://www.en.wikipedia.org/wiki/It_Takes_a_Village>. Retrieved May 5, 2011.

It's Time to Take One Giant Step for Womankind; [Northwest, FNW Edition]. <http://quickproxy4.chipublib.org/ YVDgO147 /url =http://proquest.umi.com/pqdweb? index=1>. Retrieved August 3, 2010.

James Farmer, Civil Rights Giant in the 50's and 60's. <http://www. interchange.org/jfarmer.html>. Retrieved August 24, 2010.

James Farmer Project. <http://jamesfarmer.umwblogs.org/>. Retrieved August 31, 2010.

John Donne quotes. <http://www.goodreads.com/author/quotes/ 77318.John_Donne>. Retrieved August 9, 2010.

Julian Bond: Official Biography. <http://a-s.clayton.edu/mlking/ Julian %20Bond%20Official%20biography.htm>. Retrieved October 1. 2010.

Julian Bond. Speaker Profile and Speaking Topics. <http://www. apbspeakers.com/speaker/julian-bond>. Retrieved October 1, 2010.

Knowledge Is the Key. (WAK) 2011.

Kwanzaa. A Celebration of Family, Community, and Culture. The Founder's Message 2000. <http://www.officialkwanzaa website.org/origins1.shtml>. Retrieved July 6, 2010.

Kwanzaa. A Celebration of Family, Community, and Culture. The Founder's Message 2000. <http://www.officialkwanzaa website.org/NguzoSaba.shtml>. Retrieved July 6, 2010.

List of African American firsts. <http://en.wikipedia.org/wiki/List_of_African- American_firsts>. Retrieved November 6. 2010.

Mae Jemison, "I recall looking at the stars, knowing I'd go up there some day. <http://quickproxy4.chipublib.org /YVDgO147 url=http://proquest.umi.com/pqdweb?index=3...>. Retrieved August 3, 2010.

Mae Jemison Quotes.<http://womenshistory.about.com/od/quotes/ a/mae_jemison.htm>. Retrieved July 30, 2010.

Mae Jemison. <http://www. notablebiographies.com/Ho-Jo/ Jemison-Mae.html>. Retrieved July 30, 2010.

Mae Jemison, Phones Home While In Orbit. Science Students Talk To Astronaut. <http://quickproxy4.chipublib.org /YVDgO147/url=http://proquest.umi.com/pqdweb?index=3 >. Retrieved August 3, 2010.

March on Washington. All about the March on Washington, August 28, 1963. <http://www.infoplease.com/spot/ marchonwashington.html>. Retrieved September 3, 2010.

Margaret Taylor Burroughs: Biography from Answers.com. <http:// www.answers.com/topic/margaret-taylor-burroughs>. Retrieved August 14, 2010.

Medgar Evers. Wikipedia, the free encyclopedia. < http://en. wikipedia.org/wiki/Medgar_Evers.>. Retrieved October 14, 2010.

Medgar Evers. < http://www.africanwithin.com.bios.medgar_evers. htm >. Retrieved October 14, 2010.

Murder of Emmett Till. <http://...wikipedia.org/.../Murder_ of_ Emmett...>. Retrieved January 10, 2011.

My Space-Dorothy Wright Tillman. <http://www.mysapce.com/ dorothytillman>. Retrieved August 23, 2010.

NAACP. Our Mission. <http://www.naacp.org/pages/our- misssion>. Retrieved July 29, 2010.

Pullman Porters Helped Build Black Middle Class. <http://www.npr
.org /templates/story/story.php?storyId=103880184>.
Retrieved August 14, 2010.

Real Men Cook. Gimme Five. <http://www.realmencook.com/
Gimme5.html>. Retrieved August 18, 2010.

Real Men Cook. Real Men Charities Presents Real Men Cook in
Multiple Cities across the Country. <http://www.realmen
cook.com/RMCharities.html>. Retrieved August 18, 2010.

Real Men Cook-Chicago Event Page. <http://www.realmencook.
com/Chicago.html>. Retrieved August 21, 2010.

Real Men Cook. <http://www.realmencook.com/History.html>.
Retrieved August 18, 2010.

Real Men Cook .Mission Statement. <http://www.realmencook.com
/Mission.html>. Retrieved August 18, 2010.

Rosa Louise Parks Biography. <http://www.rosaparks.org/bio.
html>. Retrieved. July 30, 2010.

Rosa Parks, Black History Month. <http://www.gale.cengage.com
/free_resources/bhm/bio/parks_r.htm>. Retrieved July 30,
2010.

Rosa Parks. <http://www.africanonline.com/rosa_parks.htm>.
Retrieved July 30, 2010.

Selma to Montgomery marches. Wikipedia, the free encyclopedia.
<http://en.wikipedia.org/wiki/Selma_to Montgomery
_marches.> Retrieved October 14, 2010.

Segregated Lunch Counters. <http://www.spartacus.schoolnet.
co.uk/USAsitin.htm>. Retrieved September 6, 2010.

16th Street Baptist Church Bombing. Wikipedia, the free
encyclopedia.<http://en.wikipedia.org/wiki/16th_Street_Ba
ptist_Church_bombing>. Retrieved September 6, 2010.

Still I Rise by Maya Angelou. <http://www.poets.org/viewmedia. php/prmMID/15623>. Retrieved August 9, 2010.

10 Reasons Why Congress Should Back A Reparations Commission.<http://news.newamericamedia.org/news/view article.html?article_id=74afaa2bd8a36dc137...>. Retrieved August 30, 2010.

The King Center. The Beloved Community of Martin Luther King, Jr.<http://www.thekingcenter.org/ProgServices/Default. aspx>. Retrieved August 10. 2010.

The Ethics of Reparations: Engaging the Holocaust of Enslavement. <http://www.africawithin.com/karenga/ethics.htm>. Retrieved September 8, 2010.

The Final Call. Reparations Resolution Passed in Chicago. <http:// www.finalcall.com/national/reparations5-30-2000.htm>. Retrieved August 23, 2010.

The History Makers. Margaret Burroughs Biography. <.http://www. the historymakers.com/biography/biography.asp?bioindex =39>. Retrieved July 2, 2010.

The History of Black History Month. <http://www.asalh.org/black historymonthorigins.html>. Retrieved October 21, 2010.

The Salem to Montgomery March: The Struggle for Voting Rights. <http://www.byways.org/stories/73679>. Retrieved October 14, 2010.

The Silent Protest: Parade Organized By Harlem Religious and Civic Leaders and the NAACP, 1917. <http://www2.si umich.edu/ chico/Harlem/text/silentprotest.html>. Retrieved September 5, 2010.

UNCF Breaks Ground in D.C. on New National Headquarters. <http://www.diverseeducation.com/article/14730/>. Retrieved April 22, 2011.

Urban Prep Academies. Wikipedia, the free encyclopedia. <http://

en.wikipedia.org/wiki/Urban_Prep_Charter_Academy-for - Young_Men>. Retrieved October 18, 2010.

When in the Course of Human Event. Thomas Jefferson. <http://www.humanevents.com/article.php?id=21399>. Retrieved September 5, 2010.

The White House Historical Association/White House History/ Timelines. <http://www.whitehousehistory.org/whha_ timelines/timelines_africanamericans-04.html>. Retrieved August 4, 2010.

The White House Historical Association/White HouseHistory/ Timelines. <http://www.whitehousehistory.org/whha_ timelines/timelines_african-americans-03.html>. Retrieved August 4, 2010.

Women of the Hall. National Women's Hall of Fame. <http://www. greatwomen.org/women.php?action=viewone&id=117>. Retrieved July 30, 2010.

You've been had. Been took! Hoodwinked. Bamboozled! Led astray...<http://foreclosureblues.wordpress.com/2011/02/28 /you%E2%80%99v...>. Retrieved April 20, 2011.

Yvette Moyo Gillard. <http://www.linkedin.com/in/marketing innovatoryvettemoyo1>. Retrieved August 21, 2010.

Decosta-Willis, Miriam. *The Memphis Diary of Ida B. Wells: An Intimate Portrait of the Activist as a Young Woman.* Boston: Beacon Press, 1995.

Feldman, Eugene Pieter. *The Birth and the Building of the DuSable Museum.* Chicago: DuSable Museum Press, 1981.

Hughes, Lyn. *An Anthology of Respect-The Pullman Porters National Historic Registry of African American Railroad Employees.* Chicago: Hughes Peterson Publishing, 2007.

James, Michael. *ABSENT-The Assimilation of African American*

Males Into Nonbeing. Chicago: HOPE Publishing (Helping Oppressed People Emerge), 2006.

James, Michael. *Brother to Brother-A Message of Hope.* Chicago: HOPE Publishing (Helping Oppressed People Emerge), 2008.

Kunjufu, Jawanza. *Countering the Conspiracy to Destroy Black Boys.* Chicago: African American Images, 1994.

Reef, Catherine. *Black Explorers-American Profiles.* New York: Facts on file, Inc., 1990.

Turner, James (Introduction). *David Walker's Appeal.* Black Classic Press, 1993.

Notes

Notes